SCIENCE
AND THE
AFTERLIFE EXPERIENCE

"The evidence in favor of an afterlife is vast and varied. The evidence from near-death experiences and deathbed visions was described in two previous books by Chris Carter. *Science and the Afterlife Experience* is the final work of his trilogy, and one will see in this wonderful book that we do indeed have strongly repeatable evidence for the continuity of consciousness after physical death, based on children who remember previous lives, reports of apparitions, and communication from the deceased. What all these cases show is that human personality survives death and, by implication, human consciousness can exist independently of a functioning brain. When one has read the overwhelming evidence as described in this excellent book, it seems quite impossible not to be convinced that there should be some form of life after death. Any continuing opposition to the evidence is based on nothing more than willful ignorance or ideology. Highly recommended."

PIM VAN LOMMEL, M.D., CARDIOLOGIST AND
AUTHOR OF *CONSCIOUSNESS BEYOND LIFE*

"Chris Carter addresses the question that is, or should be, the single most important question for any being who considers himself—or suspects himself to be—mortal. He argues that this is not the case. If he is right then this is not only the single most life-transforming realization for a mortal or perhaps immortal being but also one of the most potent realizations that could prompt such a being to enter on a better path during his or her known life."

ERVIN LASZLO, PH.D., AUTHOR OF
SCIENCE AND THE AKASHIC FIELD
AND *THE NEW SCIENCE AND SPIRITUALITY READER*

". . . some of the best evidence offered by the near-death experience. This book is informative, interesting, intriguing, and inspirational."

MICHAEL TYMN,
AUTHOR OF *THE AFTERLIFE REVEALED*
AND *THE AFTERLIFE EXPLORERS*

"This third volume of Chris Carter's trilogy may be the best. Reincarnation, ghostlike visions, and messages from the dead make for some very stimulating reading. As an historical chronicle alone this would be a valuable work. But Carter's historical treatment also combines philosophy and analysis into an always interesting and well-organized treatise."

ROBERT BOBROW, M.D.,
AUTHOR OF *THE WITCH IN THE WAITING ROOM*

"The statement 'Survival of human consciousness past the point of biological death is a fact' will seem an extraordinary claim to some, and they may reasonably demand extraordinary evidence to support it. Carter has both made the claim and provided the evidence."

GUY LYON PLAYFAIR, AUTHOR OF *THIS HOUSE IS HAUNTED, IF THIS BE MAGIC,* AND *TWIN TELEPATHY*

"Carter boldly concludes that the survival of consciousness after the death of the body is a scientific *fact*—as well established as any other scientific fact."

NEAL GROSSMAN, PH.D., PROFESSOR EMERITUS
OF PHILOSOPHY, UNIVERSITY OF ILLINOIS AT CHICAGO

"Chris Carter has produced a compelling synthesis and brilliant analysis of some of the best evidence for life beyond physical death. This book should be required reading for believers and skeptics alike."

GARY E. SCHWARTZ, PH.D., PROFESSOR OF PSYCHOLOGY
AND MEDICINE AT THE UNIVERSITY OF ARIZONA AND
AUTHOR OF *THE AFTERLIFE EXPERIMENTS*

"Chris Carter establishes the existence of the afterlife beyond a reasonable doubt. I congratulate him on such a solid synthesis of the relevant data and arguments—both for and against."

EBEN ALEXANDER III, M.D.,
AUTHOR OF *PROOF OF HEAVEN: A NEUROSURGEON'S
NEAR-DEATH EXPERIENCE* AND *JOURNEY THROUGH THE AFTERLIFE*

"In this wonderful book, a work of great erudition, Chris Carter succinctly examines the works of giants in the field of survival of consciousness. . . . Carter's careful analysis of evidence for survival promptly lays super-ESP counterarguments to rest. . . . I highly recommend this book to the serious student."

JOHN L. TURNER, M.D.,
AUTHOR OF *MEDICINE, MIRACLES, AND MANIFESTATIONS*

SCIENCE
AND THE
AFTERLIFE
EXPERIENCE

Evidence for the
Immortality of Consciousness

CHRIS CARTER

Inner Traditions
Rochester, Vermont • Toronto, Canada

Inner Traditions
One Park Street
Rochester, Vermont 05767
www.InnerTraditions.com

SUSTAINABLE Certified Sourcing
FORESTRY
INITIATIVE www.sfiprogram.org
SFI-00854

Text stock is SFI certified

Library of Congress Cataloging-in-Publication Data
Carter, Chris.
  Science and the afterlife experience : evidence for the immortality of consciousness / Chris Carter.
     p. cm.
  Summary: "Reveals the evidence of life beyond death"—Provided by publisher.
  Includes bibliographical references (p.   ) and index.
  ISBN 978-1-59477-452-2 (pbk.) — ISBN 978-1-59477-499-7 (e-book)
  1. Future life. 2. Immortality. 3. Parapsychology. 4. Occultism. I. Title.
  BF1999.C293 2012
  133.901'3—dc23

                                                                2012007915

Printed and bound in the United States by Lake Book Manufacturing, Inc. The text stock is SFI certified. The Sustainable Forestry Initiative® program promotes sustainable forest management.

10   9   8   7   6   5   4   3   2   1

Text design by Priscilla H. Baker
Text layout by Virginia Scott Bowman
This book was typeset in Garamond Premier Pro and Gill Sans with Swiss and Gill Sans used as display typefaces.

To send correspondence to the author of this book, mail a first-class letter to the author c/o Inner Traditions • Bear & Company, One Park Street, Rochester, VT 05767, and we will forward the communication, or contact the author directly at **webslinger_999@yahoo.com**.

Dedicated to the memories of Curt Ducasse,
John Eccles, and Frederic Myers, three remarkable
individuals who never let fashion dictate their opinions.

Contents

The answer to human life is not to be found within the limits of human life.

CARL JUNG

Foreword

By Robert Almeder

I am a philosopher, and skeptics on the possibility of life after death occasionally defend their skepticism with reasons that are philosophical. Take, for example, three of the most popular philosophical arrows in the skeptic's quiver.

The first is that the very idea of humans existing independently of their bodies is inconceivable or incoherent. It makes no sense, they say, to talk about personal survival after death, either because we cannot imagine what a human person is if it is not at least partially identifiable with a unique human body or else because the very idea of surviving one's death is conceptually incoherent. We are our bodies, so they say. In the end, of course, this objection is rooted in the mistaken belief that just because we may not be able to imagine what a disincarnate human is like without a human body, there cannot be any.

However, the history of science shows again and again that a failure of imagination provides no compelling reason to doubt claims that are supported by the evidence. Reports of rocks that fall from the sky—what we today call meteorites—were rejected by scientists for decades on the grounds that there are no rocks in the sky to fall. Continental drift was ridiculed by geologists for decades because they could not imagine any means by which the continents could drift. The incredible claims of quantum mechanics may forever defy our ability to imagine them. And, finally, we might just find very strong evidence for accepting the *ancient* belief in the existence of disincarnate persons even if they are not physical bodies as we generally describe them in natural science.

The second objection is that even if human survival of death were logically and factually possible, we still have no scientific knowledge of anybody ever surviving biological death, because we have no experimental evidence for it that will hold up under serious scientific scrutiny. We cannot, so the objection goes, generate at will compelling case studies; we cannot control disembodied spirits in order to make them appear under empirically desirable conditions. Any evidence offered for the survival of humans or human consciousness after death is not repeatable under controlled conditions. Unless the evidence can be repeated at will under controlled conditions, the belief cannot transcend the anecdotal into the realm of human knowledge.

However, there are many things we know exist that cannot be repeated at will. The fact that home runs cannot be repeated at will does not mean that home runs do not occur. We now know that rocks do sometimes fall from the sky, even though we cannot produce at will the evidence for this belief. Unique historical events cannot ever be repeated. Even so, as you will see in this wonderful book *we do indeed have strongly repeatable evidence* based on reincarnation studies, reports of apparitions, and apparent communication from the deceased via mediums.

The third objection is that the evidence for personal survival is persuasive only if the ever-present possibility of fraud or hoax can be clearly excluded. But the possibility of fraud or hoax can never be completely excluded in any field. Even so, we do not need to completely exclude all logical possibility of fraud. We only need the continual widespread emergence of cases that have the same characteristics as the ideal cases (of the sort you will find in this book). When enough cases continue to occur and are examined by many different researchers who are incapable of finding any fraud, over time the probability of fraud becomes remote, just because such cases are repeating themselves in widely differing contexts and in the hands of different researchers. As the esteemed Cambridge philosopher Henry Sidgwick remarked in his presidential address to the British Society for Psychical Research in 1882, "We have done all we can when the critic has nothing left to allege except that the investigator is in the trick."[1]

This is not the place to examine closely all the arguments offered by the skeptics who advance them against the more persuasive arguments for personal survival. But the author of this book has written two other books on the skeptical arguments, and he has done an admirable job in showing just how terribly superficial the skeptical arguments are, primarily because skeptics typically come to the discussion with a deeply rooted bias that undermines the spirit of inquiry based on the facts.

This sort of bias is nothing new. It is a tribute to William James to keep in mind his claim that progress in the area of paranormal research and belief in life after death will be a slow process more likely to occur incrementally as the product of sustained research in the area. James suggested that skepticism in this area dies slowly because of the deep cultural and religious influences on the formation of belief. Even so, for those who have studied carefully the various bodies of evidence for belief in some form of human survival it is something of a mystery why some members of the scientific community still resist serious research into this belief.

The author of this book, like so many others, is less motivated by some need to refute skeptics than he is in reaching those who come to the issue with an open mind and who are not fearful of learning that which may challenge their present beliefs. Even so, as you will see, his careful criticisms of the skeptical position are more than enough to put the typical skeptic in his or her place.

As a matter of fact, when you finish reading this book, you will probably find the arguments for survival and against the skeptics so compelling that you will come to view death not as a sad extinction of one's personality but rather as a joyful beginning in a different dimension of existence. As philosopher Alice Bailey put it:

> We can live in the consciousness of immortality, and it will give an added coloring and beauty to life. We can foster the awareness of our future transition, and live with the expectation of its wonder. Death thus faced, and regarded as a prelude to further living experience, takes on a different meaning.[2]

Even so, the ultimate question may not be whether we are strongly justified in believing some form of life after death, although that is certainly an important question. Rather the question is more properly whether that belief is more rationally justifiable than its denial quite independent of whether one believes or disbelieves it. In the meantime, we can continue to argue that not only is it reasonable to believe in some form of life after death, but more interestingly, *that it is irrational not to believe,* based purely on the force of the available evidence.

ROBERT ALMEDER, PH.D., is a professor of philosophy at Georgia State University. A former Fulbright scholar, he is the author of *Truth and Skepticism* and *Death and Personal Survival: The Evidence for Life after Death.*

Introduction

The major problem of our time is decay in the belief in personal immortality.

GEORGE ORWELL

The manner in which we live our lives depends, to a large extent, on what we believe comes after it. Men and women throughout history have willingly gone to their deaths for their spiritual beliefs. Critics may point out that human beings have also committed grave atrocities and even launched wars motivated, at least in part, by "spiritual" beliefs inspired by the various religions. On the other hand, however, those who believe that death is nothing but oblivion often lead selfish and ruthless lives, concerned only with momentary pleasures, status, and the pursuit of material wealth.

Orwell's grim vision of the future, portrayed in his novel *1984,* fortunately did not come to pass. However, we may now face a future even worse than anything Orwell imagined. Philosopher David Griffen recently issued this dire warning:

> I believe the human race now faces the greatest challenge in its history. If it continues on its present course, widespread misery and death of unprecedented proportions is a certainty. Annihilation of

human life and of millions of species of non-human life as well is probable. This is so because of polluting technologies, economic growth-mania, out-of-control population growth, global apartheid between rich and poor nations, rapid depletion of non-renewable resources, and proliferation of nuclear weapons combined with a state of international anarchy that makes war inevitable and sufficient measures to halt global ecological destruction impossible.

What seems clear is that a transition in world *order,* if it is to occur, will have to be accompanied by a shift in world *view,* one that would lead to a new sense of adventure, replacing the modern adventure of unending economic growth based on the technological subjugation of nature. Only if we come to see human life as primarily a spiritual adventure, an adventurous journey that continues beyond this life, will we have a chance of becoming sufficiently free from destructive motivations to affect a transition to a sustainable global order.[1]

Griffen and I both agree that the belief in an afterlife offers several practical benefits:

◄ Such a belief can help overcome the fear of death and annihilation.

◄ If people are convinced that they are ultimately not subject to any earthly power, this can increase their courage to fight for freedom, ecologically sustainable policies, and social justice.

◄ If people believe that this life is not the final word, and that justice will prevail in the next life, this can help them withstand the unfairness they encounter in the here and now.

◄ The idea of life as an unfolding journey, which continues even after death, can lead to a greater sense of connection with the universe as it unfolds into the future.

◄ The belief in life after death can help counter the extreme degree of materialism that has pervaded every niche of modern civilization.

◄ The belief that we are on a spiritual journey, and that we have time to reach our destination, can motivate us to think creatively about what we can do now—socially, internationally, and individually—to move closer to what we should be in the here and now.

But for many of us these practical benefits alone are not sufficient to compel belief. We seek hard *evidence* that stands up to the most rigorous critical scrutiny. Years before I even considered writing this book, I sought to find such evidence, and after combing through numerous books and journals, I was surprised by the sheer quantity and variety of the evidence for an afterlife. Some of the reports dated back hundreds and even thousands of years. But the most rigorous evidence by far has been gathered in modern times by respected scientists and scholars, beginning in the closing years of the nineteenth century, and continuing to the present day.

However, as a philosopher, I was not content to merely examine the evidence in favor of the survival of death; I knew that any counterarguments must also be fairly and closely examined if we are to arrive at any solid conclusions. I was aware that several philosophers and scientists have doubted or denied that we survive the death of our bodies, and so I began an in-depth study of the skeptical literature. Through reading, discussion, and the occasional debate, I eventually came to understand not only the "skeptical" arguments, but also the motivations of those who deny so vehemently that there is more to human beings than material bodies.

The idea that our minds survive the deaths of our bodies is known as the survival hypothesis, and although many people today associate belief in an afterlife with religious faith, it is important to remember that this belief long predates any organized religion. It is found in the old shamanic spiritual beliefs of hunter-gatherers from around the world, and dates back at least to the Neanderthals, who buried their dead with flowers, jewelry, and utensils, presumably for use in the next world. Reports of phenomena suggesting the continued existence of those who once lived on Earth have come from virtually all known cultures, and have continued into the modern age. As we will see, the most convincing evidence has been gathered under rigorous conditions over the last 125 years.

The evidence in favor of an afterlife is vast and varied, and comes from near-death experiences, deathbed visions, children who remember previous lives, apparitions, and communications through mediums. In my previous book, *Science and the Near-Death Experience,* I discuss the first two lines of evidence in depth. In this book I concentrate on the even more impressive last three lines of evidence.

Part 1, "Reincarnation," explores this ancient idea by examining contemporary reports of children who claim to remember previous lives. Although most people associate a belief in reincarnation with the religions of the Far East, it is shown that this belief has historically been found among cultures all over the Earth. As such, modern reports from children in a variety of cultures and locations are critically examined in order to see how such evidence stands up to critical scrutiny.

Part 2, "Apparitions," considers the ancient and widespread belief that the departed sometimes return to visit the living in the form of apparitions. We carefully examine accounts of apparitions, including accounts in which they are reported by numerous eyewitnesses, accounts in which animals also seem to perceive them, and accounts in which the apparitions behave with a purpose of their own and sometimes convey information unknown to the living. Skeptics have challenged the testimony of these witnesses, and we carefully scrutinize these challenges.

Part 3, "Messages from the Dead," evaluates the evidence that the departed are capable of detailed, two-way communication with the living through talented human mediums. Although this idea can also be traced to ancient times, modern scholarly researchers have rigorously and thoroughly examined the validity of communication through mediums for well over a century. We carefully examine alternative explanations in order to see how well they stand up to the best cases, and the reader will see why mediumistic communication is considered the most convincing single line of evidence for survival.

Finally, part 4, "Conclusions," summarizes the case for survival as it stands today, based on all of the available lines of evidence. The book concludes with a sample of messages purporting to come directly from the afterworld.

The experiences described in the pages that follow have important implications for humanity. Based upon my own experience and that of many others, I sincerely believe that deeply beneficial changes in our view of the universe and our place within it will be gained by those who read about these strange and often wonderful experiences, and then take their profound lessons to heart.

Most people base their beliefs regarding the afterlife on religious or materialistic faith. But there is a third alternative, one that requires neither a leap of faith nor the denial of evidence. However, as philosopher Carl Becker has written, this third alternative comes with an unusual requirement:

> We must always walk a tightrope: we are examining data often ignored by the scientific community and embraced by the religious community, but we are using methodology that is advocated by the scientific community and ignored by much of the religious world. Therefore we should expect to be criticized by dogmatists from both sides of the fence.[2]

The purpose of this book is to examine the most convincing ancient and modern evidence for the existence of the afterlife; to carefully consider all the skeptical objections; and finally, to arrive at a solution to this deep and ancient mystery.

Psychic Phenomena and the Near-Death Experience

Background

Although this is the third and final book in a trilogy, it is not necessary to read the first two books before reading this one. However, because the first two books contain much of the background for many of the main points of this book, it is useful to summarize here some of their conclusions. Those readers who are interested in pursuing these issues in more depth may always consult the original texts.

It is a curious fact that most—although by no means all—of those who doubt or deny the survival of mind past the point of bodily death also deny the existence of psychic abilities, such as telepathy. As such, my first book, *Science and Psychic Phenomena,* was primarily concerned with understanding why a substantial minority of the scientific community has been vehemently denying the existence of psychic abilities such as telepathy for well over a century. At first glance, this may seem very puzzling: Reports of psychic abilities date back to the dawn of history, and come from cultures all over the world. Surveys also show that most working scientists accept the possibility that telepathy exists,[1] and many leading scientists have endorsed and supported psychical research.[2]

Those who call themselves "skeptics" assert that there is no replicable, experimental evidence for the existence of psychic abilities, now commonly called *psi* (pronounced "sigh"). However, as I described at length in my first book, high-quality, consistent, replicable experimental evidence for the existence of psi has in fact been provided for decades.[3] If this were any other field of inquiry, the controversy would have been settled by the data decades ago. However, parapsychology is *not* like any other field of inquiry. The data of parapsychology challenge deeply held worldviews, worldviews that are concerned not only with science, but also with religious and philosophical issues. As such, the evidence arouses strong passions, and for many, a strong desire to dismiss it.

BASIS OF THE CONTROVERSY

It is impossible to fully understand this controversy without realizing that it has a strong ideological component. The ideology involved is a product of the unique history of Western civilization. Until the eighteenth century, the great majority of our philosophers and scientists took for granted the existence of psychic phenomena. Among educated people, all of this changed with the dawn of the Scientific Revolution, spanning the period between the birth of Galileo in 1564 and the death of Newton in 1727. During this period the universe came to be viewed as a gigantic clockwork mechanism, operating as a self-regulating machine in accordance with inviolable laws.

These views became prevalent in the eighteenth century, during what became known as the Enlightenment, which can be thought of as the ideological aftermath of the Scientific Revolution. Its most striking feature was the rejection of dogma and tradition in favor of the rule of reason in human affairs, and it was the precursor of modern secular humanism. Inspired by the dazzling success of developments in physics, prominent spokesmen such as Diderot and Voltaire argued for a new worldview based on an uncompromising materialism and mechanism that left no room for any intervention of mind in nature, whether human or divine.

The horrors of the religious wars and of the Inquisition were still fresh in people's minds, and the new scientific worldview, can be seen partly as a reaction to the ecclesiastical domination over thought that the church held for centuries. The Scientific Revolution of the seventeenth century completely transformed the outlook of educated people, so that by 1750 the picture of a mechanistic universe governed by inviolable laws had established its hold on the minds of Enlightenment thinkers; now such things as sorcery and second sight seemed incredible at best, and vulgar superstition at worst. Lingering widespread belief in the reality of these phenomena was considered to be the unfortunate legacy of a superstitious, irrational, prescientific era.

The counteradvocates of parapsychology at the present time are those who see themselves as heirs of the Enlightenment, guardians of rationality who must at all costs discredit any dangerous backsliding into religious fanaticism and superstition.

The science of Newton, Galileo, and Kepler had breathed new life into the ancient philosophy of materialism. It is the materialistic worldview that is defended by modern secular humanists, which they rightly see as threatened by the claims of parapsychology. For many secular humanists the widespread acceptance of these claims would be the first step in a return to religious fanaticism, superstition, and irrationality.

Modern secular humanists and other militant atheists are the direct descendants of the Enlightenment thinkers, the *philosophes,* and their thinking is, for the most part, still based on the materialism implied by classical physics. And materialism simply cannot accommodate the reality of psi phenomena. If materialism is proven false by the data for psi, then one of the foundations of their opposition to religion and superstition is thereby removed. Hence, their vehement denial of any evidence for the existence of psi.*

---

*There is a deep connection between the ideology of secular humanism and the so-called skeptical movement. For instance, the world's leading "skeptical" organization, the Committee for the Scientific Investigation of Claims of the Paranormal (CSICOP) was formed in 1976 at a meeting of the American Humanist Association by atheist philosopher Paul Kurtz (in 2006 CSICOP shortened its name to Committee for Skeptical Inquiry).

The doctrine of materialism is one of the implications of taking classical physics to be a complete description of all of nature, including human beings.* It is essentially the idea that all events have a physical cause: in other words, that all events are caused by the interaction between particles of matter and force fields. It follows from this that mind has no causal role in nature but is at most merely a useless by-product produced by the brain, and so in short, all that matters is matter.

Considered as a scientific hypothesis, materialism makes a bold and admirable prediction: psychic abilities, such as telepathy, simply do not exist. If they are shown to exist, then materialism is refuted.† Of course, in practice, followers of a theory do not always admit defeat so easily, as the philosopher of science Karl Popper reminded us.

> We can always immunize a theory against refutation. There are many such immunizing tactics; and if nothing better occurs to us, we can always deny the objectivity—or even the existence—of the refuting observation. Those intellectuals who are more interested in being right than in learning something interesting but unexpected are by no means rare exceptions.[4]

Immunizing a theory against refutation turns it into an ideology, a belief held as an article of faith: a belief whose truth is simply not questioned, because it is considered so important. This is just what the critics of parapsychology have done, for the so-called skeptics have gone to extraordinary lengths to try to dismiss and explain away the data.

Remarks to the effect that "the existence of psi is incompatible with

---

*Newton did not subscribe to this view but instead followed Descartes on this matter, viewing humans as the sole exception in an otherwise deterministic universe. As mentioned above, this doctrine was popularized by Newton's followers, such as Voltaire and Diderot, both of whom were strongly motivated by opposition to religion.

†Note that materialism can be refuted independently of parapsychology. See Beauregard, *The Spiritual Brain*, 125–153; Carter, *Science and Psychic Phenomena*, 165–80; Popper and Eccles, *The Self and Its Brain*, 98–99.

modern science" are common in the skeptical literature. However, it is rare for a critic to ever back up this criticism with specific examples. On those rare occasions when they do,[5] they invariably invoke the principles of classical physics, which have been known to be grossly and fundamentally incorrect since the early years of the twentieth century.

MODERN PHYSICS DOES NOT PROHIBIT PSI PHENOMENA

However, a number of leading physicists, such as Henry Margenau, David Bohm, Brian Josephson, and Olivier Costa de Beauregard, have repeatedly claimed that nothing in modern physics prohibits psi phenomena. Costa de Beauregard even maintains that the theory of quantum physics virtually *demands* that psi phenomena exist.[6]

There is no longer any conflict on a theoretical level between physics and reports of psychic abilities. Objections based on an incompatibility with physics are grounded in a theory of physics that has been known to be obsolete for over a century.

It is important to remember that most so-called skeptics of parapsychology are not physicists, but psychologists. In one of the surveys mentioned above, Evans found that only 3 percent of natural scientists considered ESP "an impossibility," compared to 34 percent of psychologists. And many of the most prominent "skeptics"—such as Richard Wiseman, Susan Blackmore, Ray Hyman, and James Alcock—are psychologists.

Accordingly, the great psychologist Gardner Murphy, a president of the American Psychological Association and later of the American Society for Psychical Research, has urged his fellow psychologists to become better acquainted with modern physics.

[T]he difficulty is at the level of physics, not at the level of psychology. Psychologists may be a little bewildered when they encounter modern physicists who take these phenomena in stride, in fact, take them much more seriously than psychologists do, saying, as physicists, that they are no longer bound by the types of Newtonian energy distribution, inverse square laws, etc., with which scientists used to regard themselves as tightly bound . . . [P]sychologists probably will witness a period of slow, but definite, erosion of the blandly exclusive attitude that has offered itself as the only appropriate scientific attitude in this field. The data from parapsychology will be almost certainly in harmony with general psychological principles and will be assimilated rather easily within the systematic framework of psychology as a science when once the imagined appropriateness of Newtonian physics is put aside, and modern physics replaces it.[7]

Genuine skepticism is an important part of science. New claims must be subjected to the most severe critical scrutiny and rigorous testing if we are to minimize our chances of mistakenly accepting false claims. However, genuine skepticism involves the practice of *doubt,* not of *denial.* And so I argued in my first book that most of the so-called skeptics of psi are not true skeptics, but merely deniers.

One final point needs to be made here regarding the relevance of psi abilities to the survival hypothesis. I mentioned earlier that most of those who doubt or deny the survival of mind past the point of bodily death also deny the existence of psychic abilities. However, there are skeptics of survival who do *not* doubt the existence of psi; neither do they try to dismiss the evidence for survival as fraudulent. Rather, they argue that a combination of telepathy and clairvoyance* can explain the data better than the idea of survival.

Hence, one of the other reasons I started this series with a book on the controversy over the existence of psi is that I wanted to fully explore and discuss the nature of psi abilities, in order to effectively deal with

*Telepathy refers to the exchange of information between minds without use of the ordinary senses. Clairvoyance, also called "remote viewing," refers to information about the physical environment received from a distance, beyond the reach of the ordinary senses. Together with precognition—seeing the future—these three abilities are collectively referred to as extra-sensory perception, or ESP. ESP plus psychokinesis —mind/matter interaction—are collectively termed "psi."

this skeptical objection. The present book fully explores and discusses the nature of the survival evidence and also contains a critical examination of the idea that ESP—or even *Super*-ESP—can explain the evidence better than the hypothesis of survival.

THE RELATIONSHIP BETWEEN MIND AND BRAIN

My second book, *Science and the Near-Death Experience,* began by examining the question of whether or not consciousness depends on the brain. Obviously, if consciousness depends for its existence on a material brain, then our minds cannot survive the destruction of the brain. So, various materialist theories to that effect were examined, and it was shown that all the arguments for the dependence of the mental on the physical—such as the effects of age, disease, brain damage, and drugs on the mind—are all based on an unstated assumption.

The implicit assumption made in all the materialist arguments was that the relationship between brain activity and consciousness was always one of *cause to effect,* and never that of *effect to cause.* But this assumption is not known to be true, and it is not the only conceivable one consistent with the observed facts mentioned above. Just as consistent with the observed facts is the idea that the brain's function is that of an intermediary between mind and body. In other words, that the brain's function is that of a two-way receiver-transmitter: sometimes from body to mind, as in sense perception; and sometimes from mind to body, as in willed action.

THE TRANSMISSION HYPOTHESIS

The idea that the brain functions as an intermediary between mind and body is an ancient one. But it has been discussed and endorsed by modern thinkers, such as Henri Bergson, William James, and Ferdinand

Schiller. The form of interactive dualism implied by this relationship has also been endorsed by several modern philosophers, including Curt Ducasse, Karl Popper, Robert Almeder, and Neal Grossman, and by several prominent neuroscientists, including renowned brain surgeon Wilder Penfield and Nobel Laureate Sir John Eccles.

In addition, an entire chapter in my second book is devoted to showing why many physicists now believe modern physics supports a dualistic model of mind-brain interaction. Several of these physicists have gone even further, and have advanced hypothetical quantum mechanical models that propose to explain precisely *how* a nonphysical mind may interact with a brain. Ironically, these days it is possible to be a materialist only by ignoring the most successful theory of matter the world has yet seen.

I argued in the second book that the transmission hypothesis can explain everything the production hypothesis explains, such as the effect of drugs and brain injury on the mind. For any change in brain functioning, such as that resulting from intoxication or a stroke, should be expected to affect its capacity as a receiver-transmitter just as certainly as its capacity as a producer.

If the mind must inhabit a biological machine in order to operate in and manifest itself in the material world, then as long as it is bound to this machine we should expect its operation and manifestation to be affected by the condition and limitations of the machine. If the machine is impaired, then under both the production hypothesis *and* the transmission hypothesis, so too will be the operation and manifestation of mind.

However, the dualistic theory that the mind plays a genuine, causal role in nature has the advantage of also being able to explain many phenomena that are simply inexplicable under any doctrine of materialism in which mind is at most only a useless by-product produced by the brain. These would include the placebo effect, cognitive behavioral therapy, and psychic abilities such as telepathy.

THE PRODUCTION HYPOTHESIS

The most dramatic phenomena that remains utterly inexplicable by the theory of materialism is the Near-Death Experience (NDE), in which people near death sometimes report leaving their bodies, observing the surrounding scene in detail, traveling through a tunnel, and sometimes meeting deceased friends and relatives, or a mysterious "being of light." In many of these cases, people accurately described details of their surroundings, yet medical personnel present at the time later testified that the person was deeply unconscious, with little if any brain activity possible.

Many attempts have been made to explain the NDE within a materialist framework, and these were dealt with in the second book. All the attempts to explain away the NDE as the product of a malfunctioning brain were closely examined, and ultimately *not one* stood up to critical scrutiny. The conclusion finally arrived at was that the NDE is exactly what it appears to be: a genuine separation of mind from body during the early stages of biological death.

The second book demonstrated that the idea that the mind depends on the brain has been conclusively refuted, and so it is a hypothesis that no longer has the support of scientific evidence. Hence, it is unscientific to continue to accept it. Any continuing opposition to the evidence that falsifies materialism is based on nothing more than ignorance or ideology.*

DENIERS, DEBUNKERS,
AND MILITANT ATHEISM

In summary, the deniers and debunkers tend to be militant atheists who are motivated by allegiance to an obsolete worldview, by ignorance of the implications of the new physics, and by a hatred of religion and superstition. If they admitted to the reality of psychic abilities, such as

---

*Nor is there any evidence that memories are stored within the brain. Chapters 5 and 6 of *Science and the Near-Death Experience* deal with this issue.

telepathy, and of near-death experiences as involving a genuine separation of mind from body, then the materialistic foundation of their worldview would crumble. The deniers fear that the demise of materialism would usher in a return to an age of religious persecution and irrationality. This fear is evident in the apocalyptic strain to some of the Committee's writing. For instance, the announcement of the founding of CSICOP stated:

> Perhaps we ought not to assume that the scientific enlightenment will continue indefinitely . . . like the Hellenic civilization, it may be overwhelmed by irrationalism, subjectivism, and obscurantism.[8]

But these fears seem to be absolutely groundless. As mentioned above, surveys show that most scientists accept the likely existence of psychic abilities. Among the general public, belief in the reality of psi phenomena is widespread, but polls have also shown that over 90 percent of the public regard scientists as having "considerable" or even "very great" prestige.[9] And many of the leading NDE researchers are respected cardiologists and neuroscientists. So, society is unlikely to return to the Dark Ages because of widespread interest in psychic phenomena and the NDE.

One last point about the NDE is worthy of mention: most of the individuals who have had an NDE feel that it has been the single most significant event in their lives. The nature of the near-death experience may be controversial, but there is little disagreement that the experience usually has profound, life-changing aftereffects. These typically include a thirst for knowledge; increased compassion and tolerance for others; reduced competitiveness; reduced interest in material possessions; an increased interest in spirituality, coupled with a decreased interest in sectarian religion; a greater appreciation for life, coupled with a greatly reduced fear of death; and most strikingly, a greatly increased belief in an afterlife.

People who have had an NDE are often changed for the better by the experience, and return with a vital message for humanity: after death there is more, and the purpose of life is to grow in love and knowledge.

Similarly, there seem to be important messages contained in the experiences described in the pages that follow. But it is not necessary to directly experience these phenomena in order to learn from them.

If you are encountering these lines of evidence here for the first time, then you may perhaps be astonished at the variety and quantity of the evidence for survival. If, on the other hand, you are somewhat familiar with this evidence, then you may be surprised to find out how well the best evidence holds up to close and careful scrutiny. Our pre-scientific ancestors accepted survival of death as a matter of course, until the scientific revolution of the seventeenth century seemed to provide theoretical support for the ancient doctrine of materialism. Modern science—as opposed to classical science—provides no such support for materialism. Ironically, the twenty-first century application of the scientific method of empirical hypothesis testing may now restore the idea of survival to a position stronger than any it has ever occupied.

PART I

Reincarnation

Were an Asiatic to ask me for a definition of Europe, I should be forced to answer him: It is that part of the world which is haunted by the incredible delusion that man was created out of nothing, and that his present birth is his first entrance into life.

ARTHUR SCHOPENHAUER

ONE

Evidence from India to England

Reincarnation is an ancient belief, one found in many widely separated parts of the world. Westerners frequently associate the belief in reincarnation exclusively with the Hindus and Buddhists of Southeast Asia, but this is a misconception. Despite the best efforts of Christian missionaries, a belief in reincarnation persists among the tribes of east and west Africa, the native tribes of northwest North America, the Eskimo of the arctic, the Trobriand Islanders of the South Pacific, the Ainu of northern Japan, the Druses of Lebanon, and the Aborigines of central Australia. There *are* some religions outside the scope of the Judeo-Christian tradition that do not include a belief in reincarnation; but as one leading researcher in the field wrote, "Nearly everyone outside the range of orthodox Christianity, Judaism, Islam, and Science—the last being a secular religion for many persons—believes in reincarnation."[1]

At one time the belief in reincarnation was also common in parts of the Western world. The Pythagoreans of ancient Greece taught a doctrine of reincarnation, and Plato expounded the idea of reincarnation in *Phaedo* and the *Republic*. The Celts of Great Britain believed in reincarnation, as did the Vikings of Scandinavia. In southern Europe at least some Christians believed in reincarnation up until the sixth century. Although it was not part of official instruction, leaders of the church appear to have tolerated the belief as acceptable, until the Council of Nice in 553 CE. It has been argued that the actions of this council did not constitute a binding official ban, as the council was not called by the pope.[2] However, a decline in the acceptability of the idea set in among orthodox Christians at about this time and has persisted ever since.*

The late twentieth century did witness something of a renaissance in the belief in reincarnation in the West. A Gallup poll conducted in 1968 showed that 18 percent of people in eight countries of Western Europe believed in reincarnation, and a survey a year later showed that 26 percent of Canadians questioned said they believed in reincarnation. In a 1982 survey, 23 percent of American respondents claimed to hold this belief.[3] By the late 1960s reincarnation even began to appear in popular culture, and has appeared as a theme in literature, film, and music.†

How did reincarnation come to be such a widespread belief in the premodern world, shared by people separated by enormous distances over land and sea? The belief in reincarnation can be traced in India to at least 1000 BCE, and it does seem possible that the belief in Asia can be traced to a common source. It seems far less likely that an Eskimo in northern Canada and a villager of the Ganges Valley acquired their beliefs from a common source; and even less likely that the belief in reincarnation spread from south Asia to west Africa, the Celtic British Isles, and to central Australia.

If the belief did not arise in a single location and then spread to other regions, it must have arisen independently in several locations. How could this have occurred?

<hr />

*This is even more puzzling when we realize that there are at least two references to reincarnation in the New Testament. At one point the disciples ask Jesus if a blind man sinned in a previous life, and Jesus did not rebuke them (John 9:1–2); at another point Jesus describes John the Baptist as the prophet Elijah reborn (Matthew 11:11–15).
†Examples include the novel (and later film) *The Reincarnation of Peter Proud* by Max Erlich; the song "Déjà Vu" by Crosby, Stills, Nash, and Young; "Cosmic Dancer" by T. Rex; and "Highwayman," performed by the group Highwayman.

A skeptic could argue that the belief in an afterlife is comforting to those left behind, and that this is sufficient to account for the widespread belief in an afterlife. But this does not seem sufficient to account for the specific belief that the deceased will be reborn into this world, as opposed to simply spending eternity in some otherworldly realm. Some additional factor seems to be required. One such possibility is that some individuals in different parts of the world have claimed to remember having lived before.

There are several ancient accounts of claims to remember previous lives: for instance, both Pythagoras and Apollonius claimed to remember having lived before. In the sixteenth century, Tulsi Das, the translator of the *Ramayana,* claimed to remember a previous life. In the eighteenth century, the Mogul Emperor Aurangzeb, although a Muslim who did not believe in reincarnation, was sufficiently open-minded to interrogate witnesses to a case in the manner of a modern investigator. In the early nineteenth century, a Japanese boy named Katsugoro seemed to remember the life of a farmer's son. After this case, no other cases appeared to have been documented until 1898, when the summaries of six Burmese cases appeared in print.[4]

Between 1900 and 1960 a number of cases, mostly from India, were reported in newspapers, magazines, journals, and books. Most were reports of only a single case, and so were easily dismissed as superstitious tales of imagination. But in the 1950s, psychiatry professor Dr. Ian Stevenson began to collect and systematically compare such accounts. After finding forty-four reasonably detailed accounts that could not be easily dismissed as fraudulent, Stevenson published an article in 1960 that startled many of his readers with the conclusion that the cases provided sufficiently strong evidence for reincarnation to justify further research of similar cases.[5] He did not have long to wait. In 1961 he learned about a new case in India, received a small research grant to go there, and thus began his field investigations.

Nothing prepared Stevenson for the abundance of cases of claimed memories of past lives that he found in India after he arrived—during his first five weeks in India he learned of no fewer than twenty-five cases. Since then, Stevenson and his colleagues have investigated thousands of reincarnation cases, with over 250 cases intensively investigated. In 1966 he published his landmark book *Twenty Cases Suggestive of Reincarnation,* and has followed up this book with several others. The resurgence of interest in reincarnation in the West since 1960 is, in large part, due to the research of Stevenson and his colleagues.

Stevenson employs research methods that have been used by lawyers and historians for centuries. His primary method is to interview the subject and all firsthand witnesses. Repeated interviews are usually held with the most important informants in order to check the consistency of their reports, and to study details previously missed. In addition, Stevenson locates and copies birth certificates, hospital records, and reports of post-mortem examinations in order to substantiate details of the witnesses' accounts.

In a typical case, a child between the ages of two and five begins to speak of a previous life. In some cases this occurs as soon as the child is able to speak, although it is often triggered by an incident or observation that is related to those memories. Often the child will use adult expressions and behave in a way that is strange for a child, but which seems entirely appropriate for the previous personality. The memories of the previous life usually begin to fade by ages five or six, and are usually gone by age eight, although there are exceptions to this rule. The unusual behavior and dispositions generally persist for some time after the specific memories have disappeared, although these too seem to fade with time and maturity.

Let us now consider some specific cases Stevenson has collected.

The Case of Corliss Chotkin Jr.

This case started with a prediction by an elderly Tlinget fisherman named Victor Vincent, who, shortly before his death in Alaska, told his niece, Irene Chotkin, that he would be reborn as her son. He showed Mrs. Chotkin two scars, one on his nose and one on his back, and told her that she would recognize him by birthmarks on his body corresponding to these scars. Victor Vincent had become very fond of his niece and told her: "I know I will have a good home."

In the spring of 1946, Victor Vincent died. About eighteen months later, on December 15, 1947, Mrs. Chotkin gave birth to a baby boy, who was named after his father. Corliss Chotkin Jr. had two birthmarks, which his mother said were of exactly the same shape and location as the scars Victor Vincent had pointed to in his prediction of his rebirth.

One day when Corliss was thirteen months old, his mother was trying to get him to repeat his name. Instead, he replied petulantly, "Don't you know me? I'm Kahkody." Victor Vincent had been a full-blooded Tlinget, and *Kahkody* had been his tribal name. When Mrs. Chotkin told one of her aunts about the boy's claim to be Kahkody, the older woman claimed that she had dreamed shortly before Corliss's birth that Victor Vincent was coming to live with the Chotkins. Mrs. Chotkin was sure that she had not told her aunt about Victor Vincent's prediction before she heard about this dream.

When Corliss was two years old and being wheeled along the docks by his mother, he spontaneously recognized a stepdaughter of Victor Vincent. They were not there to meet her, and neither Mrs. Chotkin nor her other child had noticed the woman before Corliss pointed her out. Corliss showed great excitement on seeing her, jumping up and down, saying "There's my Susie." Corliss hugged her affectionately, called her by her Tlingit tribal name, and kept repeating "My Susie."

On another occasion when he was two, Corliss spontaneously recognized Victor's son William, saying, "There is William, my son." On another he recognized the widow of Victor Vincent, and on several other occasions he recognized old friends of Victor Vincent. All these recognitions occurred by the time Corliss was six years old.

According to Corliss's mother, he had also mentioned two events in Victor Vincent's life that she did not think he could have learned about normally. In addition, he shared several behavioral traits with Victor Vincent: Corliss combed his hair in a very similar manner; like Victor, Corliss also stuttered; both were left-handed; and both had a strong interest in boats and being on the water. Corliss also showed a precocious aptitude for handling and repairing engines, and, according to his mother, had taught himself to run boat engines without lessons.

After the age of nine, Corliss made fewer remarks about the previous life he seemed to remember, and when Stevenson interviewed him in 1962, when he was fifteen, he said he remembered nothing of the previous life. By 1972, when Stevenson met him for the last time, Corliss had almost completely overcome his stuttering, although he maintained his interest in boat engines.[6]

The Case of the Pollock Twins

On May 5, 1957, a crazed automobile driver deliberately drove her car onto the sidewalk of a street in Hexham, England, killing two sisters, Joanna and Jacqueline Pollock, who had been walking to Sunday school. Joanna was eleven years old, Jacqueline six. The driver had been distraught over losing her own children in a custody battle, and was later confined to a mental hospital.

The parents grieved, but John Pollock believed that the girls had survived death, and felt that they remained close to the family. When his wife Florence became pregnant again early in 1958, he confidently asserted that the two deceased sisters would be reborn as twins. Despite the opinion of her physician that she would have a single baby (he could only hear one fetal heartbeat), on October 4, 1958, Florence Pollock gave birth to twin girls.

John and Florence soon noticed that Jennifer, the younger twin, had two birthmarks that corresponded in location and size to two marks on Jacqueline's body. One was on her forehead, and matched a scar that persisted on Jacqueline's forehead after she had fallen and cut herself. The other was on her left side, and matched a similar congenital mark that had been on Jacqueline.

Both Gillian and Jennifer were a little slow in acquiring speech, not really speaking coherently until they were about three years old. Between the ages of three and six they made a few statements about the lives of their deceased sisters, and recognized some objects that their deceased sisters had owned. One incident concerned a couple of dolls that had been packed in a box and put in an attic after the deaths of Joanna and Jacqueline. Years later the box was opened and the dolls were given to Gillian and Jennifer, who identified them as "Mary" and "Susan," the names the dead girls had given them. Gillian claimed the one that had belonged to Joanna, and Jennifer claimed the one that had belonged to Jacqueline.

When the twins were less than a year old, the family had moved away from Hexham. The twins did not return there until their parents took them there on a trip when they were about four. According to their father, the twins spontaneously mentioned two places—a playground and a school—before these came into view. John Pollock did not believe that there was any normal way the girls could have acquired knowledge of the school or the park.

The behavior of the twins also corresponded in some respects with that of their deceased sisters. Jennifer was somewhat dependent on her older twin, Gillian, just as Jacqueline had been on her older sister, Joanna. Gillian gave the general impression of being more mature than Jennifer, and like Joanna, was very generous, and more interested in playacting with costumes than her sister.

Comments on the Case of the Pollock Twins

Stevenson first learned of this case through newspaper publicity it received in the spring of 1963, and met the family at their home in the fall of that year. Critics of the case have pointed out that since John Pollock believed in reincarnation, and that his deceased daughters would return to the family, he may very well have talked about the dead girls in front of the twins. When a journalist raised the objection that his prior belief in reincarnation may have biased his observations and reports, he replied that if he had *not* believed in reincarnation, he would not have noted and remembered the remarks and behaviors of his twin daughters that most other Western parents would have ignored or ridiculed.

Stevenson remained in touch with the Pollock family until 1985, and by that time Gillian and Jennifer had grown up to become normal young women. Long before that, they had completely forgotten the memories they had of other lives, and were mildly skeptical about whether or not reincarnation did occur. However, they did not challenge or deny the testimony of their parents, and willingly participated in a television program that was almost entirely devoted to their case.[7]

In these two cases the children did not repeat anything that their family members did not already know. But the following two cases are very different in this regard.

The Bishen Chand Case

Bishen Chand Kapoor was born in 1921, in Bareilly, India. As he gradually gained the power of speech, he began to speak of a previous life in Pilibhit, a town approximately fifty kilometers east of Bareilly. No one in Bishen's family knew anyone there.

But by the time Bishen Chand was five, he had mentioned many details of a previous life. He claimed that his name had been Laxmi Narain, and that he had an uncle named Har Narain. He also claimed that his father had been a wealthy landowner, and frequently expressed disdain for his present family's poverty. His father earned the meager salary of a clerk in the railway service, and could only support his family with difficulty. Bishen Chand reproached his father for his poverty, tore cotton clothes off and demanded silk ones, and complained that even the servants in his previous life would not touch the food they insisted he eat.

Once, when Bishen Chand was about five, his older sister caught him drinking brandy, which finally explained the diminishing supply of brandy that his family kept in the house for medicinal purposes. When this matter was discussed with him, he claimed that he was accustomed to drinking. On another occasion around this time, he recommended that his father acquire a mistress. He claimed to have had a mistress in his previous life, and boasted that he had once killed a man he had spotted coming out of her apartment. The influence of his wealthy family, he said, had enabled him to escape punishment.

Bishen Chand's father mentioned his son's statements to another man, who, in turn, informed K. K. Sahay, a prominent and respected attorney in Bareilly. Sahay became interested in the case, and visited Bishen Chand's family in the summer of 1926, writing down twenty-one statements the boy made about the life he claimed to remember. He persuaded Bishen Chand's father to undertake a visit to Pilibhit to verify the boy's statements, and on August 1, 1926 the two men took Bishen Chand and his older brother to Pilibhit.

Once in Pilibhit, Bishen Chand recognized various places and made additional statements about his previous life. A crowd of curious onlookers gathered, and someone produced an old photograph of Laxmi Narain and Har Narain. In the presence of the crowd Bishen Chand put his finger on the photograph of Har Narain and said "Here is Har Narain and here I," which seemed to establish his identity as Laxmi Narain, although Har Narain turned out to be his father, not his uncle.

Laxmi Narain had been the spoiled son of a wealthy landowner, who had died two years before Bishen Chand was born. After Har Narain had died when Laxmi was about eighteen, Laxmi had squandered the family fortune on high living and debauchery, although, like his father, he also seems to have been generous in donating his money to the needy. He had been involved with a prostitute who still lived in Pilibhit, and in a jealous rage had once killed a man he spotted coming out of her apartment. His family was influential enough to get the charges dropped, but he died of natural causes a few months later, at the age of thirty-two.

The attorney Sahay published his account of that remarkable day in the national newspaper *The Leader* in August 1926. According to this account, Bishen Chand recognized the house of Sander Lal, which he had previously described as having a green gate. Sahay verified that the gate was painted with a faded varnish, but was still green. He also recognized the house of Har Narain, which, much to his distress, had fallen into a state of disrepair and had been abandoned. He pointed out the courtyard where parties had been held, noted where a collapsed staircase had once stood, and pointed to where the women's quarters once existed. People in the crowd following the boy repeatedly asked him for the name of the prostitute he had associated with in the previous life. Bishen Chand reluctantly answered "Padma," which people in the crowd certified was correct.

When the boy was presented with a set of *tabla*—a pair of drums— he surprised his family by playing them skillfully, as Laxmi Narain had been fond of doing. His father said that Bishen had never even seen tabla before. The mother of Laxmi Narain was still living, and when the boy was brought to her she asked him a series of test questions that convinced her that he was her surviving son. The most dramatic example concerned some treasure that it was thought Har Narain had hid in his house before he died. When Laxmi's mother asked Bishen about this, he led the way to a room in the old house. After a subsequent search, the treasure was found in this room, and turned out to consist of gold coins.

Nearly all of Bishen Chand's statements that could be verified were correct. Of the twenty-one statements that Sahay had written down before verification was attempted, fourteen were subsequently verified. Six items were not verified, but most of these were thought to be almost certainly correct.[8] Only one item was wrong—the name of Har Narain was given correctly, but turned out to be Laxmi's father, not his uncle.

Bishen Chand claimed that Laxmi Narain had known how to speak Urdu, a variant of Hindi that civil servants in India at that time were required to use. As Laxmi Narain had worked in government service for a time, this does seem likely. Bishen's older brother, Bipan, said that when Bishen was a child he could read Urdu despite not receiving any instruction. Bishen's father told how Bishen unexpectedly used two Urdu words when he was a child: *masurate* instead of the Hindi word *zenana* ("women's quarters") and *kofal* instead of the Hindi word *tala* ("lock").

At any rate, following the first visit to Pilibhit at the age of five, Bishen established affectionate relations with Laxmi's mother, and after she moved to Bareilly he would visit her frequently. He also attempted to establish a relationship with Padma, although she quite naturally considered this inappropriate.

When Bishen was a child, he had a quick temper. As mentioned earlier, his childhood behavior was that of a rich spoiled young man: he would frequently boast of the murder he remembered committing, would rebuke his parents for their poverty, and would demand food and clothing that his parents could not afford. However, as he grew older, his attitude gradually changed. The memory of the murder persisted long after other memories of the previous life had faded. It gradually occurred to Bishen that perhaps he had been born into poverty because of the murder that Laxmi Narain had committed. He became a reformed person, and when Stevenson knew him in later life, he showed no trace of violent behavior. Remorse had replaced haughtiness; and Stevenson felt himself in the presence of a generous person of limited means, who had learned that material goods and carnal pleasures do not bring happiness.[9]

Comments on the Bishen Chand Case

In his detailed review of this case, Stevenson considers it to be of considerable significance. Numerous statements were written down by a respected attorney before verification was attempted, and many people who had personally known the previous personality were still alive to verify Bishen's claims. In addition, two skills were shown—playing the tablas and understanding Urdu—which Bishen apparently had no way of acquiring normally. As for the possibility of fraud, no financial gain was possible: it was well known that Laxmi Narain had squandered the family fortune, leaving the surviving members almost destitute, and unable to maintain the family home. Finally, can we reasonably suppose that a father would want his son to boast of a murder, and to scoff at his family's poverty?

The Case of Swarnlata Mishra

Swarnlata Mishra, daughter of Sri M. L. Mishra, was born on March 2, 1948. When she was three years old, her family lived in Panna, and one day her father took her with him on a trip 170 miles south. On the way back, as they passed through the city of Katni—about a hundred miles south of Panna—Swarnlata unexpectedly asked the driver of the truck to turn down a road toward "my house." The driver did not follow her request, of course. A little while later, when the group was taking tea in Katni, Swarnlata told her father that they could have much better tea at "her house" nearby. As puzzling as these statements were, Sri Mishra became even more puzzled when he learned that Swarnlata later told other children in the family further details about a previous life she claimed to remember in Katni, as part of a family named Pathak. At the time, the Mishra family did not know anyone by the name of Pathak in Katni.

Two years later, the Mishra family moved forty miles west to Chhatarpur. When she was about five, Swarnlata began performing unusual songs and dances, in a language incomprehensible to her parents. In 1958, when she was ten and had been talking about a previous life for about six years, Swarnlata met a woman from the area of Katni that she claimed to recognize from a previous life in that city. Sri Mishra was now able to confirm some of his daughter's statements, and began to take them more seriously. In March 1959, Sri H. N. Banerjee investigated the case, and wrote down nine statements that Swarnlata made about the Pathak residence in Katni before attempting verification. Stevenson investigated the case in 1961, and checked the details that Banerjee had reported.

Guided by Swarnlata's statements, Banerjee had found the Pathak residence, and confirmed the nine statements. He found that her statements corresponded closely with the life of Biya, daughter of a family called Pathak in Katni, and deceased wife of a man named Pandey. Biya had died in 1939, nine years before Swarnlata was born. Some of Swarnlata's statements—such as her description of the family house being only partly finished—were no longer true, but had been true twenty years earlier when Biya was living.

In the summer of 1959, members of the Pathak family and of Biya's marital family traveled to Chhatarpur to meet her. Without introductions, Swarnlata recognized all of them, called them by their correct name, and related personal incidents concerning them that Biya would have known. The Pathaks came to accept Swarnlata as Biya reborn. Shortly after these visits, Swarnlata and members of her family traveled to Katni and then to Maihar, where the deceased Biya had lived much of her married life and had died. In these towns she recognized additional people and places, and commented on the changes that had taken place since the death of Biya. On one instance, she recognized a friend of the Pathak family, and then correctly pointed out that the man did not wear spectacles when Biya knew him; on another occasion, she inquired about a parapet at the back of the Pathak residence in Katni, which had been removed since the death of Biya. All together her witnessed recognition of people amount to twenty, and despite several attempts to mislead her, she was never fooled.

As mentioned earlier, Swarnlata began performing songs and dances when she was about five, in a language that was incomprehensible to her parents. The language of the songs was identified as Bengali by Professor P. Pal, a native of Bengal. This seemed to present a problem: both Swarnlata and Biya spoke Hindi, and neither had learned Bengali. Swarnlata claimed that she had learned the songs and dances from a friend named Madhu, during a previous life in between the lives of Biya and Swarnlata. She stated that after her life as Biya, she was reborn as a girl named Kamlesh in Sylhet, lived to about nine, and was then reborn into the Mishra family. Although Stevenson could not identify a child whose life corresponded with the fragmentary information given by Swarnlata, he did think that her account of life in Sylhet contained several plausible features, such as details of geography. Perhaps of more importance, the people of Sylhet speak mostly Bengali. Although the name Kamlesh is unusual for a Bengali family, a non-Bengali speaker could, of course, learn a song from a Bengali friend. It should be noted that Swarnlata could not translate the words for her parents, and that Swarnlata's parents were certain that she had not had contact with Bengali-speaking persons from whom she could have learned the songs.* Although the songs had been recorded and played in certain films, Swarnlata's parents had not heard these songs before. Since female children in Asia are kept under close surveillance by their families, it seems very doubtful that Swarnlata could have learned these songs and dances without her parents' knowledge.

As mentioned, the Pathak family accepted Swarnlata as Biya reborn. Among members of her present family in Chhatarpur, Swarnlata behaved like a child, although she was somewhat more serious and mature than the average child her age. But among the Pathaks, she behaved like an older sister of men forty or more years her senior, who completely accepted her as their older sister returned. One of her brothers, Rajendra Pathak, stated that he had no convictions regarding reincarnation prior to Swarnlata's visit, which had completely changed his mind.

Swarnlata's behavior around Biya's children depended on who was present. If the parents or elders of her current family were around, she was reserved. But Murli Pandey reported that if Swarnlata was alone with him or her brother, she relaxed and treated them as a mother would treat her sons—despite the fact that he was thirty-five in 1961 and Swarnlata was twelve. He and his brother did not find this behavior inappropriate, as they, too, accepted her as Biya reborn. Like his uncle, Sri Murli Pandey also said that he did not believe in reincarnation until he met Swarnlata.

---

*Professor Pal made the following comment in his report on Swarnlata's songs: "Some of the words are blurred, modified, or changed by Swarnlata, though the sound, meter, and tune are maintained fairly intact, just as would happen to someone who does not understand English, but learns an English song sung by an English singer from his singing. The original singer might also have deviated from the original song at places as is sometimes done by singers" (Stevenson, *Twenty Cases Suggestive of Reincarnation*, 85).

As Swarnlata grew older she spoke less about a previous life as Biya, but unlike most other children who claim to remember previous lives, her memories did not seem to fade. Her parents had done nothing to suppress her statements, and as the years went by she remained close to both her own and the Pathak family.

TWO

Characteristics of Reincarnation Cases

As mentioned earlier, in the typical case the child begins speaking about a previous life between the ages of two and five. This seems to be true regardless of the culture into which the child is born. An analysis of 235 cases in India carried out by Stevenson and his associates showed that the average age at which the child began to speak about a previous life was thirty-eight months; a sample of seventy-five American cases also showed an average age of thirty-eight months, almost the same as cases from five other cultures.[1]

The children almost always stop talking about previous lives between the ages of five and eight, although some seem to preserve their memories into adulthood. However, with few exceptions, a child who claims to remember a previous life has little more than three years to communicate his memories to other persons, and he often has less.

Children who claim to remember a previous life are easily found in certain areas of the world. These include northern India, Sir Lanka, Burma, Thailand, Lebanon, Syria, West Africa, and the northwestern region of North America. Regions of the world in which the inhabitants believe in reincarnation tend to have a high density of reported cases, but it would be a mistake to assume that cases are not to be found in other regions. Such cases seem to occur in Western countries much more frequently than the average Westerner realizes, and Stevenson and his colleagues have investigated many cases in Europe and North America. They have also found some cases in Asia among groups of people who do not believe in reincarnation, such as the Christians of Lebanon and Sri Lanka.

However, cases of reincarnation are much more frequently reported in countries in which most of the population believes in reincarnation. One obvious explanation for this is simply that such cases are much more likely to be suppressed in cultures where the majority of people do not believe in reincarnation. Parents of the subject may think the child is talking nonsense or telling lies, and tell him or her to shut up. But Stevenson has also found that even in cultures with a strong belief in reincarnation, parents sometimes try to suppress a child's statements about a previous life. This seems particularly likely when the parents dislike what the child is saying, or dislike the behavior that corresponds with the child's statements.

In some cultures the case frequently begins with a prediction, usually by an elderly person, that he will be reborn into a particular family after he dies. Such cases occur rarely in most cultures, but Stevenson found in ten of forty-six Tlinget cases (22 percent) he investigated the previous personality had indicated his desire to be reborn into a particular family.

More common are dreams in which a deceased person appears to the dreamer and announces his desire or intention to be reborn into a particular family. The person having such a dream is usually an expectant mother, although the dream may also occur to her husband, a relative, or a friend. Announcing dreams are reported in all cultures, but more frequently among the Burmese, the Alevis of Turkey, and the tribes of northwestern North America. Stevenson realizes that such announcing dreams, occurring before birth or before conception, lessen the value of evidence that may appear later in the case, as it tends to bias the attitudes of the parents; it may also cause them to influence the child to adopt the behavior of the deceased person, even without being aware that they are doing so. Nevertheless, some announcing dreams do seem to indicate a determination of some individuals to be reborn into a particular family. Stevenson describes one such case in India:

> A daughter of the family was killed in an accident. Later, her mother had a dream in which the daughter seemed to announce her wish to be reborn to her. Rajani's mother, however, did not wish to have another child and induced an abortion. The deceased child appeared again in a dream and rebuked the mother for not letting her reincarnate. Eventually, the mother consented and gave birth to Rajani, who later remembered the life of her older sister.[2]

The amount of detail included in each child's statements seems to vary widely, with some remembering little of a previous life, and others, such as Swarnlata, claiming almost total recall. But in the majority of cases, the most vivid memories tend to concern events in the last year of the life of the person remembered. For instance, more than three-quarters claim to remember how the previous personality died. But the subject also usually remembers the name of the previous personality, and of some members of his circle of family and friends.

Most subjects have nothing at all to say about events between the death of the previous personality and their own birth. Their memories of anything in between are usually a complete blank. A few subjects, however, do claim to have memories of the intermediate period, and these take two forms: memories of terrestrial events and memories of a life in a discarnate realm.

In the first type, the subjects claim to have stayed near where the previous personality had lived and died, and to have monitored local events. One subject in Asia claimed that he watched his murderers drag his body into a field, and then stayed in a bamboo tree near the murder site for years, until he saw his present father pass by, and followed him to his new home. A Thai monk claimed to remember attending his own funeral, although he was invisible to the guests.[3]

The second type of memories is more common: subjects claim to remember spending the time between lives in another world. These subjects recall with nostalgia spending some time in a pleasant environment, and sometimes claim that they eventually met a sagelike man who befriended them, and advised them on their next rebirth.

On rare occasions, subjects will claim to remember a previous life as a nonhuman animal. Hindus and Buddhists believe that nonhuman animals reincarnate, and are capable of reincarnating as human beings. However, Stevenson has found that claimed memories of a previous life as a nonhuman animal are very rare in Asia and almost completely absent elsewhere: his investigations have uncovered fewer than thirty such cases. For obvious reasons, most of these claims are simply impossible to verify.

BEHAVIORAL SIMILARITIES

It must be stressed that many subjects who claim to remember a previous life show much more than mere memories of facts and events in the previous person's life: they also show forms of behavior that may be unusual in the child's family, but that correspond to traits the previous personality was known to have had.

These behavioral traits are in the form of fears, likes, interests, and skills. Stevenson has found that in about 50 percent of the cases in which the previous personality died violently, the subject shows a phobia corresponding to the way in which the previous personality died. If the previous personality died from drowning, the subject may show a fear of water; if from gunshot wounds, he or she may show a fear of firearms. Favoring (or having an aversion to) particular foods also seems common. It could be argued that many children share a particular fear, like, or interest; but many of the children in Stevenson's cases show a *cluster* of behaviors that set them apart from their family, but which characterized the person the child claims to have been. Ma Tin Aung Myo, a girl in Burma, claimed to have been a Japanese soldier stationed in Burma who was killed after being strafed by an enemy airplane. As such, she showed masculine traits, had a phobia of airplanes, played at being a soldier, and longed for Japan.[4] Bishen Chand disliked the food his family insisted he eat, complained about having to wear cotton clothes, showed a fondness for alcohol and meat, and generally behaved like a spoiled and arrogant young man. These behaviors often persist long after the subject has forgotten most or all of the previous memories. Bishen Chand, for instance, continued to eat meat whenever he was away from his vegetarian family long after he had almost completely forgotten the life of Laxmi Narain.

Children who claim to have lived a previous life as an adult often seem to their elders to be more mature than other children their own age. Some of these children adopt an attitude of condescension toward other children, and even toward some adults. Their parents may discover that they can trust these children with greater responsibility at an earlier age than they can with their other children.

Most of the children who claim to have been a member of the opposite sex in a previous life will show, in varying degrees, habits of dressing and manners of play appropriate for the sex of the person whose life they claim to remember. The Burmese girl Ma Tin Aung Myo is a rather extreme example: even though she was born a girl, she continued to insist that she was a Japanese man, and dressed as a man into adulthood.

FACTORS INFLUENCING REINCARNATION

Time between Death and Rebirth

The interval between the previous personality's death and the subject's birth is usually less than three years. In 616 cases from ten different cultures, Stevenson found that the median interval was fifteen months, although Stevenson says that in the cases he has examined, the intermission length varies from a few hours to more than twenty years.[5]

Incidence of Violence

In several cultures, people believe that a violent death leads to a more rapid reincarnation, and Stevenson's data supports this idea. In an analysis of cases in both North America and India, there was a statistically significant shorter interval between death and presumed rebirth in those cases in which the previous personality had died a violent death.[6]

In fact, one of the most prominent features of Stevenson's cases is the high incidence of violent death among the previous personalities. In 725 cases from six different cultures, Stevenson and his colleagues found that 61 percent of subjects remembered lives that ended violently.[7] This incidence far exceeds the rate of violent death in the countries in which these cases occurred.

Unfinished Business

Another prominent feature of Stevenson's cases seems to be a sense of unfinished business in the lives of most of the previous personalities— even of the minority who died a natural death. Considering the majority of his cases, Stevenson writes:

> [W]e can see that . . . their lives ended in a state of incompleteness. At the time of death they might all, for different reasons, have felt entitled to a longer life than the one they had had, and this in turn might have generated a craving for rebirth, perhaps leading to a quicker reincarnation than that among persons who died replete with life, so to speak, and at its natural end.[8]

Karma

Finally, for many people the concept of reincarnation is linked with the Hindu and Buddhist concept of karma, according to which our conduct in one life determines the circumstances we will find in a subsequent incarnation, although not necessarily the incarnation immediately following the current life. The idea of retributive karma is mostly peculiar to Hindu and Buddhist cultures, although several other cultures with a belief in reincarnation do contain the belief that there may be some causal links between lives. However, Stevenson writes:

In the cases that I have investigated, I have found no evidence of the effects of moral conduct in one life on the external circumstances of another. When I examine the cases that include the feature of a marked difference in socioeconomic status between the families concerned, I can discern no pattern indicating that the vicious have been demoted in this respect and the virtuous promoted.[9]

Stevenson has found only a few hints of retributive karma, such as the case of Bishen Chand, who came to believe that his present life of poverty was due to his behavior in a previous life. However, despite the paucity of evidence, Stevenson has concluded:

Although the cases provide no evidence for a process like retributive karma, this does not mean that conduct in one life cannot have effects in another. Such effects, however, would not occur *externally* in the material conditions of successive lives, but *internally* in the joys and sorrows experienced. In this respect—and in it alone, I think—the cases provide hope for improvement in ourselves from one life to another. The subjects frequently demonstrate interests, aptitudes, and attitudes corresponding to those of the persons whose lives they remember. These similarities occur not only in matters of vocation but also in behavior toward other persons, that is, in the sphere of moral conduct. One child counts every rupee he can grasp, like the acquisitive businessman whose life he remembers; but another gives generously to beggars, just as the pious woman whose life she remembers did. One young boy aims a stick at passing policemen, as if to shoot them, as did the bandit whose life he remembers; but another solicitously offers medical help to his playmates in the manner of the doctor whose life he remembers.

The children just mentioned, however, did not all remain set in the attitudes of the previous lives, and I have had the pleasure of hearing about, and occasionally observing, the development of different habits in some of them. In these evolutions we see the effect of new environments perhaps; but I think we also see the inner growth of personalities, accomplished only by the self working on itself. There is a deep truth in a remark made by Friar Giles, one of St. Francis of Assisi's close companions: "Everything that a man doeth, good or evil, he doeth to himself." There is then—if we judge by the evidence of the cases—no external judge of our conduct and no being who shifts us from life to life according to our deserts. If this world is (in Keats's phrase) "a vale of soul-making," we are the makers of our own souls.[10]

THREE

Alternative Explanations for Reincarnation Evidence

Several explanations for these reports, which do not involve reincarnation, have been proposed. Before we deal with these, let us first address a commonly proposed objection to the very idea of reincarnation.

POPULATION INCREASE AND REINCARNATION

Some have objected to the idea of reincarnation by noting that the world's population has increased from roughly 5 million in 8000 BCE to its present level of roughly 5 billion. It is argued that there just do not seem to be enough human minds to account for the explosion in the world's human population.

Of course, this argument is based on the assumption that the number of persons there are or can be is somehow fixed or limited, or that the duration between incarnations is fixed. However, there are other possibilities that are consistent with the population increase. One possibility, of course, is that minds presently incarnated in human bodies have been promoted from previous lives in nonhuman bodies. Another is that the interval between lives has not remained fixed, but has fluctuated. There may have been periods in which many discarnate minds were waiting for an opportunity for a terrestrial incarnation, or to perhaps avoid one. The concept of reincarnation does not, in and of itself, imply any particular assumptions regarding the number of minds available, what sorts of bodies they may inhabit, or the length of the interval between incarnations. The objection based on the fact that the human population has increased carries no weight whatsoever.

FRAUD

A more serious objection to the evidence is fraud on the part of participants in the cases. Critics point to cases in which the child claims to remember a previous life in more prosperous circumstances, and raise the possibility of fraud, with potential financial gain as the motive.

Stevenson does not deny that fraudulent cases may in fact occur: he has uncovered one such case himself in India that was definitely a hoax (perpetrated by the subject), and has learned of two other faked cases—one in Israel and one in Lebanon.[1] But critics point out that perhaps Stevenson's naïveté and sloppy methodology account for the fact that he has failed to uncover evidence of fraud in the other cases in which there is an obvious disparity of wealth between the present circumstances of the subject and the previous life he or she claims to remember.

However, there are several reasons to question this simple interpretation of the evidence. First of all, it is important to remember that even some of Stevenson's critics admire his research methods.[2] Anthropologist P. K. Bock, past chairman of the of the Anthropology Department at the University of New Mexico and former editor of the *Journal of Anthropological Research,* reviewed Stevenson's work and wrote that Stevenson "has had to find ways to verify interview data that many readers would accept if the topic were less controversial."[3]

Second, it is also important to remember that Stevenson's results have been replicated by others. Stevenson is sometimes portrayed as a lone fanatic, but this is simply misleading. We have already seen that the Bishen Chand case was first investigated by local attorney K. K. Sahay, and the Swarnlata Mishra case was first investigated by Sri H. N. Banerjee. More recently, anthropologist Antonia Mills studied ten new cases in northern India and concluded that "an independent investigator, using Stevenson's methods of investigation, finds comparable results. Some aspects of these cases cannot be explained by normal means. I found no evidence that the cases I studied are the result of fraud."[4] Mills later joined psychologists Erlendur Haraldsson and Jurgen Keil in another replication study of 123 cases in Burma, Thailand, Turkey, Sri Lanka, and India, which concluded, "Some children identify themselves with a person about whom they have no normal way of knowing. In these cases, the children apparently exhibit knowledge and behavior appropriate to that person."[5]

Third, the hypothesis of fraud for material gain can hardly account for the many cases in which the subject remembers a life in *poorer* circumstances. Differences in wealth between the subject and the previous personality are most apparent in countries such as Sri Lanka and India, in which widespread variation in wealth can easily be found. Yet in thirty of the forty cases Stevenson studied in Sri Lanka, there was no clear difference in the circumstances of the two families. In the ten cases in which there was a distinct difference, seven found the previous person in better circumstances, and three in worse.*[6]

However, in India Stevenson found that two-thirds claim to recall lives in better conditions, and one-third in worse conditions.[7] A replication study by Satwant Pasricha found that 58 percent of Indian subjects reported lives in better circumstances, and another study by David Barker and Satwant Pasricha found that only 53 percent claimed to recall a more prosperous previous life.[8] And where a difference was reported, the difference was often slight. So, while there does seem to be a tendency for Indian subjects to recall a previous life in more prosperous circumstances, this is by no means always the

---

*Stevenson writes: "One child of rather prosperous parents recalled a life in a lower class family of definitely inferior, almost squalid circumstances. And another child born in a family of well-to-do, well-educated professional persons remembered a life as a child in a peasant family living at a level of bare subsistence in a village not far from where she was born" ("Characteristics of Cases of the Reincarnation Type in Ceylon," 34–35).

case, and the actual percentage may be even less than the two-thirds Stevenson reports.

Fourth, it is also important to remember that a child, or his family, does not necessarily benefit from claiming to remember a life in more prosperous circumstances. A child in India who does so will be judged to have done something sinful in the previous life that earned the demotion. Subjects may also cause trouble for themselves by complaining about their family's poverty, refusing to eat food they are given, and so forth. We have already seen that, in the Bishen Chand case, no financial gain was possible, as it was well known that the previous personality had squandered the family fortune, leaving the surviving members almost destitute. And although Swarnlata Mishra also fondly recalled living in more prosperous conditions, she did not struggle to return to the Pathak family. Her father also seems to have declined offers of financial aid from the Pathaks.[9]

Finally, even in cases in which a motive for fraud can be seen to exist, this in and of itself cannot explain how a child came to know intimate details of a deceased stranger's life. Opportunity as well as motive must be established in order to make a solid case for fraud. In connection with this, Stevenson concedes that he may have been the victim of a hoax on occasion; but he remains confident that this may only have happened rarely, if ever, because of the circumstances of the people among whom these cases are usually found.

> The average villager in Asia and Africa does not have time to devise and perpetrate a hoax. He sometimes begrudges the time we take for our interviews; a hoax and its related cover-up would take far longer. One can see no profit in money from a case and usually none, or only the slightest, in local fame. Moreover, with the multiple interviews that I usually conduct, a fraud would require the cooperation of numerous witnesses, any one of whom might forget his rehearsed lines or defect from the other conspirators.[10]

CULTURAL FANTASY

The most popular rival to the reincarnation interpretation of Stevenson's cases has been the hypothesis that all such cases can be explained in terms of culturally conditioned fantasies, combined with unconscious distortions of memories regarding what the child actually said. Several writers have stated this hypothesis in one form or another, but Dr. Eugene Brody's statement has probably been the most concise.

Brody, a physician, is content to rule out fraud, praising Stevenson's work as "meticulous," and writing that "it seems to me unlikely that the complex effort necessary to construct a fraudulent picture, or the rewards from so doing, have occurred with sufficient frequency to account for the bulk of the observations."[11] Brody is confident that Stevenson has established that we are dealing with a real phenomenon, but thinks that the claimed memories of a previous life can be accounted for by normally transmitted information. He admits that the exhibition of skills, interests, and habits of the previous personality cannot be a consequence of the normally transmitted information, but writes

> The problem here, if fraud is discounted, would either be one of parental interpretation and reporting of the behavior, or reorganization of both the subject's and parents' perceptions with increasing information about the other family. It is not impossible, either, that some shred of information about similar characteristics in another recently deceased person or his family—reinforced by cultural expectations—could serve as an organizing event. In this instance, the child's odd behavior would be more apt to be perceived as evidence of reincarnation. More important, the "previous" family could actually be unwittingly selected by the immediate family to fit the child's behavior patterns and statements.[12]

Brody himself considers these proposed explanations far-fetched and speculative, but has advanced them largely because of what he perceives as the difficulties of reconciling reincarnation with the accepted body of scientific knowledge. "The problem lies less in the quality of the data Stevenson adduces to support his point," he says, "than in the body of knowledge and theory which must be abandoned or radically modified in order to accept it. . . . [P]aranormal phenomena in general and the theory of reincarnation are intrinsically unacceptable—there is no way to make them compatible with the total accumulated body of scientific knowledge."[13]

Unfortunately, Brody does not specify in detail just what scientific knowledge "must be abandoned or radically modified" in order to accept reincarnation as an explanation of Stevenson's data. The only specific difficulty that he mentions is with Stevenson's statement that "memories may exist in the brain and in a 'somewhere else' that may endure after physical death."[14] Brody appears to believe that the idea that memories are stored in the brain is part of the accumulated body of scientific knowledge, and that reincarnation is therefore unacceptable because it would imply that memories can exist apart from a brain. However, as we saw in chapter 5 of my previous book, *Science and the Near-Death Experience,* we do not "know" that memories are stored in the brain. The idea that memories are stored in the brain is only an *assumption* that follows from the philosophy of materialism. All surgical attempts to localize memory traces in the brain have failed, leading one researcher to the untestable conclusion that "memory seems to be both everywhere and nowhere in particular." That researcher published his findings *fourteen years* before Brody wrote his critique of reincarnation. A testable—and therefore scientific—biologist's theory of how memories are stored outside the brain was also outlined. Great pains were taken in this chapter to show that there is nothing intrinsically incompatible between the facts and theories of modern science and the idea that memories may survive the death of the brain. This issue is purely one for the testimony of the facts to settle. Neither Brody nor any other critic has succeeded in specifying the precise nature of the incompatibility between reincarnation and modern science. Until they do so, the claim that the idea of reincarnation is somehow "intrinsically unacceptable" remains no more than an empty piece of rhetoric.

However, despite the spurious nature of Brody's rationale, the cultural fantasy hypothesis *is* a viable counterexplanation for Stevenson's data. Stevenson himself considers a version of this hypothesis to be the most serious objection to the reincarnation interpretation of his data. Brody's case is for "culturally influenced unconscious parental selection" of a previous personality as an alternative to reincarnation. Stevenson lays greater emphasis on *paramnesia,* which is the technical term for distortions and inaccuracies in the informants' memories.

> To understand how paramnesia may occur . . . we need to consider again a child's first utterances about a previous life that he seems to remember. Let us suppose that his parents, hearing him make a few statements, begin to give them a coherence that they may not have had. They think of the sort of person whom the child might be talking. Then they start searching for such a person. They find a family having a deceased member whose life seems to correspond to the child's statements. They explain to this family what their child has been saying about the previous life. The second family agrees that the child's statements might refer to the deceased member of their family. The two families exchange detailed information about the deceased person and about what the child has been saying. From enthusiasm and carelessness, they may then credit the child with having stated numerous details about the identified deceased person, when, in fact, he said very little, and perhaps nothing specific, before the two families met. In this way, a myth of what the child had said might develop and come to be accepted by both the families.[15]

Problems with the Cultural-Fantasy Hypothesis

There is a good deal of data that does not fit very well with the cultural-fantasy hypothesis. In many cases the families lived far apart and had no contact before the case developed. Contact came about because of claims by the child, and not before. Yet in many of these cases the child talked about the previous life in considerable detail for several years before a meeting occurred between the families. Such repetition would tend to fix what the child said firmly in the minds of his or her listeners, making the case for memory distortions more difficult.

The cultural-fantasy hypothesis also requires the parents of the subject to *want* to find evidence that their child has reincarnated, and, in fact, this is often the case. But in many other cases, the families concerned are either indifferent to the child's claims, or adopt a hostile attitude toward them. They may worry about losing the child to another family; may dislike what the child is saying about his current family's living standards; and may worry that verification of the child's statements will only encourage behavior in the child that the parents find unattractive or inappropriate. Such people would not actively seek to identify a deceased individual whose life matches the child's statements. On the other hand, the members of the previous personality's family may also not wish to endorse the case, particularly if they are wealthy and wary of being taken in by a hoax. For all these reasons, the adults in these cases would tend to minimize, not exaggerate, the accuracy of the child's statements.

The cultural-fantasy hypothesis also has difficulty explaining cases with similar features in places where reincarnation is a foreign concept, such as Europe and the United States. Stevenson has found numerous cases in Europe and the United States, and about the latter has written:

> Some American cases of this type occur in families already believing in reincarnation, but many others do not. In these families the child's statements about a previous life are often puzzling and even alarming to his or her parents. The child is sometimes involved in conflict over the apparent memories with members of his or her family. In turn, the family members immediately involved often fear that other members of the family or other persons in the community will consider the child abnormal.[16]

It is difficult to see how culturally influenced fantasy could play any role in such cases.

Cultural fantasy also has difficulty explaining birth marks on the child corresponding with marks or wounds that were on the body of the deceased previous personality, especially when the subject and the previous personality were not related, and when the subject's family had no contact with the previous person's family before the case developed. The only way around this difficulty is to argue that the subject's family searched for a deceased individual who had wounds resembling birth-marks on their child, and on these birthmarks built their case.

Another problem with this hypothesis is that the details of cases do not always conform to the beliefs of the culture in which they appear. It is true that the characteristics of cases often *do* conform to the beliefs of their culture: for instance, sex-change cases are only found with extreme rarity in cultures in which it is believed to be impossible to change sex between lives. However, several other common beliefs are usually *not* reflected in the cases. The Hindus and Buddhists believe in the pos-sibility of nonhuman animals reincarnating as humans, but memories of previous lives as nonhuman animals are only rarely reported, even among Hindus and Buddhists. And as mentioned earlier, evidence of karma—at least in the narrow sense of retribution in the present life for misdeeds in the previous one—is also scarce. If past-life memory cases are only fantasies derived from cultural beliefs, we should expect to find such important cultural beliefs more often reflected in cases.

Also, several features of reincarnation cases occur universally, inde-pendent of cultural beliefs. Everywhere such cases are found, subjects begin mentioning memories of a previous life at a very early age, between two and five; and everywhere such cases are found subjects nearly always stop talking about previous lives a few years later, between ages five and eight. In almost every culture, male subjects outnumber female subjects, and the proportion of previous personalities who died violent deaths greatly exceeds the incidence of violent death in the culture.

It is worth noting that the fact that we find cultural variation in some of the characteristics of the cases does not, in and of itself, necessarily imply that the cases can be explained as cultural fantasy. This point was made clearly by James Matlock, who

> proposes that reincarnation be thought of in psychological rather than mechanical terms. Perhaps the dying person has some (albeit usually unconscious) control over the process. If one believed firmly that one could not change sex between lives, one might not be inclined to try. If one believed that one ought to be reborn in one's family, that is where one might chose to go. If one believed that the period before one's next life ought to be of a certain length, one might strive to make it as close to this length as possible. The Tlingit and other Northwest Coast tribes believe they have control over the process, and some of their cases suggest that they do in fact have such control. Control is also suggested in those cases in which subjects claim to recall having chosen their parents in the interval between lives. . . . Reincarnation may be a natural process; we may not have control over the process as such, but merely over some aspects of its operation.[17]

Finally, cultural fantasy cannot explain those cases, such as those of Bishen Chand and Swarnlata Mishra, in which written records were made of what the child said *before* the child's statements were verified. In these cases—assuming the absence of a conspiracy of fraud—we know what the child said before the families met. Such cases are admittedly only a small fraction of the total: one percent, or 24 in number at last count.[18] But their relatively small number does not by itself detract from their evidential value.

FOUR

The Objections
of Paul Edwards

Paul Edwards, a philosopher of materialism has probably written more material criticizing the idea of reincarnation than anyone. His most recent work on the subject is a book-length critique of the idea of reincarnation in general—but the writer most frequently criticized in the book is, not surprisingly, Stevenson.

Edwards lays great stress on what he calls "the initial presumption against reincarnation." By this he means that, regardless of the evidence, the very *idea* of reincarnation involves a set of assumptions that are just too preposterous for a rational person to take seriously.

In his own words,

A believer in reincarnation is committed to a host of collateral assumptions the most important of which I will now enumerate. When a human being dies he continues to exist not on the earth but in a region we know not where as a "pure" disembodied mind or else as an astral or some other kind of "non-physical" body; and although deprived of his brain he retains memories of life on earth as well as some of his characteristic skills and traits; after a period varying from a few months to hundreds of years, this pure mind or nonphysical body, which lacks not only a brain but also any physical sense-organs, picks out a suitable woman on earth as it mother in the next incarnation, invades this woman's womb at the moment of conception of a new embryo, and unites with it to form a full-fledged human being; although the person who died may have been an adult and indeed quite old, when he is reborn he begins a new life with the intellectual and emotional attitudes of a baby; finally, many of the people born in this way did not previously live on the earth but (depending on which version of reincarnation one subscribes to) in other planes or on other planets from which they migrate (invisibly of course), most of them preferring to enter the wombs of mothers in poor and over-populated countries where their lives are likely to be wretched. The collateral assumptions listed so far are implied by practically all forms of reincarnationism, but in Stevenson's case there is the additional implication that the memories and skills that the individual took over from the person who died and that are transmitted to the new regular body appear therefore a relatively short time during childhood to disappear forever after.

If Stevenson's reports are evidence for reincarnation they must also be evidence for the collateral assumptions just mentioned. These assumptions are surely fantastic if not indeed pure nonsense; and, even in the absence of a demonstration of specific flaws, a rational person will conclude either that Stevenson's reports are seriously defective or that his alleged facts can be explained without bringing in reincarnation. An acceptance of the collateral assumptions would, to borrow a phrase from Søren Kierkegaard, amount to the "crucifixion" of our intellect.[1]

Edwards then approvingly quotes Brody's statement about how the problem lies less with the quality of Stevenson's data, "than in the body of knowledge and theory which must be abandoned or radically modified in order to accept it," and sums up his "initial presumption" against reincarnation:

In simplified form, the question before a rational person can be stated in the following words: which is more likely—that there are astral bodies, that they invade the wombs of prospective mothers, and that the children can remember events from a previous life although the brains of the previous person have long been dead, or that Stevenson's children, their parents, or some of the other witnesses and informants are, intentionally or unintentionally, not telling the truth: that they are lying, or that their very fallible memories and powers of observations have led them to make false statements and bogus identifications.[2]

Philosopher Robert Almeder writes that Edwards's assertions "have the disturbing ring of dogmatic materialism committed to showing that, owing to the incredible nature of the reincarnationist thesis, the cases offered by Stevenson *must* be instances of fraud, or hoax, or cultural fabrication, or delusional imagining on the part of Stevenson himself."[3] If Stevenson's cases are seriously flawed, then of course the case for reincarnation collapses. But deciding in advance that memories, skill, and traits cannot survive the death of one brain and become associated with another, and then using this prejudgment to dismiss the evidence is just another example of a priori dogmatism. We do not know—in advance of examining the evidence—that consciousness and memories cannot exist in the absence of a brain. We know nothing of the sort. As Almeder writes in his thorough review of Edwards's work,

> In the absence of our being able to document that the case studies are flawed, what the cases do show is that human personality (whatever it is) survives death and, by implication, human consciousness can exist independently of brains, flourish for a period without a body as we know it, and reincarnate. So, the charge that all this is just too incredible for any rational person to believe is a blatant bit of question begging, unworthy of a reasoned response.[4]

The fact that we cannot specify a mechanism for the transfer of minds from one body to another does not, in and of itself, invalidate the evidence, nor does this, in and of itself, make the case for reincarnation less plausible. The fact that we could not specify how rocks could fall from the sky, or how continents could drift across the face of the earth, did not mean these phenomena were not real. No doubt had Edwards lived in an earlier era, he would have been one of those skeptics asking: What is more likely: that rocks fall from the sky, or that the individuals reporting these events are lying?

Edwards describes the main characteristics of Stevenson's child cases and writes that "if one reads his books and articles without knowing what the critics have to say, one can hardly fail to be impressed."[5] Edwards then turns his attention to some of the actual cases Stevenson has endorsed.

The first case he discusses did not involve a child, but rather an elderly Englishman named Edward Ryall who wrote a letter to the *Daily Express* in May 1970, in which he claimed to remember the life of a farmer in the seventeenth century named John Fletcher. After the letter came to Stevenson's attention, Stevenson paid Ryall two visits to his home, concluded that the case may be authentic, and wrote an introduction to Ryall's book *Second Time Round*. It should be noted that thirteen years before Paul Edwards's book appeared, Stevenson publicly modified his position on this case.*[6] But before mentioning this, Edwards writes, "Ryall was eventually exposed as either a hoaxer or the victim of delusions, or very possibly, a combination of the two. Credit for his exposure belongs to Michael Green, an architectural historian, . . . Renee Haynes, . . . and to Ian Wilson, whose *Mind Out of Time* . . . presented the full details of the story for the first time."[7]

Edwards points out that Haynes and Wilson found that while some of Ryall's recollections did check out, others did not. The most damaging of these was that the parish records of Weston Zoyland do not list

---

*The reason Stevenson changed his mind was that the names of John Fletcher and his family were not found in the parish and other records. The search had only just begun when Ryall's book was published in 1974.

a John Fletcher for the period of Ryall's story—for his marriage, for the baptism of his two sons, or for his death. However, Edwards writes, "What finally proved the undoing of Ryall's claims were the investigations of Michael Green." In Green's opinion, no farmhouse could have stood where Ryall located John Fletcher's farm in the late seventeenth century.

Although Stevenson has modified his position on the case, and concedes that the absence of parish records is damaging, he is not prepared to discard it altogether, pointing out, "Critics have focused on Ryall's mistakes without addressing the question of where he obtained all the more numerous *correct* details that he included in *Second Time Round*.[8] At the time Stevenson wrote this, he noted that he had been waiting eight years for Michael Green to provide the grounds for saying there could have been no farm where Ryall said Fletcher lived in the seventeenth century. In the meantime, Stevenson also noted that Dr. Robert Dunning, editor of the *Victoria History of Somerset,* has gone on record as stating that he thinks it quite possible that a farm did indeed exist at the site indicated by Ryall as that of Fletcher's farm.[9]

Stevenson has also pointed out several mistakes in the review of Haynes, and several writers—including Alan Gauld, James Matlock, and Stevenson—have pointed out numerous mistakes of fact and reasoning in Wilson's book.[10] Edwards, however, seems to have relied entirely on Wilson in his critique of the case, and even repeats Wilson's mistaken spelling of the title as *Second Time Around.*

At any rate, Edwards's persistent focus on this case is puzzling. Because it involves an adult, it is highly atypical of Stevenson's cases. Stevenson also expressed reservations about the case many years *before* Edwards did. Finally, as Matlock pointed out, "it is arguably the weakest case Stevenson has endorsed."[11]

One more example should serve to illustrate the quality of Edwards's criticisms of Stevenson's data. Edwards devotes an entire paragraph to the only case on record in which there is a clear disagreement between two researchers, both of whom conducted interviews with the witnesses.

The case concerns an East Indian boy named Rakesh Gaur, who claimed to remember a previous life as a carpenter in the city of Tonk. Researchers Satwant Pasricha and David Barker investigated the case together shortly after learning of it in a newspaper, and came to different conclusions regarding the best interpretation of the case. Although Barker conceded that Rakesh may have shown some paranormal knowledge about the previous person's life, Barker interpreted the case "largely as a product of Indian social psychology and the widespread belief in the possibility of remembering a previous life." Pasricha disagreed, thinking that the case is best explained as *either* due to extrasensory perception or memories of a previous life. These differing opinions were carefully presented in a jointly written paper, consisting of three parts. In the first part, the authors summarized the facts of the case that they both agreed on, and the other two parts contain their separately written evaluations.

Edwards mentions only the barest details of the case, and writes, "Anybody sufficiently interested should read all three parts of the article. I have no doubt that, unless one is already a passionate believer in reincarnation, one will find Barker's conclusion vastly more reasonable. I should add that Pasricha strikes me as a person of truly staggering credulity . . ."[12]

The Case of Rakesh Gaur

Both researchers agreed on the key facts of the case. Rakesh Gaur was born on March 15, 1969, into a family of the Brahmin caste. When he was a little more than five years old, he began to tell his parents that in a previous life he had been a member of the carpenter caste who had lived in the Chhippa neighborhood of Tonk, a city about 225 kilometers northwest of the family's home in Kankroli. He said that he had been married to a woman named Keshar, and that he had died after having been electrocuted. Three informants told Pasricha and Barker that Rakesh had mentioned the name *Bithal Das* before the two families met, but three other informants said that he had not done so in their presence.

Several informants agreed that Rakesh had shown an interest in carpentry and repeatedly asked to be taken to Tonk. Although family friends urged Rakesh's father to take him to Tonk, S. N. Gaur did not appear to take his son's statements seriously, and hesitated to take the one-day trip.

In the summer of 1976 a bus driver from Tonk named Chhittarji stopped in Kankroli. Chhittarji said that Rakesh spontaneously recognized him and described several details of their friendship in Tonk. The bus driver was so impressed that when he returned to Tonk he told the family of Bithal Das that he had been reborn in Kankroli. S. N. Gaur was also impressed by this chance encounter, and wrote to the Tonk Electricity Board to inquire if any employee belonging to the carpenter caste had been electrocuted. At the urging of friends, Gaur finally took Rakesh to Tonk in October 1976, to see if any of his son's assertions could be verified.

As their bus entered Tonk late in the afternoon, Rakesh pointed to an electricity pole and said that he had died while repairing it. At the post office, they encountered some difficulty in tracing the family of the person Rakesh was describing. A large crowd gradually formed, and an elderly person in the crowd recalled that a carpenter named Bithal Das had been accidentally electrocuted twenty-one years earlier, in 1955.

The crowd set off for the house of Bithal Das, but turned back before reaching it. On the way back, witnesses testified that Rakesh saw and recognized Bhanwar Lal, the son of Bithal Das. Bhanwar Lal was some distance off and leaving for Jaipur, and the two did not meet that evening. The widow of Bithal Das, a woman named Radha, was sent for. When they met at the post office, Radha cried most of the time. Close to midnight, S. N. Gaur concluded that he had seen and heard enough to confirm his son's statements, and they returned to Kankroli on a late-night bus.

Two days later Bhanwar Lal visited the Gaur family in Kankroli. When Bhanwar Lal asked Rakesh what his previous name had been, Rakesh answered "Arun," which Bhanwar Lal understandably took to be a mistake. But when Bhanwar asked Rakesh to describe his house,

Rakesh did so accurately, mentioning such details as the number of rooms, that his room was painted green and had two doors, and that in a table he had kept 1,500 rupees. The visit lasted only four hours, but was sufficient to convince Bhanwar Lal that Rakesh was the reincarnation of his father.

Bithal Das had been born in Tonk in or about 1922, and had worked as a carpenter. He also enjoyed electrical work and used to do it privately, but was never formally employed as an electrician. For most of his life, he seems to have been rather poor, but he did manage to save some money. Bithal Das died on August 15, 1955, during the rainy season. He was trying to clear a blocked drain with an iron rod when the rod accidentally touched a live electric wire, killing him instantly. He was about thirty-four years old when he died.

Tonk is a small city of about 70,000, located about 225 kilometers northeast of Kankroli. There is no regular exchange of goods or people between the two cities. Barker and Pasricha learned of this case about a month after Rakesh's visit to Tonk, and conducted interviews with the principal witnesses shortly afterward. In all, they conducted thirty-six interviews with twenty-four informants, and not a single informant indicated that there had been any kind of contact whatsoever between the two families before Rakesh began to speak of a previous life.

Comments on the Case of Rakesh Gaur

All in all, of the twenty-eight statements said to have been made before the families met, twenty-two were deemed correct, five proved wrong, and on one key point there is some uncertainty. The correct details corresponding with the life of Bithal Das included the home city of Tonk, membership in the carpentry caste, death by electrocution, the recognition of the bus driver and knowledge of their relationship, and the accurate details about the house of Bithal Das, including the fact that Bithal Das had kept 1,500 rupees in a table in his room. The mistakes were the name of the wife as Keshar (it was Radha); that Bithal Das had died while wiring a pole; that he had lived in the Chhippa neighborhood of Tonk; that he had lived in a house of clay (it had been mostly brick); and answering "Arun" when Bhanwar Lal asked Rakesh what his previous name had been.

The disagreement between Barker and Pasricha hinged primarily on whether or not Rakesh actually gave the name of Bithal Das before the first visit to Tonk. Three informants claimed that Rakesh did provide the name, and three others, including Bithal Das's son, said that he did not mention the name in their presence. Rakesh's father and the bus driver Chhittarji both claimed that Rakesh had spontaneously mentioned the name in their presence. Unfortunately, the only written record that could decisively settle the issue—the postcard that S. N. Gaur had sent to the Electricity Board in Tonk, asking if a carpenter had been electrocuted—had been thrown out. The postcard had been turned over to two clerks, named Phool Chand and Bhol Chand. They searched their records, found no employee of the Board who had been electrocuted, and threw the postcard away. When Barker and Pasricha interviewed the two men in November 1978, Phool Chand insisted that Bithal Das's name had been given in the postcard. He added that several employees of the Electricity Board knew of Bithal Das's death, but that he had not been an employee of the Board. Bhol Chand remembered the postcard and said that it had included the name of the person inquired about, but also said that he could not remember the name.

Barker considered the question of whether or not Rakesh had mentioned the name of Bithal Das the "most serious point of disagreement among the informants." The events of the first visit to Tonk suggested to him that Rakesh had not mentioned the name of Bithal Das before going to Tonk:

He and his father spent about six hours searching Tonk for his house in the previous life. It seems to me extremely unlikely that the boy would have been asked to do this if the name Bithal Das had been attached to his other statements from the moment of their arrival; the postmaster would have simply sent someone the 500 meters to

Bithal Das's house to tell a member of his family to come immediately. This is what eventually happened, but only hours later, after an elderly person in the large crowd thought of Bithal Das, whose wife was then brought to the post office.[13]

This, combined with the other mistakes in Rakesh's statements, led Barker to conclude:

I interpret the case of Rakesh Gaur largely as a product of Indian social psychology and the widespread belief in the possibility of remembering a previous life. As I reconstruct the case, Rakesh as a young child repeatedly made a few general statements about a "previous life." He was taken to Tonk in order to "confirm" these statements by leading his father to the family of his previous life. He could not do this because many of his statements and recognitions did not correspond to anyone known to have existed. After two or three hours of searching, a large crowd gathered. A person in the crowd thought of Bithal Das, a man who matched enough of Rakesh's statements to satisfy nearly everyone that Rakesh had been talking about this man from the beginning. From that moment Rakesh was provided with abundant clues for appropriate behavior, and Rakesh, an unusually intelligent and observant child, quickly learned to become Bithal Das. . . . Rakesh became the reincarnation of Bithal Das because he identified himself fully with Bithal Das's life and because other people supported him and rewarded him in this identification.[14]

However, although Barker did not interpret this particular case as evidence that a previous life can be recalled, he did think that there was "at least one instance of what might be called paranormal knowledge" on the part of Rakesh: his recognition of Chhittarji, and the fact that he managed to convince Chhittarji that he was indeed Bithal Das reborn. At any rate, Barker concluded:

I hope that as the importance of these cases is perceived by scientists, qualified investigators can begin before the two families meet. Had we been able to accompany Rakesh during his first visit to Tonk, we might have acquired stronger evidence that reincarnation actually occurs.[15]

Pasricha laid less emphasis on Rakesh's mistakes. Although she thought there were more mistakes and inconsistencies in this case than in other cases she had investigated, she also thought that some of them had a valid explanation. For instance, Bhanwar Lal had asked Rakesh what his name had been "before," and Rakesh had answered "Arun," which Bhanwar Lal understandably took to be a mistake. But Pasricha pointed out that *Arun* was a name that Rakesh had been given when he was younger. It seemed to Pasricha that Rakesh simply misinterpreted Bhanwar Lal's use of the word *before*.

Pasricha also conceded that three witnesses reported that Rakesh had not mentioned the name of Bithal Das in their presence before the journey to Tonk, but commented:

If informant A reports that the subject made a particular statement to him, but informant B says that the subject did not say the same thing in his presence, their testimonies are not discrepant unless both were referring to the same occasion when both were present. A subject may make one remark to one person, but not repeat this in the presence of another person on some other occasion.[16]

But if Rakesh had mentioned the name of Bithal Das before going to Tonk, why did it take his father and post office employees several hours to locate the correct family? Pasricha thought that there might be several likely explanations for the delay. Bithal Das had died about twenty years earlier, so young people would not know of him. Rakesh had also given the wrong neighborhood of residence, and had wrongly stated that he had been doing electrical wiring at the time of his death.

Pasricha felt that these mistakes by Rakesh may have put false scents on the trail. Also, the assistant postmaster at Tonk stated that during the search for a family matching Rakesh's statements, "One elderly carpenter said, 'Certainly there was a person of that name who used to work at the Electricity Board who died of electric shock.'"[17] Although the deceased person they were searching for did not, in fact, work for the Electricity Board, Pasricha considered this as some evidence that Rakesh or his father did mention the name of Bithal Das in Tonk.

Pasricha laid greater stress than Barker on the correct details Rakesh had mentioned. Pasricha pointed out that not only did Rakesh correctly identify the bus driver from Tonk, but he also recognized Bithal Das's son from a distance. Pasricha also pointed out that Bhanwar Lal said that when he asked Rakesh about the house, he had expected Rakesh to make only a simple statement about its structural quality. But Rakesh spontaneously went on to provide several correct details about the houses interior, including the detail that 1,500 rupees had been stored in a table in Bithal Das's green room. His son acknowledged as correct both the amount of money and its location inside a table in the green room. Pasricha later pointed out that a normal explanation for this requires us to assume either that Rakesh learned all these details during the single meeting with Bithal Das's widow in Tonk two days earlier, or that Bhanwar Lal grossly distorted what Rakesh had told him when interviewed a few weeks later. She wrote that "although they seem improbable, neither can be ruled out as impossible."[18]

Barker concluded that this case is best explained as cultural fantasy, with at least one element that may be an example of extrasensory perception. Pasricha disagreed with Barker's cultural-fantasy interpretation, but hesitated to consider the case solid evidence for reincarnation. Instead, she wrote, "It seems wiser to close this discussion with the expression of my belief that some paranormal process—not otherwise definable at present—should be considered the most likely source of the correct information that Rakesh showed about the life of Bithal Das."[19]

When Pasricha and Barker wrote their article in 1981, they wrote,

"We do not regard the investigation of this case as completed." Pasricha subsequently reexamined the case two years later. In their jointly written article, both Barker and Pasricha had noted that all the informants agreed that Rakesh said three things corresponding to Bithal Das's life: that he had belonged to the carpenter caste, that he had lived in Tonk, and that he had been electrocuted. The main point of disagreement was over whether or not it was likely Rakesh had mentioned the name of Bithal Das before the first visit to Tonk. Consequently, Pasricha set out to determine the odds that Rakesh's statements could have correctly applied to someone other that Bithal Das, even if Rakesh had never mentioned the name of Bithal Das before visiting Tonk.

Essentially, her method involved estimating the number of carpenters in Tonk who had died after being electrocuted during the fourteen years between 1955 (the year of Bithal Das's death) and 1969 (the year of Rakesh's birth). Using conservative assumptions regarding the number of deaths by electrocution and the total number of deaths in Tonk, she concluded that "there is a probability of less than 1 in 1,500 that Rakesh's statements could have correctly applied to someone other than Bithal Das."[20] She therefore felt confident that Barker's cultural-fantasy hypothesis could be rejected, whether or not Rakesh did or did not mention the name of Bithal Das before the first visit to Tonk. However, she still did not think that the case provided strong evidence for reincarnation.

I have only examined and described this case in detail in order to illustrate the shallowness and poor quality of Edwards's examination of the empirical evidence. Edwards writes, "The entire 1981 article is highly instructive because it clearly illustrates Chari's view that the kind of case investigated by Stevenson is a cultural artifact and nothing else."[21] But Edwards does not bother to mention that this is *not* one of Stevenson's cases—it was investigated directly only by Pasricha and Barker. Pasricha and Barker say that they reported on this case only because it was the case they studied most thoroughly together *without* Stevenson's participation. The case itself is not particularly impressive: the only record of Rakesh's statement written down before the families met was thrown out, Rakesh made an unusual number of errors, and there were several discrepancies in the accounts of the informants. One may wonder why Edwards would point to *this* case as indicating that "the kind of case investigated by Stevenson is a cultural artifact and nothing else." But it is consistent with his habit of focusing on the weakest cases while ignoring the strongest.

Closing Remarks

In closing, it may be interesting to note the manner in which Edwards refers to Stevenson in his book. When he first introduces Stevenson in any depth, Edwards refers to him as "an investigator and spokesman whose presentations deserve to be taken seriously. . . . It should be remarked that he is an excellent writer and that the presentation of his cases is always lucid, systematic, and extremely detailed. . . . I . . . wish to record that I have the highest regard for his honesty."[22]

However, three rambling chapters later, he refers to Stevenson as "a sincere, but deluded man," and to Stevenson's work as "absurd nonsense."[23] Later in the book he is even more effusive in his "praise," writing that "Stevenson evidently lives in a cloud-cuckoo land."[24]

However, insults aside, open-minded people who read Stevenson's book, *Children Who Remember Previous Lives,* will conclude that Stevenson is a much more sensible and coherent writer than Edwards. And despite the way Edwards describes reincarnation as absurd nonsense that no rational person could take seriously, he is oddly reluctant to publicly defend his views against those who live in a cloud-cuckoo land. His fellow philosopher, Robert Almeder at the University of Georgia, has written a good deal of material on the subject of reincarnation and has come to conclusions diametrically opposed to those of Edwards. In Almeder's words:

> I once invited Edwards to come here for a large stipend and defend his views publicly. He told me he had a sore back and would get back to us later. He never did. (personal communication, October 27, 2003)

FIVE

Reincarnation in Review

Reincarnation provides a rational and coherent explanation for the data from past-life memory cases. At this point, it would also appear that reincarnation provides the *best* explanation of the data. As with all empirical hypotheses, we cannot claim that reincarnation has been proven beyond all possible doubt; but the best cases have not been proven false. The competing explanations all have serious shortcomings, and—despite the dogmatic assertions of Edwards—they do not explain the data nearly as well.

Precisely *what* it is that reincarnates is difficult to say: we may call it a mind, a center of consciousness, or a soul, but more than that we cannot say at present. Precisely *how* reincarnation works is likewise a mystery. But the fact that we cannot specify the details of the process does not logically prevent us from concluding *that* reincarnation occurs, at least to some people. The fact that until recently men did not know how the sun shone does not imply that it did not shine.

Some skeptics say that reincarnation is not a scientific hypothesis. But it should be clear that the reincarnation hypothesis *can* be formulated as a scientific hypothesis; that is, one that is capable of being tested. The blanket statement "Reincarnation occurs" is obviously not capable of being disproved, for the simple reason that even in the complete absence of evidence it may possibly be true. But Stevenson and the other researchers do not formulate their hypothesis in this dogmatic manner. Instead, they propose reincarnation as the best explanation *for the data*. In astronomer Carl Sagan's words, it is the hypothesis "that young children sometimes report the details of a previous life, which upon checking turn out to be accurate and which they could not have known about in any other way than reincarnation."[1] Stated this way, it can be disproved as an explanation in any particular case whenever (1) the details of the children's reports do not turn out to be accurate, or (2) the details are accurate, but could have been known about by other means.

The reincarnation hypothesis predicts that cases of accurate past-life memories will sometimes be found. It is true, of course, that such cases cannot be produced *on demand*. But this is also true of home runs and earthquakes, and does not mean that home runs and earthquakes do not occur.

Finally, it should be pointed out that the reincarnation hypothesis does not stand in opposition to current biological and psychological explanations of personality. Past-life-memory theorists do not propose reincarnation as an alternative to heredity and environment, but as a *supplement* to them. Reincarnation is proposed as a third factor contributing to the formation of personality, in addition to heredity and environment.*

---

*It is worth mentioning that many genetic biologists are not at all impressed by the influence of heredity on personality. For instance, Paul Ehrlich and Marcus W. Feldman recently wrote: "Many other cases illuminate the failure of genes to 'control' behavior. The original Siamese twins, Chang and Eng, were joined for life by a narrow band of tissue connecting their chests. Despite their identical genomes, they had very different personalities. One was an alcoholic, the other sober; one was dominant, the other submissive. Equally fascinating is the story of the Dionne quintuplets, five genetically identical little girls who, in the 1930s, were essentially raised in a laboratory under the supervision of a psychologist. When the girls were only five, the psychologist wrote a book that expressed his astonishment at how different the little girls were—something confirmed by their very different life trajectories. One had epilepsy, the others did not; some died young, the others old; some married, others remained single; and so on. Similarly, the identical Marks triplets grew up with different sexual orientations, two straight and one gay; one of the two identical Ferez girls chose to change her sex with hormones and surgery and married a woman, while the other twin remained female and married a man" ("Genes, Environments, and Behaviors," 9–10).

DOES TELEPATHY OR ESP ACCOUNT FOR REINCARNATION EXPERIENCES?

There is only one remaining alternative explanation for these cases that does not involve reincarnation. Some critics of reincarnation accept the existence of extrasensory perception and object to the reincarnation interpretation on the grounds that such cases can be explained by the telepathic or clairvoyant abilities of the children. These critics assert that the children are unconsciously clairvoyant: that is, without being aware of their unusual powers, the children have knowledge of past events and the persons involved without having been told about them. These critics also assert that, for some reason, the child unconsciously identifies with a certain deceased individual, and then subconsciously impersonates that person.

But there are several things wrong with telepathy or clairvoyance as an explanation of past-life cases. First of all, the errors made by the subjects are far more consistent with the characteristics of memory than ESP. For instance, ESP cannot explain why subjects have difficulty recognizing persons or places that have changed since the death of the previous personality, and cannot explain why the subjects are unaware of changes in the previous personality's environment they have not yet seen.

Second, information acquired clairvoyantly or telepathically is not typically experienced as something remembered. Also, the best clairvoyants and telepaths make a predictable number of mistakes, but we have seen that Swarnlata and Bishen Chand made virtually no errors.

Third, the ESP hypothesis would predict that we would occasionally find more than one child claiming to remember the life of a certain deceased person, and making statements about the deceased person's life that, upon checking, turn out to be accurate. But we have not found cases with more than one child making such claims.

Fourth, while ESP can explain the acquisition of knowledge, it cannot explain the acquisition of skills requiring a great deal of practice. That is, ESP can explain knowing *that* something is true, but cannot explain knowing *how* to do something. But we have seen two cases in which the subjects exhibited skills that they did not have the opportunity to learn: Bishen Chand apparently knew how to skillfully play the tablas without being taught, and Swarnlata knew how to perform complicated songs and dances, in a language neither she nor her parents spoke.

Fifth, in most cases, the operation of ESP appears to be goal-directed, operating to satisfy some desire or need of the experient. But in many cases of the reincarnation type, we can find no plausible motive on the child's part to imitate the deceased person. On the contrary, the child's statements and behavior frequently cause the child trouble with his or her family.

Sixth, there is simply no evidence, apart from these cases, of young children having the ability to impersonate a person they have never met. As Almeder writes:

> Apart from the fact that there is no known evidence of children ever mistakenly identifying themselves with other people whom they have never met, the argument that these children successfully impersonate deceased people whom they mistakenly identify with is ad hoc in the extreme. After all, can anybody honestly believe that Swarnlata, an eight-year-old child, was so good at impersonating Biya that nobody in Biya's family (brother, sisters, father, mother, and husband) could detect it as a clever bit of impersonation? It seems very unlikely that she could have duped the whole family.[2]

Finally, the ad hoc nature of this explanation is apparent when we consider the fact that we have no evidence of ESP abilities in most of these children *apart* from their claimed memories of a previous life. Stevenson explains that the super-ESP hypothesis . . .

> does not adequately account for the fact that the subjects of cases of the reincarnation type show no evidence of having powers of ESP apart from the claimed memories of a previous life. It may reason-

ably be asked why a child with paranormal powers of this sort that would be required to obtain all the correct information that many of these children show would not manifest such powers in other situations or with regard to other persons besides the single deceased person whose life the subject claims to remember.[3]

PART II

Apparitions

Controversial data . . . tend to lay bare the decision process. They reveal, if you will, a scientist's "boggle threshold," beyond which he or she will accept no more. For many scientists the thought that there might be yet unknown forces operating in the universe is simply too much to accept. They feel that any normal explanation for allegedly paranormal events is preferable, regardless of how strong or weak the evidence to support it. For other scientists the possibility of unknown, "paranormal" forces presents no problem, but discarnate entities? Spirits? That is asking too much.

RICHARD BROUGHTON,
THE CONTROVERSIAL SCIENCE

If, like most contemporary Western philosophers and scientists, I were completely ignorant of, or blandly indifferent to these phenomena, I should, like them, leave the matter there. But I do not share their ignorance, and I am not content to emulate the ostrich.

C. D. BROAD,
LECTURES ON PSYCHICAL RESEARCH

I shall not commit the fashionable stupidity of regarding everything I cannot explain as a fraud.

CARL JUNG,
JUNG ON SYNCHRONICITY AND
THE PARANORMAL

SIX

Strange Visits

Reports of apparitions come from virtually all societies of which we have records. It is said that they are portrayed on Egyptian papyri, and St. Augustine wrote about them as familiar occurrences. Accounts presented as genuine also appear in classical literature.

Pliny the Younger tells the story of Athenodorus the philosopher, who one day heard that a house was going cheaply in Athens because it was haunted by the specter of an old man, described as skinny and dirty, with fetters on his legs and clanking chains on his wrists. Considering the house a curious bargain, the philosopher decided to rent it. The first night, as he sat reading a book, he first heard the chains, and then saw the figure. It beckoned him into the garden, and the philosopher followed. After pointing to a spot on the ground, the specter suddenly vanished. Athenodorus marked the spot with some grass and leaves, and on the next day had the local magistrates dig there. A skeleton in chains was found, and given a proper burial. From that time on, we are told, the haunting ceased.[1]

Ghost stories of this kind continued to be reported down through the centuries, but by the nineteenth century it was becoming unfashionable to admit believing them—even after personally experiencing the phenomena. Fearing ridicule, even people who had been personally convinced of the reality of apparitions often declined to testify for the benefit of the Society for Psychical Research. As the next account illustrates, this reluctance caused several researchers a great deal of frustration.

When Ernest Bennett was gathering material for his book *Apparitions and Haunted Houses,* he received a letter from the University of Leeds, describing how "Mr H," cycling home one night, spotted a strange lady walking along, wearing a crinoline-shaped ankle-length dress. Later, a friend told him that this apparition was well known to local residents, and the man gave Bennett the names of four local men who claimed to have seen her. However, try as he might, he could not get the men to attest to the story. Normally, Bennett did not include accounts that were not formally attested to by witnesses; but he included this one just to show how difficult it was to obtain corroboration for such stories out of fear of ridicule, even when witnesses were assured that their identities would not be disclosed. *Gegen Dummheit kampfen die Gotter vergebens!* he thundered: Against stupidity even the gods battle in vain.[2]

REPORTS FROM CHILDREN

Children have reported encounters with apparitions and, unlike their adult counterparts, typically show no reluctance to relate their story. They often also seem to show neither distress nor disbelief with regard to the experience. Karlis Osis and Erlendur Haraldsson tell of a seven-year-old boy dying of mastoid infection who was being rebellious, refusing to take his medicine. Then one day:

> The boy insisted that Uncle Charlie [a doctor] came, sat beside him and told him to take his medicine. He also told the boy that he would get well. The boy was very sure that Uncle Charlie had sat in the chair and told him these things. After this experience, the patient was cooperative. He was not excited, and he took the deceased doctor's "visit" as a matter of course. The next morning, the boy was much better—a dramatic change had occurred in his condition.[3]

This case is somewhat unusual, as it includes a report of spoken communication with the apparition. But it does illustrate a typical feature of apparition reports: unlike the misty, translucent figures of fiction, apparitions are typically reported as appearing completely lifelike, so much so that witnesses frequently report mistaking them for living persons. The following case, involving an Icelandic housewife who had lost her eight-year-old boy two years earlier, is much more typical of apparition reports.

> I was washing the wooden floor in our living room when I looked
> up a moment to pause. Then I saw him standing some distance
> away from me looking toward me. I looked for a while and did not
> immediately realize that he had died. I ran toward him saying, "My
> Beggi," but then he disappeared. He was dressed in the clothes he
> had on when he drowned. I saw him on two occasions, both times
> on the same spot. His grandmother also saw him once at her home.[4]

Occasionally, apparitions are seen at the same time by more than one person. In 1919, Horace Traubel, a close friend and biographer of the poet Walt Whitman, lay dying in a remote vacation lodge in Ontario owned by a Canadian mining family, the Denisons. Lieutenant-Colonel Musgrave was present at the deathbed, and gave the following account of what happened.

> [On September 6, 1919, two days before Traubel's death] about 3
> a.m. he grew perceptably weaker, breathing almost without visible
> movement, eyes closed and seemingly comatose. He stirred restlessly
> towards the further side of the bed, his lips moved, endeavoring to
> speak, I moved his head back, thinking he needed more air, but . . .
> his eyes remained riveted on a point some three feet above the bed.
> My eyes were at last drawn irresistibly to the same point in the dark-
> ness, as there was but a small shaded night lamp behind a curtain on
> the further side of the room. Slowly the point at which we were both
> looking grew gradually brighter, a light haze appeared, spread until

it assumed bodily form, and took the likeness of Walt Whitman, standing upright beside the bed, a rough tweed jacket on, an old felt hat upon his head, and his right hand in his pocket . . . he was gazing down at Traubel, a kindly . . . smile upon his face. He nodded twice as though reassuringly, [his] features quite distinct for at least a full minute . . . toward the end of his appearance, while Horace and I were gazing at him, [Whitman] moved closer to Horace, from the further side of the bed, [and] Horace . . . said, "There is Walt." At the same moment, Walt passed apparently through the bed towards me, and appeared to touch my hand, as though in farewell. I distinctly felt it, as though I had touched a low electric charge. He then smiled at Horace, and passed from sight.[5]

APPARITIONS OF ANIMALS

Apparitions of animals have also been reported, such as the following by Celia Green and Charles McCreery from their book, *Apparitions*.

In the beginning of the summer of 1884 we were sitting at dinner at home as usual, in the middle of the day. In the midst of the conversation I noticed my mother suddenly looking down at something beneath the table. I inquired whether she had dropped anything, and received the answer, "No, but I wonder how that cat can have gotten into the room?" Looking underneath the table, I was surprised to see a large white Angora cat beside my mother's chair. We both got up, and I opened the door to let the cat out. She marched round the table, went noiselessly out of the door, and when about half way down the passage turned round and faced us. For a short time she regularly stared at us with her green eyes, and then she dissolved away, like a mist, under our eyes.[6]

In Green and McCreery's study of apparitions, the great majority of animal apparitions were of dogs and cats. However, apparitions of a wide variety of other species were reported to them, such as apparitions of horses, a deer, and a tiger. The following case involves a rabbit.

> I had gone to bed and had slept for a couple of hours and had to get up to visit the bathroom. As I was about to leave the bedroom, the door of which opens inwards, I happened to see a fluffy white rabbit sitting at the foot of the door. I stood there for a couple of seconds to make sure of what I was seeing. I then bent down in an attempt to touch the back of the rabbit and it disappeared. I even found myself turning the light on and running my hand over the carpet where the rabbit had been sitting.[7]

Some apparitions are of a purely auditory nature, such as the following.

> For some fifteen years I owned a working Sheep Dog, which I had destroyed because he was suffering, due to old age. Two hours after his death I was sitting in the lounge after lunch when I heard distinctly the pad of his feet and his characteristic snuffling at the bottom of the door, sounds which I had heard hundreds of times before when he wanted to come into the room. I half rose from the chair to go and open the door, realized I was imagining things and sat down again.[8]

Although the previous case might be dismissed as an auditory hallucination, perhaps brought on by habit and sorrow, the following case is more difficult to explain in that manner. But whatever it is a case of, it is an extremely unusual report, since it involves much more than a mere sighting.

> Thirteen years ago, I was in the army, stationed in Germany, and coming home on leave by ship, and train, usually meant arriving home somewhere during the early hours of the morning. My parents

knew on which day I was arriving, and left the back door open. This meant going through a dark passage between the two houses . . . I had made good friends with the next-door neighbor's dog "Bobby," a large black mongrel. Before I went in the army, we had grown very fond of each other, and an outsider would have thought he was my dog—I would take him for walks every day without fail. I volunteered for the army to be a regular soldier, but my attachment to the dog was so great, that I almost didn't "join up." Nevertheless, I did, but don't mind admitting I suffered a lot of emotional upset over the dog.

On the night in question, I arrived home at about 2 a.m., and sure enough, as soon as I opened the side gate, "Bobby," who normally slept in a kennel outside the house, bounded up to me, and made a terrific fuss of me, nuzzling and licking my face. I stayed with him for some ten minutes or so, and then went indoors. There is no question in my mind, to this day, that I played with "Bobby" for that short time. I knew and loved him so well that there couldn't possibly be any mistake about his identity. As he left me, he disappeared out of sight into my neighbor's large dahlia bed, and that was the last I saw of him.

The following morning after an enjoyable reunion with my family, I made my usual visit to my neighbor, the dog's owner, who was a very great friend of ours. I told him about meeting Bobby the previous night, and remarked quite casually that he was out of his kennel (he was normally kept chained in). My neighbor was thunderstruck, and said, "Bobby died three months ago, and is buried in the middle of the dahlias."[9]

SEVEN

Characteristics and Theories of Apparitions

Reports of apparitions are not as uncommon as one might think. In 1975 Erlendur Haraldsson asked a representative sample of people in Iceland: "Have you ever perceived or felt the nearness of a deceased person?" Thirty-one percent of respondents replied in the affirmative.[1] In 1979 parapsychologist John Palmer surveyed the residents of Charlottesville, Virginia, and found that 17 percent of 622 respondents claimed to have had the impression of an apparition, and about three-quarters of these acknowledged more than one experience.[2]

Apparition reports are not necessarily visual; people may say the apparition was only heard, or somehow "sensed" as a presence. Palmer found that about half the reports seem to be visual: 44 percent, or 7.5 percent of the original sample. However, Haraldsson found that 67 percent of reports were visual,[3] and Green and McCreery's study found that 84 percent of experiences were primarily visual, with about a third of these cases also having an auditory component; only about 14 percent of their cases were entirely auditory.[4] In this chapter we will be primarily concerned with visual apparitions.

The duration of the reported experience is variable. In Green and McCreery's 1975 survey, about half considered their experience to have lasted less than one minute, while 20 percent estimated its duration to exceed five minutes.[5] Apparitions only rarely are reported to have been seen in gloomy or dark conditions. Haraldsson found that slightly more than half the experiences (52 percent) occurred either in daylight or full electric light, and only 10 percent occurred in darkness.[6]

As mentioned earlier, apparitions typically appear real and solid, so much so that they are frequently mistaken for actual living persons. Green and McCreery state that only 46 percent of their sample realized immediately they were experiencing an apparition; 18 percent realized this before the experience ended, 6 percent as it ended, and 31 percent only *after* it ended. In other words, *over half* did not immediately distinguish the apparition from a living person, and nearly a third thought they were seeing an ordinary person throughout the entire experience.[7]

There are several reasons for this perceived realism. Apparitions may cast a shadow, and be reflected in a mirror. They typically show awareness of their surroundings, avoiding furniture and people, and they may turn to follow a person's movements. Some are reported to speak, although this is not common; if the apparition does speak, there are usually only a few words. However, in other respects apparitions do not resemble ordinary living persons: they may appear and disappear in locked rooms; vanish while being watched or fade away in front of the percipient; pass through physical objects; and be visible to some people in a room, but not to others. Most attempts to touch an apparition are unsuccessful, but most who do report their hands simply passing through the figure. Only rarely do people report apparitions that are capable of being felt. Sometimes a feeling of cold is reported, especially when the figure is nearby. Typically, they leave behind no physical traces, such as footprints. At the end of the experience the figure usually vanishes instantly, although it may fade gradually or simply walk out of the room.

In Haraldsson's survey, most apparitions were of persons recognized by the respondents. Almost half, or 47 percent, of the apparitions were of deceased persons related to the experient; 24 percent were recognized as acquaintances; and the remaining 29 percent were complete strangers (some of whom were later identified).

A prominent characteristic of apparitions of the dead is the high frequency of persons who died violently. Haraldsson found that 30 percent of his Icelandic cases involved encounters with persons who had died violently, almost identical to the 28 percent frequency of violent death found among the nineteenth-century British cases of *Phantasms of the Living.*[8] Haraldsson also pointed out that the percentage of persons identified with apparitions who died violently is *4.6 times* the percentage of persons in Iceland who died violently over the same period (6.5 percent).[9]

TYPES OF APPARITIONS

Various types of apparitions have been reported, and the following categories are usually used to classify the cases.

Crisis Apparitions

In crisis cases, an apparition is perceived at a time the person represented is undergoing some sort of crisis. By convention, a case qualifies as a crisis case only if the crisis occurs within twelve hours before or after the person's apparition is perceived. Often the crisis is death, so the apparition is reported as having been seen shortly before or after the person's death. According to Alan Gauld, this is the most frequent type of *veridical* apparition, that is, the most frequent type of apparition that conveys information later verified as correct but not known to the experient at the time it was conveyed. In terms of all cases, though, crisis cases are in the minority.

Postmortem Apparitions

These cases involve an apparition of a person who has been dead for at least twelve hours before the experience. About two-thirds of recognized apparitions are of the dead.[10]

Apparitions of the Living

Apparitions are sometimes reported of people who turn out to have been very much alive at the time someone reported seeing an apparition in their form. They seem to occur when the agent is asleep or in a trancelike state, although there are a few cases on record of people trying, allegedly with success, to make an apparition of themselves appear to a friend.[11]

Hauntings

Ghosts are apparitions that are seen in the same vicinity over and over again, sometimes by the same person, and often by a number of different persons. They seem to show less awareness of their surroundings and of people than do other apparitions. Although they are frequently assumed to be deceased persons, their identity is often a mystery.

THEORIES OF APPARITIONS

The modern study of apparitions began with Edmund Gurney, Frederic Myers, and Frank Podmore in 1886. Since that time, three main categories of explanations have been advanced: the first is that apparitions can be explained as mistaken eyewitness testimony, ordinary hallucinations, or fraud. The second is that apparitions are telepathically induced hallucinations; and the third is that apparitions are, in some sense, physically or quasiphysically real. The first is the simple skeptical position: any apparition that is not simply a case of fraud or misperception is a purely subjective hallucination. Only the last two allow for the possibility that some discarnate agency is responsible for the apparition.

The Skeptical Theory

The simple skeptical position is probably the easiest to deal with. Back in 1886, Gurney, Myers, and Podmore, in their landmark book *Phantasms of the Living,* presented in great detail over 700 reports of apparitions. The three researchers tried very hard to exclude any cases that might be due to mistaken eyewitness identity, faulty memories, or fraud. They argued that their cases must be explained away in detail, and went on to describe the sheer number of improbable hypotheses that must be advanced if the best documented cases are to be explained away.

> We must . . . make suppositions as detailed as the evidence itself. We must suppose that some people have a way of dating their letters in indifference to the calendar, or making entries in their diaries on the wrong page and never discovering their error; . . . that when [a man] says that he is not subject to hallucinations of vision, it is through momentary forgetfulness of the fact that he has a spectral illusion once a week; that that when a wife interrupts a husband's slumbers with words of distress or alarm, it is only her fun, or a sudden morbid craving for undeserved sympathy; and when people assert that they were in good health, in good spirits, and wide awake, at a particular time which they had occasion to note, it is a safe conclusion that they were having a nightmare, or were the prostrate victims of nervous hypochondria. Every one of these improbabilities is, perhaps, a possibility; but as the narratives drive us from one desperate expedient to another, where time after time we are compelled to own that deliberate falsification is less unlikely than the assumptions we are making, and then again when we submit the theory of deliberate falsification to the cumulative test, and see what is involved in the supposition that hundreds of persons of established character, known to us for the most part and unknown to one another, have simultaneously formed a plot to deceive us—there comes a point where . . . reason rebels.[12]

One hundred years later, Henry Gordon, magician, newspaper columnist, and member of CSICOP, briefly reviewed the work of sociologist Ian Currie on apparitions, and wrote:

> I find one basic weakness in Currie's arguments: His "evidence" is based on personal anecdotes and eyewitness testimony. To accept

such evidence you have to agree that most people are reliable witnesses, that they have perfect memories, that they can trust the evidence of their senses. It's an illusion to believe this. There have been a great number of psychological studies done in the past few years on the subject of eyewitness testimony. It is flimsy. It is often unreliable. Apart from what these studies have revealed, it is also well known that eyewitness testimony has caused tragic errors to be made in some court cases.[13]

On this point, philosopher David Lorimer has written:

Recently the unreliability of human testimony has been the subject of psychological experiments in which a sequence of staged events suddenly takes place during a psychology lecture, and the students are asked to write a description. In many cases this proves to be inaccurate in its details, sometimes wildly so. The result of this is then used to justify a wholesale rejection of the validity of human testimony. But we do not take human testimony at its face value. The law has an elaborate procedure of cross-questioning of witnesses, whose accounts are expected to square with other facts pertinent to the case, including the alleged perpetrators' own description. If the testimony reveals a discrepancy, then this is followed up in turn, so that either a more comprehensive account is arrived at, or some part of the evidence or testimony is rejected. In the end there are generally a number of facts and testimonies which support a particular hypothesis as the most plausible account of the event, even if it is recognized that absolute certainty is ruled out.[14]

Yes, tragic errors have occurred in courtrooms because of mistaken eyewitness testimony. But this fact does not imply that *all* eyewitness testimony is seriously flawed, and that courts should therefore rule all such evidence inadmissible. Juries are only asked to decide based on guilt beyond *reasonable doubt,* not beyond all doubt, and wrongful convictions are frequently overturned on appeal.

It is important to remember that although eyewitness accounts of an event, actual or staged, may differ in detail, eyewitnesses may all agree *that the event took place.* That is, eyewitnesses may differ as to whether the assailant was wearing a blue shirt or a green one, whether he had red hair or brown, fired three shots or four, and so forth; yet they all may agree that a shooting occurred.

And just how reliable is eyewitness testimony in real-life situations? Almost all the studies indicating that eyewitness testimony is often flawed have involved staged events in psychology classrooms. Because of the unrealistic nature of staged events, the response of the judicial system to most psychological studies done on the subject of eyewitness testimony has been lukewarm.[15] Staged events cannot duplicate the seriousness of actual events, and in many of the studies the subjects are told beforehand that they are witnessing a contrived event. This problem can be avoided by deceiving observers, but this raises obvious ethical problems.

Acutely aware of the limitations of staged events, psychologists John Yuille and Judith Cutshall examined eyewitness accounts of an actual shooting that occurred on a city street in broad daylight, in full view of several witnesses. A thief had robbed a gun store, and the owner picked up a revolver and followed the thief into the street. At a distance of six feet, the thief fired two shots at the owner, who, after a slight pause, emptied his revolver in the thief's direction. Both men fell, but only the thief was mortally wounded.

Twenty-one witnesses to the shooting were interviewed by police. Five months later, Yuille and Cutshall interviewed thirteen of the fifteen principal witnesses, and compared their statements with the police reconstruction of the incident,* and with the statements the witnesses had given five months earlier. The statements given to the police were

---

*This reconstruction was done by combining the eyewitness reports with photographs of the scene, location of bloodstains, reports from ambulance attendants, and forensic evidence.

found to be highly accurate, and five months later, there was virtually no reduction in the level of accuracy. Yuille and Cutshall concluded

> We take issue with the essentially negative view of the eyewitness that has been consistently presented by most eyewitness researchers. . . . In the present research . . . a different picture emerges. Most of the witnesses in this case were highly accurate in their accounts, and this continued to be true 5 months after the event.[16]

But Gordon does not dismiss all accounts of apparitions as due only to mistaken eyewitness testimony. He thinks that many people who have reported seeing apparitions may have had a genuine experience—of sorts. Gordon writes that "the most common psychological explanation for seeing ghosts is that of hallucination." What about cases in which more than one person reports seeing an apparition at the same time? Here Gordon also has a ready answer: "The fact is, once again, that *studies have shown that collective hallucinations do take place*. And the power of suggestion is the explanation (emphasis added)."[17]

What studies? Gordon provides no references. In researching this chapter I combed through the entire *PsychInfo* database, from 1887 to the time of writing, and could find only one article on collective hallucinations. It appeared in the *Royal Naval Medical Service Journal* in 1942, and it described the experiences of the shipwrecked survivors of a torpedoed ship in Arctic waters. Out of the hundreds of men who managed to make it to rafts and lifeboats, only thirty-six survived, and two of these died shortly after being rescued. The men were without food and water for three days before help arrived. The mortality rate was so high, and the exhaustion of the men so great, that they were finally unable to jettison the dead.

The shipwrecked survivors told a horrific tale of hunger, thirst, bitter cold, and despair. By the third day, some of the men in the floats started to hallucinate. They claimed to see land, a dockyard, and ships on the horizon. Although some of the other men remained skeptical, others began to think they also saw these things. Most of the visions were seen on the horizon, at what seemed to be a distance of several miles, and no humans were seen. Most of the visions only lasted a few minutes, although some seemed to have lasted an hour or so. After each vision ceased, most of the men realized what they had seen was only an illusion, and their depression returned.

I found absolutely nothing in this single study that is in any way relevant to the vast majority of reports of apparitions. The author of the study, Surgeon Lieutenant-Commander E. W. Anderson, would almost certainly have agreed: he wrote, "It is hardly necessary to state that visual hallucinations in a setting of clear consciousness are rare, if indeed they ever occur. It is certain that in some of the cases described here consciousness was not always clear, and in some cases the subject was actually delirious."[18]

Anderson briefly mentions psychical research, and quickly adds that "the observations here contain little relevant to this discussion."[19] Indeed, it seems preposterous to argue that the hallucinations experienced by these desperate and miserable men—which seemed to spread to some of those around them by the power of suggestion—could throw any light whatsoever on most reports of collectively perceived apparitions. As Anderson concludes:

> Powerful affects, in this case, hope, expectation and trust in delivery set against a background of despair, and the imminence of death, in a series of small communities shut off from contact with the outer world, with no diversions, together with gradually increasing exhaustion, the result in part of the absence of food and drink and exposure to the rigours of the Arctic climate, which in turn influenced the state of consciousness in many if not all, and lastly the diminishing daylight and probably cloud formation, are the essential factors involved. The inevitable increase in the suggestibility of each individual needs no underlining, and no psychiatrist would, therefore, be surprised to hear of the occurrence of collective sense-deception in these circumstances.[20]

With mistaken eyewitness testimony and ordinary hallucinations eliminated from consideration, the simple skeptical position is left only with fraud as an explanation. As we will see, although fraud is always a possibility, in several cases it can be shown to be a very implausible explanation. Human testimony is certainly far from perfect. But it is important to remember that *all* knowledge not due to our own direct experience ultimately depends on the testimony of others. As we review several of the more impressive cases, it will quickly become apparent to the reader that the simple skeptical position can only be maintained by ignoring the objectionable evidence.

The Telepathic Theory

A more sophisticated theory of hallucinations was first advanced by Edmund Gurney, and was meant to explain how the appearance of some apparitions could convey information that later turns out to be accurate. Basically, Gurney contends that apparitions are telepathically induced hallucinations. According to Gurney's theory, if you perceive an apparition of someone you know, but in clothing or circumstances of which you could have no normal knowledge, then the information has been telepathically acquired, and dressed up in the form of an apparition. Collectively perceived apparitions were explained as telepathically shared hallucinations. One person would acquire the extrasensory information and then telepathically communicate the hallucinatory figure to other people present in a form of "contagious telepathy."

Gurney's theory was originally designed to explain crisis apparitions and apparitions of the living, but was extended to cover apparitions of the deceased by postulating impedances in the percipient's mind, which allowed an "arrived" communication to work its way into consciousness slowly. Gurney's theory does not necessarily preclude the possibility that the source of the telepathic hallucination is the deceased personality; but it does not necessarily point to it either. According to his theory, the only source could be the mind of the original percipient, who then "infects" those around him with his hallucination.

G. N. M. Tyrell, former president of the Society for Psychcial Reasearch, agreed with Gurney that apparitions were telepathic hallucinations, but thought Gurney's theory did not adequately explain collective sightings, in which different individuals did not merely see the same thing, but saw the figure as correct from their own perspective and distance. Tyrell proposed that the subconscious minds of the witnesses collaborated together to produce a hallucination that was appropriate for each observer, so that the figure is seen as though it were a real, physically present person. As in Gurney's theory, the mind of the person represented by the apparition is not necessarily involved.

Tyrell advanced his modification of Gurney's theory because he emphatically believed that apparitions could not be material objects. He stated the following differences between apparitions and physical objects:

1. Apparitions appear and disappear in locked rooms.
2. They vanish while being watched.
3. They sometimes become transparent and fade away.
4. They are often seen and heard by some of those present, but not all.
5. They disappear into walls and closed doors, and pass through physical objects.
6. People have put their hands through them, and have walked through them without encountering resistance.
7. They leave behind no physical traces.[21]

However, physicist-philosopher C. D. Broad was quick to note that some physical phenomena share a number of these properties. Gases and rainbows, for instance, have properties 2, 3, 4, and 7; and electromagnetic fields have properties 1, 5, 6, and 7.[22]

In its favor, the theory that apparitions are telepathic hallucinations does solve the problem that apparitions are almost always seen wearing clothes. This has long been seen as a stumbling block for the idea that apparitions are physically real: as one wit put it, "If ghosts have clothes, then clothes have ghosts." However, if apparitions are, in fact, physically real, then it seems unclear to me why the materialization of clothing should pose any greater problem than, say, the materialization of hair.

The Physically Real Theories

But a number of problems have been raised with the theory that apparitions are telepathic hallucinations. First of all, why should only people in one small area share in the hallucination? In my first book, I presented evidence that telepathy does not seem to be affected by distance. Second, why should complete strangers sometimes share the experience? We also saw in the first book that telepathy only seems to operate between people who share some common rapport.

These and other problems have led some theorists to support the idea that apparitions are, in some sense, physically real. One ancient idea is that everyone has an "astral body"; that is, a second body made up of some quasiphysical substance that is attached to one's physical body during life and endures after death. According to this view, an apparition is the literal appearance of the astral body—one that is either a copy of the physical body or one that is capable of appearing as a replica.

But this is not the only possibility. Frederic Myers argued that we have no right to assume that the sight of an apparition of a deceased person literally *is* that deceased person, even if it is thought that in some cases the source of the apparition may be the mind of the deceased. He rejected Gurney's theory of telepathic infection on the grounds that if the theory were true, then we would find cases of ordinary hallucinations (from drugs or illness) spreading by telepathic infection to others in the vicinity. But according to Myers, we do not find any such cases, and Gurney came to agree that ordinary hallucinations do not seem to spread by infection.

Myers proposed a theory that the person whose apparition is perceived is not only a mere source of information, but is an actual agent in the full sense of the term. He speculated that the perceived person, living or dead, may cause changes in some nonphysical dimension of existence that intertwines with physical space. Myers referred to this other dimension of reality as the "metetherial world," and speculated that changes in the metetherial world in the vicinity of witnesses would allow them to see the figure of the agent in proper perspective, as though it were a normal person. The fact that some of those present may see the figure while others do not Myers attributed to the different sensitivities of those present. Myers was not very specific in his specification of the metetherial world, and it is difficult to see how this theory could ever be tested. But at least it is an attempt to provide an explanation for features of the reports that are troublesome under the telepathic theories. Myers also thought that the different types of apparitions may require different explanations.

Oxford philosopher H. H. Price developed a theory based on Myers's concepts, which speculates that apparitions are formed from something intermediate between mind and matter, possessing properties of both. Physicist Raynor Johnson developed this idea further, speculating on the existence of a "psychic aether" that acts as a bridge between mind and matter. He attributed the fact that some apparitions are reported as transparent and insubstantial while others are reported as capable of being felt to different degrees of materialization. On this he remarked:

> There is nothing remarkable about different degrees of materialization. . . . I regard the telepathic thought-form as the animating principle or transient mind which clothes itself in an aetheric body. This may condense enough chemical matter around it to reflect light. The extent to which it does this seems to differ greatly: sometimes the figure is transparent and the background can be seen through it; at other times it has a solidity indistinguishable from an ordinary figure.[23]

Johnson's theory is a resurrection of the ancient idea of the astral body, with a modern twist. Applying the concept of morphogenetic fields,* Johnson speculates that the materialization of apparitions "is not substantially different from that associated with creation and growth in Nature."

> How do we suppose a physical body is built? Why does a leaf or flower grow to the size, shape, colour and symmetry-pattern which in fact it does—and to no other? When repair of a wound takes place, why are the form and outline of the original pattern so closely followed? Perhaps the so-called "astral" body is a dynamic, precise and persistent thought-form, which, through the medium of the aetheric body-structure which it directly creates, in turn molds the body of ordinary matter to its form. The difference between the normal processes of growth in Nature and these paranormal processes may only be a matter of degree.[24]

One major advantage of Johnson's theory over the telepathic hallucination theory is that it accounts for the fact that apparitions are reported to be very lifelike in detail. According to the telepathic theories, the appearance of apparitions must be derived from memories. But most reports strongly suggest that apparitions are not at all like remembered images that have faded over time. There are also many reports on record of apparitions seen by strangers, who only later identified the person from a photograph. Obviously, in such cases the source of the apparition cannot be the mind of the percipient, as he or she had no memories of the appearance of the deceased. Apparitions are reported to be as lifelike in the back as they are at the front, which causes difficulty for any theory that says that apparitions are derived from memories belonging to the deceased.

However, Johnson's theory still leaves the problem of apparitional clothing unsolved. We may wonder why the materialization of clothing

---

*An extended discussion of morphogenetic fields and their relation to life may be found in Carter, *Science and the Near-Death Experience,* chapter 6; and in Sheldrake, *Morphic Resonance.*

should be harder to accept than the materialization of hair. But are we willing to extend the concept of morphogenetic fields to clothing?

We have examined the three major categories of theories: the skeptical theory, the telepathic hallucination theory, and the physical theories. We have also seen that the last two theories allow for the possibility that apparitions provide evidence in favor of life after death. Let us now see how the various theories stand up after reviewing some of the more striking cases.

EIGHT

What Underlies Ghostly Visions?

COLLECTIVELY PERCEIVED APPARITIONS

Collectively perceived apparitions are much less common than those seen by a single person. Palmer found that only about one-eighth of his cases involved several simultaneous witnesses. A major reason for this is that most people who report seeing an apparition state that they were alone at the time.

Nevertheless, there is no shortage of reports of collectively perceived apparitions. Frederic Myers wrote that when two or more persons are present at the time an apparition is perceived, in two-thirds of such cases two or more persons perceive it.[1] In a twentieth-century study, Hornell Hart and his collaborators examined forty-six cases that "reported other persons so situated that they would have perceived the apparition if it had been a normal person" and found that in twenty-six, or 56 percent of such cases, the experiences were shared.[2]

The Case of the Cheltenham Ghost

One of the most famous cases of a collectively perceived apparition concerns the haunting of a large stone house in Cheltenham, England. The Cheltenham ghost first appeared in 1882 to Rosina Despard, then a nineteen-year-old medical student living at home with her family. The earliest accounts of the haunting were written under the pseudonym of Miss R. C. Morton, and it was not until years later that the family name and location of the house were made public. Rosina did not wish to jeopardize her medical career, and her father had good reason to worry about the value of the property.

In her written account, Miss Despard describes how one night she had gone up to her room and heard someone outside her door. Thinking it might be her mother, she opened the door, but at first saw no one. Then, after stepping into the hallway, she saw the figure of a tall lady, dressed in black, standing at the top of the stairs. After a few moments the figure descended the stairs, and Rosina followed, curious as to what it might be. But the small piece of candle she was carrying went out, and she returned to her room. She wrote:

> The figure was that of a tall lady, dressed in black of a soft woolen material, judging from the slight sound in moving. The face was hidden in a handkerchief held in the right hand. This was all I noticed then; but on further occasions, when I was able to observe her more closely, I saw the upper part of the left side of the forehead, and a little of the hair above. Her left hand was nearly hidden by her sleeve and a fold of her dress. As she held it down a portion of a widow's cuff was visible on both wrists, so that the whole impression was that of a lady in widow's weeds.[3]

During the next two years Rosina saw the figure about half a dozen times, and wrote that she only mentioned these appearances to one friend, whom she believed did not speak of them to anyone. During this period it was also seen on three occasions by others. In the autumn of 1883, her older sister, while coming down the stairs for dinner, saw a tall figure in black cross the hall and walk into the drawing room. Thinking the figure was a visitor, she asked other members of the family, "Who was that Sister of Mercy whom I have just seen going into the drawing-room?" She was told there was no such visitor, and upon checking, the drawing room was found to be empty. She wrote, "This was the year before I heard of any appearance being known of in the house."[4] Next a housemaid was reported to have seen the figure, and feared that an intruder had broken into the house. Finally, in December of 1883 Rosina's younger brother, then about eight or nine years old, was playing outside with a friend when they "both saw a tall figure in black holding a handerkerchief to her face with her right hand, seated at the writing table in the window, and therefore in full light." They ran in to see who the visitor was, but found no one. Her brother later signed a statement that "it was full daylight at the time," and that prior to this sighting, "I had heard nothing about anything unusual being seen in the house."[5] After this, Rosina told the rest of the family that she had seen the figure several times in the past two years.

Her sightings began to follow a regular pattern. Often, she would first hear noises, usually slight pushes against her bedroom door, accompanied by light footsteps. If she then opened her door, she invariably saw the figure. Several times she followed the figure as it moved downstairs into the drawing room, where it usually stood to the right-hand side of a bow window. After remaining there for a variable length of time, the figure would then leave the drawing room and move along the passage to the garden door, where it always disappeared.

On several occasions Rosina attempted to speak to the figure. The first time was on January 29, 1884.

> I opened the drawing-room door softly and went in, standing just by it. She came in past me and walked to the sofa and stood still there, so I went up to her and asked her if I could help her. She moved, and I thought she was going to speak, but she only gave a slight gasp and moved towards the door. Just by the door I spoke to her again, but she seemed as if she were quite unable to speak. She walked into the hall, then by the side door she seemed to disappear as before.[6]

Attempts to touch the apparition were also unsuccessful. The figure eluded Rosina, and if followed into a corner, simply disappeared.

When Rosina told her father what she had seen and heard, he was astonished, as he had neither seen nor heard anything unusual. Captain Despard asked the landlord if he knew of anything unusual about the house. The landlord replied that he himself had only lived there for three months, and had never seen anything unusual.

During the months of July and August 1884, the sightings were at their most numerous. On August 11, at twilight, Rosina and her elder sister both saw the apparition on the balcony, looking into the window for several minutes before walking away. Later that evening, her younger sister saw the tall woman in black on the stairs. The following evening, Rosina spotted the figure outside, and watched the figure enter the open side door. She followed, as the figure walked into the drawing room to take up her usual position near the bow window. Her father entered the room, but he could not see the figure. Rosina told him the apparition was standing; when her father walked to the place indicated, the apparition quickly left the room and disappeared as before. Later the same evening, one of her younger sisters was sitting alone in the drawing room, singing, when she felt a cold shiver and saw the figure bend over her as if to turn the pages of her songbook. Another younger sister came in from the garden, saying she saw her outside. With all the sisters searching, Rosina's older sister called out from a window that the figure was walking toward the orchard. That evening then, four people reported seeing the figure.

Altogether, the specter was seen or heard by about twenty people, mostly family members, servants, or visitors. It was seen in both darkness and in daylight, inside and outside the house, and on one occasion for over half an hour. Occasionally, the lady in black was seen by two people at the same time, but more frequently, by different people at different times.

According to the reports, animals also reacted to the apparition. A large retriever who slept in the kitchen was on several occasions found by the cook in a state of terror in the morning. Rosina insisted that the dog "was kindly treated and not at all a nervous dog." She also described the reactions of a small terrier:

Twice, I remember seeing this dog suddenly run up to the mat at the foot of the stairs, wagging its tail, and moving its back in the way dogs do when expecting to be caressed. It jumped up, fawning as it would do if a person had been standing there, but suddenly slunk away with its tail between its legs, and retreated, trembling, under a sofa. We were all under the impression that it had seen the figure.[7]

However, Rosina writes:

These facts were kept quiet, on account of the landlord, who feared they might depreciate the value of the house, and any new servants were not told of them, though to anyone who *had* already heard of them we carefully explained the harmless nature of the apparition. Some left us on account of the noises, and we never could induce any of them to go out of their rooms after they had once gone up for the night.[8]

Frederic Myer of the Society for Psychical Research (SPR) joined the investigation in 1885, and offered various suggestions for the investigation. Rosina kept a camera on hand, but was unable to obtain the long exposure necessary to capture the figure on film. She glued fine strings across the stairway, and wrote that on at least two occasions the figure simply passed through the cords, leaving them intact.

Up until 1886, the figure was reported to be so solid and lifelike that it was frequently mistaken for a real person; after 1886 it seems to have gradually become less distinct. From 1887 to 1889, the figure was seldom seen, though footsteps were sometimes heard. After 1889, the figure was apparently not seen again; the footsteps lasted a little longer, but also eventually ceased.

Some unanticipated evidence came to light sixty years later, when an attorney named George Gooding wrote a letter to the SPR, indicating that he was one of the boys who had seen the tall figure in black while playing with Rosina Despard's younger brother. He mentioned that while the adults did not seem alarmed by the figure, the dogs disliked and apparently feared it. Gooding recalled seeing the apparition on two occasions: once outside in bright sunlight, and the other time inside the drawing room. On the latter occasion Gooding wrote that the boys had joined hands around the figure, "from which she appeared merely to walk out between two people and then disappeared."[9]

Comments on the Cheltenham Ghost Case

Who could she have been? After an investigation, the family concluded that the most likely candidate was Imogen Swinhoe, second wife of Henry Swinhoe, the house's first occupant in 1860. The description of the apparition fit Imogen Swinhoe, according to those who had known her, and Rosina identified a picture of Imogen's sister, who, it was said, strongly resembled her. Sadly, it does not seem that the marriage of Henry and Imogen was a happy one. The couple frequently quarreled, and Mrs. Swinhoe left her husband several months before he died in 1876. She went to Bristol, where she died in September 1878, at the age of forty-one. She was buried in the churchyard of Holy Trinity Church in Cheltenham, about five hundred yards from her former home, and there is a commemorative tablet to her in the church.

The SPR first heard about the case several years after it had apparently begun, and were not about to simply accept Despard's account without corroboration. Myers—who, as mentioned earlier, joined the investigation in 1885—interviewed all the principal witnesses and obtained several written accounts from them. Of the various accounts, he wrote: "In this case it is observable that the phenomena as seen or heard by all the witnesses were very uniform in character—even in the numerous instances where there had been no previous communication between the percipients." With the exception of one incident an elderly man could not recall six years later, he "found no discrepancy in the independent testimonies."[10]

Could it have all been an elaborate hoax? Myers could find not one shred of evidence that Rosina had reported the events inaccurately. It is hard to conceive of a possible motive for such a hoax. The original report was written under the pseudonym "R. C. Morton," partly out of fear that the report would jeopardize Rosina's medical career (at the time unusual for a woman), and partly because Captain Despard feared for the value of the house, which belonged to a friend. The family also apparently tried to keep the apparition a secret, because of the difficulty reports of it caused in attracting and retaining servants.

In 1885 Mrs. Sidgwick, one of the SPR's most skeptical investigators, examined the case. She suggested that the figure may have been another woman kept secretly in the house with the help of Captain Despard, whose wife was a partially deaf invalid. Her suggestion probably accounts for Rosina's experiments in gluing strings across the staircase, and for her attempts to touch the figure. The reports of the figure passing through the strings, and of eluding attempts to touch it count against this theory. According to the reports, the figure also did not act like someone in hiding, as it reportedly often appeared in broad daylight, and was spotted outside. For all these reasons Mrs. Sidgwick eventually rejected this explanation.

Other critics have tried to explain the case using various versions of the hallucination theory. In 1958, G. W. Lambert suggested that the noises frequently heard were caused by an underground stream running beneath the house. Lambert examined an old survey map, which indicated that a stream could have passed under the house, and speculated that the strange noises may have been caused when the flooding of the Chelt River fed the stream. In that theory's favor, Lambert pointed out that the flooding of the Chelt was reduced with the opening of the Dowdeswell Reservoirs in 1886, which corresponds with the decline in reported noises. Lambert dismissed the sightings of the apparition as a secondary effect, perhaps caused by suggestion and anxiety about the noises.[11]

Lambert himself admitted that the foregoing was inconclusive and based only on circumstantial evidence. Even so, there is much about the theory that does not seem to fit the case. It is hard to understand how rushing water could cause noises that were heard primarily on the second floor, without also causing a great deal of vibration throughout the house. The Despards' former residence was not some flimsy wooden structure, but rather a sturdy stone and brick house that still stands today. And if the phenomena were caused by running water, then why were adjacent houses not similarly affected?

Other critics have also dismissed the sightings of the apparition as due to hallucination. They argue that once Rosina reported her experience, ordinary suggestion, combined with anxiety, induced similar hallucinations in the others. However, this theory fails to account for the early instances when other people saw the apparition before Rosina reported her experiences. It also fails to account for sightings reported by maids who, for obvious reasons, had not been told about the ghost. It also needs to be remembered that several members of the family did *not* seem overly disturbed by the apparition. In his report, Myers noted that members of the Despard family "were unusually free from superstitious fears." Rosina herself seems to have taken a largely scientific interest in the apparition, and once reported seeing the figure for nearly half an hour. The simple hallucination theory seems to have too many loose ends to be considered satisfactory.

Rosina eventually became a physician, and the Despard family left the house in 1893. It was afterward used for various purposes, such as a school and a nunnery, until the house was bought and converted into apartments in 1973. At any rate, the old stone house still stands, at the corner of Pittville Circus Road and All Saints' Road, in Cheltenham.

The Butler Case

In 1826, a remarkable book was published by the Reverend Abraham Cummings, titled Immortality Proved by Testimony of Sense. Cummings says that he had heard that an apparition in the form of one deceased Mrs. Butler had made numerous appearances in a Maine village, and that he had journeyed there in order to expose what he assumed must be a hoax. However, his opinion was forced to change when he himself was met in a field by what he called "the Spectre." He wrote:

Sometime in July 1806, in the evening I was informed by two persons that they had just seen the Spectre in the field. About ten minutes after, I went out, not to see a miracle, for I believed that they had been mistaken. Looking toward an eminence, twelve rods distance from the house, I saw there, as I supposed, one of the white rocks. This confirmed my opinion of their spectre, and I paid no more attention to it. Three minutes after, I accidentally looked in the same direction, and the white rock was in the air; its form a complete Globe, white with a tincture of red, like the damask rose, and its diameter about two feet. Fully satisfied that this was nothing ordinary, I went toward it for more accurate examination. While my eye was constantly upon it, I went on four or five steps, when it came to me from the distance of eleven rods, as quick as lightning, and instantly assumed a personal form with a female dress, but did not appear taller than a girl seven years old. While I looked upon her, I said in my mind, "you are not tall enough for the woman who has so frequently appeared among us!" Immediately she grew up as large and as tall as I considered that woman to be. Now she appeared glorious. On her head was the representation of the sun diffusing the luminous, rectilinear rays every way to the ground. Through the rays I saw the personal form and the woman's dress.[12]

In his book Reverend Cummings reproduced thirty affidavits from persons who claimed to have seen or heard the apparition. Between 1800 and 1806, the apparition was seen on at least twenty-seven occasions by groups of people from two to nearly two hundred. It identified itself as the spirit of Nelly Butler, the deceased first wife of Captain George Butler. In its discourses, the apparition seemed very concerned with matters of marriage and family, urging Captain Butler to remarry, and accurately predicting the birth of a child. The apparition also seemed very concerned with establishing its identity as the deceased Mrs. Butler, and to this end repeated snatches of conversations between Nelly and her sister, husband, and mother when she was alive, and which were known only by them. Information was also conveyed to the group—such as the recent death of a man's father two hundred miles away—that they could have no normal way of knowing. One witness described the voice of the apparition as "inimitable, and the most delightful that I ever heard in my life."[13]

Reverend Cummings tells us that some of the witnesses believed the apparition was from Satan, others from God. He also tells how it presented itself "to one alone . . . sometimes she appeared to two or three; then to five or six; then to ten or twelve; again to twenty; and once to more than forty witnesses. She appeared in several apartments of Mr. Blaisdel's house, and several times in the open field . . . There, white as the light, she moved like a cloud above the ground in personal form and magnitude, and in the presence of more than forty people. She tarried with them till after daylight, and vanished."[14] The apparition also invited those present to try to touch her. On one occasion, Captain Butler "put his hand upon it and it passed down through the apparition as through a body of light, in the view of six or seven witnesses."[15]

Comments on the Butler Case

Accusations of fraud were made, most of which were directed at the new Mrs. Butler. Curiously, the apparition not only predicted that the new Mrs. Butler would soon give birth to a child, but would also die shortly afterward. Both predictions reportedly came to pass. Cummings carefully considered the accusations of fraud, but rejected them, concluding that the spirit of Nelly Butler had returned to her community, in order to bolster their belief in a life after death.

The Case of Animals Sensing Apparitions

The following case is very odd: it concerns an apparition that is unknown to the experient and is also apparently perceived by two dogs.

The account was related to the American Society for Psychical Research (ASPR) by an officer in the U.S. Navy. He had been assigned to the Naval Powder Factory at Indian Head, Maryland, in 1926, and, with his wife and two dogs, moved into half of a double house. In September 1927, another officer and his family moved into the other half, and the two families became close friends. In his letter to the ASPR, the lieutenant writes:

> Early in the following March I was sitting at a card table in the den, solving a problem in navigation. I was facing the front of the house. The time was about 12:25 a.m. Both dogs were sleeping on the floor at the end of a davenport in the living-room. I heard the spaniel growl; but as he often growls at the marine sentry as he passes the house, I paid no attention to it. Both dogs then got up, passed me in the den and went down the back hall into the dining-room where both dogs again growled and then tore madly across the hall and up the stairway. The noise they made going up the stairs awakened my wife, who was asleep on the second floor.
>
> Surprised at their actions, I looked up from my work and saw a man standing in the living-room near the hall archway. He was probably twenty-two feet from me. All outside doors and windows were closed. . . . I could see him plainly.[16]

Because of his duties, it was not uncommon for men to come to the house at all hours. However, the lieutenant was surprised that the man could have entered without his hearing the doors open and close, and the lieutenant was irritated that the man did not knock or ring the doorbell. He also did not recognize the man as an employee of the factory. The lieutenant stared at the man for about ten seconds, as the stranger seemed about to speak. Then he rose from his chair and took a few steps forward to greet the man, when the stranger vanished instantly.

After a careful search of the house, the lieutenant concluded that he had been seeing things after working too long, and turned in for the night. However, about a week later, when he was alone in the house, the lieutenant again saw the man standing in the living room, in excellent light. He appeared to weigh a little over two hundred pounds, was dressed in light gray clothing, and looked like he had a deep tan. Again the figure seemed to be trying to speak, and the lieutenant watched him for about fifteen minutes. Finally, he stepped toward the figure, and again, it simply vanished.

About ten minutes later, the lieutenant visited his neighbor in the other part of the house to get his opinion. When the neighbor's wife, Mrs. G., came into the room, her husband told him that the lieutenant had seen a ghost that he did not recognize. At this point the woman put about twenty photographs before the lieutenant, and asked him to look through them.

> I shuffled then through carelessly and at about the seventh or eighth picture I came across the portrait of the man I had seen a few minutes before. There is no doubt in my mind as to its being the same man. I would know him among a thousand.
>
> Dumbfounded, I said "That is the man. Who is he?" She replied, "My father: he has been dead for several years."[17]

The lieutenant concluded his letter to the American Society of Psychical Research with these words:

> I am willing to swear to the truth of the above statement. I hope there is some simple explanation of all this, as I would hate to have my life-long faith in a ghostless world shattered. My parents taught me from childhood that ghosts did not and could not exist, and all my life I have firmly believed that to be true. Naturally the beliefs of a lifetime are hard to shatter. Hence this letter seeking an explanation of that which to me is inexplicable.[18]

Comments on the Case of Animals Sensing Apparitions

How can this case be explained in terms of a telepathic hallucination? We would have to suppose that Mrs. G. was thinking of her late father, that the lieutenant telepathically read those thoughts, and then created the hallucination of her father. Needless to say, this would be telepathy of an astonishing degree, exercised by a person who never before had any similar experience. What about the behavior of the dogs? They became excited immediately *before* the lieutenant first saw the figure, and so could not have been merely reacting to his astonishment. Are we to say that the dogs also telepathically read Mrs. G.'s thoughts at the same moment, and also began hallucinating? Finally, what possible motive could the lieutenant—or the dogs for that matter—have for telepathically acquiring information about a deceased man they had never met?

The Case of a Father's Visit

On Christmas Eve 1869, Mr. and Mrs. P., along with their fifteen-month-old daughter, had just settled in for the night. As usual, the couple had carefully locked all the doors, including the door to their bedroom. Mrs. P. had asked her husband to leave a lamp burning in the bedroom before he got into bed, so that Mrs. P. could feed her daughter. The lamp, sitting on a set of drawers at the other end of the room, had been turned down, so that the room was dimly lit. Mrs. P. described what happened next.

> I [was] just pulling myself into a half-sitting posture against the pillows, thinking of nothing but the arrangements for the following day, when to my great astonishment I saw a gentleman standing at the foot of the bed, dressed as a naval officer, and with a cap on his head having a projecting peak. The light being in the position which I have indicated, the face was in shadow *to me,* and the more so that the visitor was leaning upon his arms which rested on the foot-rail of the bedstead. I was too astonished to be afraid, but simply wondered who it could be; and instantly touching my husband's

shoulder (whose face was turned from me), I said, "Willie, who is this?" My husband turned, and for a second or two lay looking in intense astonishment at the intruder; then lifting himself a little, he shouted, "What on earth are you doing here, sir?" Meanwhile the form, slowly drawing himself into an upright position, now said in a commanding, yet reproachful voice, "Willie! Willie!"

I looked at my husband and saw that his face was white and agitated. As I turned towards him he sprang out of bed as though to attack the man, but stood by the bedside as if afraid, or in great perplexity, while the figure calmly and slowly moved towards the wall at right angles with the lamp. As it passed the lamp, a deep shadow fell upon the room as of a material person shutting out the light from us by his intervening body, and he disappeared, as it were, into the wall. My husband now, in a very agitated manner, caught up the lamp, and turning to me said, "I mean to look all over the house, and see where he is gone." . . . [W]ithout pausing, my husband *unlocked the door,* hastened out of the room, and was soon searching the whole house.[19]

While her husband searched the house, Mrs. P. sat in bed, convinced that they had seen an apparition, and wondering what it could possibly mean. Her brother Arthur was in the navy, and she wondered if this meant that he was somehow in trouble. After her husband returned from his fruitless search, she expressed her fear that the apparition had something to do with Arthur; to which he replied "Oh! No, it was my father!"

My husband's father *had been dead fourteen years:* he had been a naval officer in his young life; but, through ill-health, had left the service before my husband was born, and the latter had only once or twice seen him in uniform. I had never seen him at all. My husband and I related the occurrence to my uncle and aunt, and we all noticed that my husband's agitation and anxiety were very great: whereas his usual manner was calm and reserved in the extreme, and he was a thorough and avowed sceptic in all so-called supernatural events.[20]

Later, Mrs. P's husband confessed to her that he had been in great financial difficulties, and was about to take the advice of a man who almost certainly would have led him into ruin, or worse. Only the apparition of his dead father had stopped him from following this course. Mrs. P.'s account was corroborated in writing by her husband, and another couple acknowledged that Mrs. P. had told them the same story years earlier. Mrs. P. concluded that the apparition was "a direct warning to my husband in the voice and appearance of the one that he had most revered in all his life, and was the most likely to obey."

Comments on the Case of a Father's Visit

If we attempt to explain this case as a telepathically shared hallucination, we would first have to suppose that Mr. P. had been brooding or dreaming about what his long-dead father would have thought about his financial difficulties. Then we would have to suppose that Mrs. P. read her husband's mind, and constructed a realistic hallucination of her husband's late father, standing at the foot of the bed. After her husband was roused, he then telepathically picked up her vision, and also began hallucinating. The purpose of the figure—to stop the actions of Mr. P.—was actually Mr. P.'s own. He knew that what he was about to do was dangerous and wrong, but he needed to hallucinate a vision of his dead father to stop himself.

Alan Gauld, commenting on this sort of explanation, has written that "a flat-earther in full cry could hardly support his hypothesis with more tortuous argumentation."[21] He believes it is much simpler to suppose that discarnate agencies shape the collective experiences in accordance with their own purposes:

That way we can avoid such bizarre notions as that persons hitherto not known to be psychically gifted can suddenly develop powers of

ESP comparable to, if not exceeding, the most remarkable that have ever been experimentally demonstrated; that two people without any conscious thought of doing any such thing can at an unconscious level telepathically link up with each other and hammer out the details of a hallucinatory figure which both shall see; that animals may to some extent share in this process; that the information thus acquired will be dressed up by processes unknown and presumably unconscious and presented to the conscious mind quite indirectly in the form of dramatic but really irrelevant interventions by deceased persons; and that the purposes promoted by the hallucinatory episodes, even when ostensibly more appropriate to the supposed deceased person, are really those of the living percipient or of some other living person whose mind telepathically influences his.[22]

Finally, it is important to stress that collectively perceived apparitions are almost invariably seen in proper perspective by the witnesses, given their position and distance from the apparition. In one reported case, a recently deceased man was seen standing on the altar steps of his church by three people in three different parts of the church, looking completely normal.[23] In another case, a woman and her daughter sleeping in the same room suddenly awoke and saw a female figure in a white garment with dark curly hair, standing in front of the fireplace, over which there was a mirror. The mother saw the face in quarter-profile; her daughter could only directly see the back of the figure, but could see the figure's face clearly reflected in the mirror.[24] In an English case from the 1930s, nine members of a family reported that together they saw the apparition of their recently deceased grandfather, which even the smallest girl, aged five, recognized.[25] These and many other similar cases can leave no doubt that collective apparitions are perceived as though they were actual living persons, obeying all the normal rules of perspective and distance for each observer. Unless we hold on to the untestable theory that the subconscious minds of the witnesses in these cases collaborated together to telepathically create a collective hallucination that was not merely identical, but correct for the perspective of each observer, it seems as though we are driven to the conclusion that collectively perceived apparitions are something objectively present.

APPARITIONS OF THE LIVING

There are several accounts in the literature of apparitions of living persons. In the following case, the woman suspected the person she saw had just died.

> My mother lived with me, and at the time of which I write was aged about eighty-three, so consequently went to bed a good deal earlier that I did. One night I was leaving the sitting room with my black cocker spaniel dog by my side, and on opening the door there was my mother standing just outside in the hall, perfectly solid and in her nightdress and with the little shawl around her shoulder that she always wore in bed. I thought she had just come to the door and spoke to her, when she immediately vanished. The dog's hackles rose slightly and I knew from his appearance that he had seen her, too. My first thought was that she had died in her sleep, and that this was her ghost, so I went at once to her room, where she was lying peacefully asleep.
>
> She lived for four years after this.[26]

The most impressive of these cases are the reciprocal cases, of which we have several examples on record. These are the cases involving a living person who claims to remember visiting the place at which was reported an apparition bearing his or her likeness. The following is a case from Sweden:

MRS. L.: We were building our summer cottage. Olle, one of the neighbor's boys, went away on holiday just when the foundation was laid, and the house went up during his absence. One evening at dusk

. . . it was still light, [and] I saw [a] man . . . striding obliquely over the rise toward the house, dressed in light blue pajamas and [looking] just like Olle. The figure walked right through the spruce trees and up to the house, where he stopped, and with hands on hips, studied the house—and then disappeared into nothing.

After a few weeks Olle strolled up just the way the figure in pajamas had, but now he avoided the spruces. He looked up at the house completely terrified and burst out, "But I've seen this before!"

OLLE: The L. family had just started leveling and grading for the foundation when I went away, so I had no way of knowing how the house was going to look when it was finished. One night I dreamed I was walking along the path that led up . . . to the L.'s [cottage site]. In the dream, when I reached the cottage I saw it absolutely clearly . . . I . . . saw Mrs. L. standing on the steps as if welcoming me.

Later, when I came back from the trip, I walked over to the L.'s to chat. I was terrified when I caught sight of the cottage; it looked exactly as I'd seen it in the dream, and Mrs. L. sat on the steps. She asked me if I'd worn a pair of light blue pajamas the night I had the dream, and in fact I did. The time corresponded, too.[27]

The SPR's *Journal* of 1891 contains the account of S. R. Wilmot, a manufacturer from Bridgeport, Connecticut. In 1863 he crossed the Atlantic in *The City of Limerick,* which ran into a fierce storm. One night the gale abated, and he slept soundly for the first time in eight days. He dreamed that his wife came to the door in her nightdress; after hesitating, as if realizing he was not alone in the cabin, she "stooped and kissed me, and after having caressed me a few moments she quietly withdrew."

When Wilmot woke up his cabin mate, William Tait, "a sedate and very religious man" was staring at him. "You are a lucky fellow to have a lady come to visit you in this way!" Tait remarked with indignation.

When the surprised Wilmot asked Tait to explain himself, Tait described what he had seen, which corresponded exactly with Wilmot's dream.

When Wilmot met his wife back in Bridgeport he was startled again, when she asked, "Did you receive a visit from me a week ago Tuesday?" She had heard of the storm and of the sinking of another ship on the Atlantic crossing, and had lain awake out of worry. At four in the morning of the day he had his dream, it had seemed to her that she had gone out to seek her husband, crossed the stormy sea, found his ship, and entered his cabin. "A man was in the upper berth, looking right at me, and for a moment I was afraid to go in, but soon I went up to the side of your berth, bent down and kissed you, and embraced you, and then went away." According to Wilmot, the description she gave of the steamer was "correct in all particulars." Wilmot's sister, who was also on *The City of Limerick,* later testified that Tait had asked her whether it was she who had come down to see her brother.[28]

In 2007, Edward Kelly, Emily Kelly, Adam Crabtree, Alan Gauld, Michael Grosso, and Bruce Greyson summarized this case in their book *Irreducible Mind.* At the end of their brief discussion they describe how Susan Blackmore and Paul Edwards (whom we met in chapter 4) have grossly misrepresented this case:

> Blackmore ["Are Out-of-Body Experiences Evidence for Survival?," 143–44] thinks she has successfully discredited the Wilmot case, and Edwards [*Immortality,* 20] agrees, asserting that "the case totally collapsed when it was investigated by Susan Blackmore." Blackmore claims that *the entire story rests on Mr Wilmot's testimony alone* and that this testimony was unreliable because he had been seasick at the time. She further claims that *"Mrs Wilmot never reported having had an OBE* [out-of-body experience] *at all."* [emphasis added]
>
> Although Blackmore claims to have read the original reports (citing Myers' reprinting of the case), she clearly did not read them carefully enough, and Edwards apparently relied entirely on Blackmore without reading the original report himself. In the report, both the

original and Myers' reprinting of it, *letters are printed not only from Mr Wilmot but also from Mrs Wilmot and Miss Wilmot,* corroborating the essential features of his account. Although Mrs Wilmot never explicitly said "I had an out-of-body experience," she did say *"I had a very vivid sense all the [next] day of having visited my husband."* [emphasis added]

She also said "I felt much disturbed at his [the man in the upper berth's] presence, as he leaned over, looking at us." She further reported that "the impression was so strong that I felt unusually happy and refreshed," in contrast to the anxiety about her husband that had preceded it. We do not unfortunately have the testimony of the man in the upper berth [who had since died], but, as mentioned above, we do have Miss Wilmot's testimony that he told her about his experience the next morning, *before* she had seen her brother and heard his account of what had happened.

The case is not perfect, but Blackmore's and Edwards's misrepresentation of the reported facts, and offhand dismissal of testimony that conflicts with their beliefs, is indefensible at best.[29]

Apparitions of the living are of special interest for what light they may shed on apparitions of the dead. Hornell Hart has provided a detailed analysis of the characteristics of apparitions. He arranged his cases of apparitions in chronological order, beginning with those occurring long before the projector's death and ending with those occurring long after the person's death. Hart argued that if consciousness is dependent on the function of a physical brain, then apparitions should show an abrupt change in character and behavior when the point of death is passed. But the observed facts do not indicate such a change except, as Hart writes, "such as might be expected from the alterations of purpose which death would produce in the appearer."[30] Hart concluded that *apparitions of the living are indistinguishable from those of the dead.* He was also able to show that in 82 percent of cases of apparitions of the living that he analyzed, these living people cited as apparitions either remembered leaving their body, or had been directing their attention to the percipient, often with the idea of "going" to him or her. If we are justified in concluding that at least some apparitions of the living are vehicles for the minds of those they represent, then it would seem that we are equally justified in concluding that at least some apparitions of the deceased are also vehicles for the minds of those they represent. The fact that apparitions of the living are indistinguishable from apparitions of the dead means that apparitions of the dead provide evidence in favor of survival.

APPARITIONS WITH THEIR OWN AGENDA

A Promise Kept

In his autobiography, Henry Brougham—later Lord Chancellor in His Majesty's Government—relates how, in December 1799, he was traveling in Sweden with friends.

Dec. 19—We set out for Gothenburg, determining to make for Norway. At one in the morning, arriving at a decent inn, we decided to stop for the night. Tired with the cold of yesterday, I was glad to take advantage of a hot bath before I turned in. And here a most remarkable thing happened to me—so remarkable that I must tell the story from the beginning.

After I had left the High School, I went with G., my most intimate friend, to attend the classes in the University. There was no divinity class, but we frequently in our walks discussed and speculated on many grave subjects—among others, on the immortality of the soul, and on a future state. This question, and the possibility, I will not say of ghosts walking, but of the dead appearing to the living, were subjects of much speculation: and we actually committed the folly of drawing up an agreement, written with our blood, to the effect that whichever of us died the first should appear to the other, and thus solve any doubts we had entertained of the "life after death." After we had finished our classes at the college G. went to India, having got an appointment there in the Civil Service. He seldom wrote to me, and after the lapse of a few years I had almost forgotten him; moreover his family having little connection with Edinburgh, I seldom saw or heard anything of them, or of him through them, so that all his schoolboy intimacy had died out, and I had nearly forgotten his existence. I had taken, as I said, a warm bath, and while lying in it and enjoying the comfort of the heat after the late freezing I had undergone I turned my head round, looking towards the chair on which I had deposited my clothes, as I was about to get out of the bath. On the chair sat G., looking calmly at me. How I got out of the bath I do not know, but on recovering my senses I found myself sprawling on the floor. The apparition, or whatever it was, that had taken the likeness of G., had disappeared.[31]

Lord Brougham wrote an account of the experience in his journal shortly after, writing, "No doubt I had fallen asleep; and that the appearance presented so distinctly to my eyes was a dream I cannot for a moment doubt." However, shortly after Lord Brougham returned to Edinburgh, a letter from India conveyed the news that G. had died on December 19, the exact date Lord Brougham had the "dream" that left him sprawling on the floor beside the bathtub.

The Case of the Doctor Making a House Call

On Saturday, October 18, 1868, Mr. and Mrs. Bacchus left some friends with whom they had been staying and went to Cheltenham to visit a sick friend. First they found rooms in a local lodging house, and left to visit their ailing friend. On their way out of the lodging house, they noticed some medicine bottles, and inquired if anyone in the house was ill. They were told that a Mrs. R., who kept a room downstairs, had been ill for some time, but that her illness was not a serious one. In the course of the evening they mentioned this woman's name to their friend, and he told them that she was the widow of a physician who formerly practiced in Cheltenham.

On Sunday morning Mr. Bacchus informed Mrs. Bacchus that Mrs. R. had suddenly died in the night, and that her body was being kept in the bedroom downstairs, directly below their own rooms. Not wishing to move on a Sunday, and being of kind disposition, the couple decided to remain at the lodging house. The day was spent with their friend and his nieces, and they returned to the lodgings late in the evening, in time to go to bed. Mrs. Bacchus wrote:

> I went to sleep quickly as usual, but woke, I suppose, in the middle of the night, not frightened by any noise, and for no reason, and saw distinctly at the foot of the bed an old gentleman with a round rosy face, smiling, his hat in his hand, dressed in an old-fashioned coat (blue) with brass buttons, light waistcoat and trousers. The longer I looked at him, the more distinctly I saw every feature and particular of his dress. I did not feel much frightened, and after a time shut my eyes for a minute or two, and when I looked again, the old gentleman was gone.[32]

Much to her surprise, Mrs. Bacchus was not frightened, and after some time fell back into sleep. The next morning:

> [W]hile dressing, [I] made up my mind that I would say nothing of what I had seen till I saw one of my nieces, and would then describe the old gentleman, and ask if Dr. R. could be like him, although the idea seemed absurd. I met my niece, Mary Copeland, coming out of church, and said, "Was Dr. R. like an old gentleman with a round rosy face," etc., etc., describing what I had seen. She stopped at once on the pavement, looking astonished. "Who could have told you, aunt? We always said he looked more like a country farmer than a doctor . . ."[33]

Her account was corroborated, in its essentials, by her husband and two of her nieces.

Comments on the Case of
the Doctor Making a House Call

This case is difficult to explain as a hallucination generated by the mind of Mrs. Bacchus. She knew neither the recently deceased woman nor her deceased husband. What possible reason could she have for telepathically acquiring details of the appearance of a man she had never met, and then incorporating them into a realistic hallucination? On the other hand, the deceased doctor—if he still existed—could reasonably be credited with a strong motive for visiting his recently deceased wife, namely, to help her through the transition of death.

The Blue Orchid Case

Arthur C. Clarke, author of *2001: A Space Odyssey,* was told the following strange tale by Englishwoman Georgina Feakes.

Before the Second World War, Georgina's sister, Beatrice, and her family had emigrated to South Africa. When hostilities broke out, Georgina's cousin, Owen Howerson, signed up, and was killed in action in 1944. Soon after, Georgina claimed, he appeared to her in England, surrounded by a golden mist. "He said his tank had been hit, but he still felt very much alive. Would I please tell his mum, and please give his love to poor Helen." Georgina claims to have been dumbstruck at first. "I tried to speak, although my lips were numb and frozen." Finally, she says she found her voice: "I said, 'Proof, give me proof.' And he said, 'Watch.'"

> To my amazement, he opened the top of his shirt, and took out a beautiful blue flower, of penetrating perfume. It was very beautiful, long and bell-like, orchid-like. A wonderful scent permeated the whole room. While I stared in amazement, he put it back in his

shirt, took it out, and put it back, and took it out. And then he said, quite loudly, "Tell mum, Table Mountain."

According to Georgina, the apparition then shimmered and vanished. With none of this making any sense to Georgina, she wrote at once to Owen's mother; back from South Africa came this curious explanation. Owen had one day gone up Table Mountain, picked a protected blue flower, and brought it home, hidden it in his shirt. The flower was a rare blue orchid that grew on Table Mountain, and since it was illegal to pick, Owen had risked prison to bring it back to her. While showing it to her, the door slammed, and he nervously hid the flower in his shirt, only taking it out again after learning it was a false alarm. Her aunt Beatrice in South Africa had kept the story secret, in order to protect Owen, who could have been imprisoned for the offense. So it does not seem likely that Georgina could have known about the incident.

Georgina claims Owen appeared a second time, again in a golden mist. But this time his manner was not friendly. "He reproached me bitterly for not contacting Helen. And I was very distressed about this, because I had tried." His mother had been through all his correspondence, and had found no letter from anyone named Helen, or any reference to anyone with that name.

But there *had* been a Helen in Owen's life, a lovely young woman with dark hair and eyes, for whom Owen had written romantic letters and poems. After reading the story of the blue orchid in the newspapers, she contacted the family, and the mystery of Helen was solved.[34]

Cases like these seem hard to explain in terms of telepathy among the living. In such cases the apparition shows a purpose that is difficult to attribute to anyone living, but which could easily be attributed to the deceased, if they still lived.

VERIDICAL APPARITIONS

We have seen several examples of apparitions that seem to convey information not known to the percipient, which upon checking, turned out to be accurate. We classify such cases as *veridical:* that is, the experiences provide information that corresponds with facts. The following apparition conveyed information about an inconsequential detail that turned out to have been correct.

The Case of a Soldier's Death

Edmund Gurney received a letter in 1886 from a British Army colonel that began:

> I am not a believer in ghosts, spirit manifestations, or Esoteric Buddhism. It has been my lot—a lot sought by myself over and over again, and never falling to me by chance—to sleep in well-known, or rather well-believed-to-be haunted rooms. I have endeavored to encounter ghosts, spirits, or beings (if you like) from another world, but like other good things that one seeks for in life, without success. When I least expected it, however, I experienced a visitation so remarkable in its phenomena, so realistic in its nature, so supported by actual facts, that I am constrained, at the request of my friends, to put my experience into writing.[35]

The colonel then described how, nearly twenty-three years earlier, he had formed a friendship with another subaltern, to whom he referred to as simply "J. P." Their friendship continued up until the Transvaal War, when J. P. was called to the scene of action. The morning he left, the two friends had breakfast together at the officers' club; at the door, J. P. told the colonel "We shall meet again," waved, and was gone.

Over a year later, the colonel awoke with a start at dawn.

> Standing by my bed, between me and the chest of drawers, I saw a figure, which in spite of the unwonted dress—unwonted, at least, to

me—and of a full black beard, I at once recognized as that of my old brother-officer. . . . His face was pale, but his bright black eyes shone as keenly as when, a year and a half before, they had looked upon me as he stood with one foot on the hansom, bidding me adieu.

Fully impressed for the brief moment that we were stationed together at C___ in Ireland or somewhere, and thinking I was in my barrack-room, I said "Hallo! P., am I late for parade?" P. looked at me steadily, and replied, "I'm shot."

"Shot!" I exclaimed. "Good God! How and where?"

"Through the lungs," replied P., and as he spoke his right hand moved slowly up the breast, until the fingers rested over the right lung.

"What were you doing?" I asked.

"The General sent me forward," he answered, and the right hand left the breast to move slowly to the front, pointing over my head to the window, and at the same moment the figure melted away. I rubbed my eyes, to make sure I was not dreaming, and sprang out of bed.[36]

Two days later the colonel learned of his friend's death, at almost the exact time he had seen the apparition. Six months later he met an officer who was at the battle, and learned that J. P. had died after being shot through the right lung, wearing the same uniform, and with a full beard, which the colonel "had never seen him wear." There seems to be no explanation for the beard if the image of the colonel's friend originated only in the mind of the colonel, due to the colonel's telepathic perception of his friend's death. A skeptic of survival could, of course, maintain that the colonel clairvoyantly perceived his dead friend's appearance, but this would be postulating a level of telepathy and clairvoyance rarely, if ever, seen, apart from apparition cases such as this. It is also worth pointing out that the colonel had never had an experience like this before or since, and considered himself "not a believer in ghosts, spirit manifestations, or Esoteric Buddhism."

Comments on the Case of a Soldier's Death

This and other veridical cases all involved information that could plausibly have been known to someone who was alive at the time, and are open to an explanation in terms of telepathy among the living. However, reports of apparitions that reveal information apparently not known by *anyone* living date back to ancient times, such as the story of the philosopher Athenodorus that served to open this section. We also have similar reports from medieval Europe, such as the story concerning Dante's lost Canto. His son, Pietro, was anxious to publish the *Divine Comedy* in its entirety, but could not find the final canto. After a long and fruitless search, Pietro dreamt one night that his father appeared at his bedside and told him that the manuscript had been hidden under a board near the window, where it was the poet's custom to sit and write. According to the story, the missing papers were then found at the spot indicated by the apparition.

Some have attempted to explain this case as due to clairvoyant perception on the part of Dante's son. They argue that Pietro was strongly motivated to find the missing manuscript, and that the information came in the form of a clairvoyant dream. According to this interpretation, the figure of his father in the dream served the purpose of providing legitimacy to the message. However, the following case is more difficult to explain in this manner.

The Chaffin Will Case

This case involves the contested will of James L. Chaffin, a farmer in Davie County, North Carolina. It is an unusual case in several respects, not the least of which is that it is unusually well-authenticated, as all known facts were carefully scrutinized in a court of justice in 1925, in the case of Chaffin v. Chaffin.

On November 16, 1905, James L. Chaffin made out a will, duly attested by two witnesses, whereby he gave his property to his third son, Marshall. To his widow and the other three sons, he left nothing. On September 7, 1921, Mr. Chaffin died suddenly, as a result of a fall. His son Marshall duly took ownership of Mr. Chaffin's farm and other possessions. His widow and the other three sons did not contest the will, as they knew of no valid reason for doing so.

Almost four years later, in June 1925, the second son, James P. (J. P.) Chaffin, began to have very vivid dreams in which his father appeared at his bedside, but without saying anything. Later that month, either in a dream, or in a state between waking and sleeping (J. P. himself was not sure):

> [H]e appeared at my bedside again, dressed as I had often seen him dressed in life, wearing a black overcoat which I knew to be his own coat. This time my father's spirit spoke to me, he took hold of his overcoat this way and pulled it back and said, "You will find my will in my overcoat pocket," and then disappeared.[37]

Convinced that his father had visited him, J. P. Chaffin visited his mother the following day, inquiring after the overcoat. The coat, he was told, had been given to his brother John. The following Monday, he traveled twenty miles to his brother's home, and found that the inside pocket of the old coat had been sewn shut. After cutting the threads, a roll of paper was found, with a message in their father's handwriting: "Read the 27th chapter of Genesis in my daddie's old Bible."

More convinced than ever that the mystery would now be solved, Chaffin recruited two neighbors—one Mr. Blackwelder and his daughter—as witnesses, and traveled back to his mother's home to examine the old family Bible. After a considerable search it was found, so dilapidated that it was broken in three pieces. Blackwelder picked up the section that contained the book of Genesis, and turned to the twenty-seventh chapter. There, within folded pages, he found the second will of the elder James Chaffin, which reads as follows.

> After reading the 27th chapter of Genesis, I, James L. Chaffin, do make my last will and testament, and here it is. I want, after giving

my body a decent burial, my little property to be equally divided between my four children, if they are living at my death, both personal and real estate divided equally if not living, give share to their children. And if she is living, you all must take care of your mammy. Now this is my last will and testament. Witness my hand and seal.

James L. Chaffin
This January 16, 1919[38]

The twenty-seventh chapter of Genesis tells how the younger brother, Jacob, supplanted the elder brother, Esau, and won his birthright. The sole beneficiary of the first will was, it will be remembered, the youngest brother, Marshall.

Marshall had died within a year of his father's death, leaving a son to inherit the family property, which had been his according to the first will. When the second will was tendered for probate, Marshall's son and his widow contested the document with a lawsuit. In December 1925, a jury was sworn in and a crowd packed the courtroom, hoping to watch the spectacle of a bitter family feud fought out in public. The court was adjourned for lunch; when the hearing continued, one of the lawyers announced that during the interval an amicable agreement had been reached, and that the new will would now be admitted to probate without opposition.

When the trial started, Marshall's widow and son had been prepared to contest the second will. However, during the lunch interval they had been shown the document. Ten witnesses were prepared to testify that the second will was in the deceased Chaffin's handwriting, and the widow and son admitted this as soon as they saw it. Their opposition was at once withdrawn, and the crowd retired, disappointed.

Comments on the Chaffin Will Case

It should be clear that this is an unusually well-researched and well-documented case. Not only were the facts put in evidence in a contested lawsuit, but they also underwent the scrutiny of North Carolina attorney J. M. Johnson, who researched the case on behalf of the American Society of Psychical Research. As part of his report, Johnson forwarded to the Society the original newspaper article on the case, official records of the proceedings from the Superior Court of Davie County, North Carolina, and sworn statements from the principal witnesses. The original documents can still be studied at the offices of the ASPR. As a result of the Court's judgment, the second will of James Chaffin was recorded in the Book of Wills of Davie County, and the first will was annulled and made void.

Nevertheless, could the second will have been a fake? If it was not, then why did the elder Chaffin hide it in the old family bible, instead of making the will public when he was alive? Evidently, there was some bitterness and acrimony in the family, which almost surely accounts for the neglect of the widow and other three sons in the first will. Possibly, Chaffin intended to reveal the existence of the revised will on his deathbed, and his sudden death as a result of an accident frustrated his intention. Ten witnesses were prepared to swear that the second will was in Chaffin's handwriting, and Marshall's widow and son agreed that it was genuine as soon as they were allowed to see it. These facts would seem to decisively counter the suggestion of a forgery. J. M. Johnson, who interviewed and questioned the Chaffins, was, in his words, "much impressed with the evident sincerity of these people, who had the appearance of honest, honourable country people, in well-to-do circumstances."

Could the surviving family members have had some subconscious knowledge of the second will, or of the note in the coat pocket? Johnson considered this explanation. "I endeavored with all my skill and ability by cross-examination and otherwise to induce some admission that possibly there was a subconscious knowledge of the will in the Old Bible, or of the paper in the coat pocket, that was brought to the fore by the dream: but I utterly failed to shake their faith. The answer was a quiet: 'Nay: such an explanation is impossible. We never heard of the existence of the will till the visitation from my father's spirit.'"[39] It should be clear that none of the surviving family members had any conscious knowledge of the second will. If the widow and three sons who were not provided for by the first will did, then they would not have allowed the first will to be proved without opposition. Nor were they likely to forget about the will during the short period (two years, eight months) between the writing of the second will and the elder Chaffin's death.

Some have argued that the case might be best explained by clairvoyant perception on the part of the son. These individuals correctly point out that the son stood to gain by the discovery of the second will. But this does not account for the fact that the message was to look for the will in the elder Chaffin's *coat pocket,* and not in the old family bible. It seems difficult to explain why the son's clairvoyant perception should focus on a scrap of paper that provided only a clue to the location of the will, and not simply on the will itself.* On the other hand, we all are familiar with the manner in which two closely related facts can become confused in memory. If the message is interpreted as coming from the deceased James L. Chaffin—motivated by a desire to rectify an injustice—then the mistaken reference to the will in the coat pocket is readily explicable.

---

*It is possible, of course, that Marshall's family knew about the reference to a second will in the coat pocket, but kept quiet, hoping it would not be discovered. Then it could be argued that J. P. Chaffin picked up this knowledge telepathically. But if Marshall's family were this selfish, dishonest, and disrespectful toward their late benefactor, then surely they would have attempted to destroy the note and the second will, rather than risk the will's discovery. But there is no evidence they attempted to do so in the four years between the death of the elder Chaffin and the discovery of the second will; instead, their first reaction was to oppose the second will with a lawsuit.

NINE

Final Thoughts on Apparitions

We have seen that theories of apparitions fall into two main categories: those that consider them purely psychic entities and those that consider them physical entities. Some features of apparitions fit the psychic model more closely, while other features seem to suggest some sort of physical reality to apparitions.

Could it be that the truth of the matter lies somewhere in between? Some writers have suggested that the distinction between the psychic and the physical is not as absolute at it appears to us, but may rather be a matter of degree. And that the reason apparitions seem to show qualities of both the mental and the material is that they share—in some sense—*both* mental and material properties. Others, such as Myers, have posited that apparitions are quasimaterial *etheric doubles* of ordinary physical objects. This would imply that they are composed of some form of matter that we do not normally perceive, or that does not normally interact with the physical universe accessible to our senses. Johnson, building on the theories of Myers and Price, speculates that materialization may be a matter of degree, and that the organizing patterns responsible for the materialization of apparitional bodies are similar to those responsible for the growth and development of biological bodies.

To solve the problem of apparitional clothing, Hart has come up with a hybrid theory. He speculates that every physical object has what he calls an *etheric* counterpart, similar to it in every detail. He also speculates that etheric objects may be created by imagination; that is, by imitating or modifying objects found in nature. In order to explain the range of characteristics of apparitions, he writes that "the differences between etheric objects and physical objects are matters of degree and may vary through the whole range between those of sheer subjective imagination and those of completely materialized forms. Collective percipience of apparitions, materializations and dematerializations, and physical phenomena in general (so far as genuine) involve relatively high degrees of approximation to physical traits on the part of etheric objects. On the other hand, 'purely mental' imaginings and dreams on the part of individuals would represent points towards the other end of the same scale."[1]

Apparitions are baffling, because there seems to be no satisfactory explanation as to what they are that will fit into the neat categories into which we fit all the other aspects of our experience. Perhaps the reason is that our categories are inadequate and incomplete.

However, we have also seen that some theories of apparitions contain the conjecture that whatever apparitions may be, they are vehicles for the consciousness of the person they appear to represent. Collectively perceived apparitions, and the fact that apparently conscious apparitions of the living are virtually indistinguishable from those of the dead, provide evidence supporting the idea that apparitions are objectively real. These characteristics also provide evidence that, at least in some cases, apparitions are also vehicles for the surviving consciousness of the deceased.

But the reports of apparitions that provide the most compelling evidence for survival are those that apparently involve the deceased person *communicating* information, unknown to anyone present, in order to fulfill what appears to be the dead person's own agenda, and in ways that are difficult to account for in terms of clairvoyance or telepathy among the living. The Blue Orchid case and the Chaffin Will case are two of the most outstanding examples of this kind. But the vast major-

ity of reports of apparitions simply do not provide evidence supporting survival nearly as strong as these cases do. It should be clear that
what makes these cases so compelling is that they seem to be evidence
of genuine *communication* with the deceased person in question. This
leads us to the final line of evidence to be examined.

PART III

Messages from the Dead

We have done all we can when the critic has nothing left to allege except that the investigator is in [on] the trick. But when he has nothing left to allege, he will allege that. . . . We must drive the objector into the position of being forced to admit the phenomena as inexplicable, at least by him, or to accuse the investigators either of lying or cheating or of a blindness incompatible with any intellectual condition except absolute idiocy.

HENRY SIDGWICK, FIRST PRESIDENTIAL ADDRESS TO THE
BRITISH SOCIETY FOR PSYCHICAL RESEARCH, 1882

The evidence is already strong, and is growing in bulk and cogency, that we are in communication with minds which are discarnate.

OLIVER LODGE, "THE UNIVERSITY ASPECT
OF PSYCHICAL RESEARCH," 1926

Unfortunately, most scientists lack the specific skills needed to distinguish fact from illusion in the world of magic. The universe does not lie; people lie. And so Lodge and other nineteenth-century psychical researchers unwittingly allowed themselves to be fooled by the tricks of professional fortune tellers and sleight-of-hand artists posing as spiritualists.

VICTOR STENGER, *THE UNCONSCIOUS QUANTUM*, 1995

TEN

Ancient Evidence

The idea that we can communicate with spirits is an ancient belief, found among many societies past and present. In tribal cultures, one of the roles of the shaman, witch doctor, or seer was to communicate with discarnate entities. Such individuals were often selected for their special role based on their perceived ability to act as intermediaries between the spirit world and their tribe.

As Western culture has relentlessly encroached on traditional societies, first-person accounts from tribal cultures are increasingly difficult to find. However, historical records show that there is a curiously consistent and genuine quality to the testimony of the phenomenon in the confessions of former shamans who had been converted to Christianity. Years later, they would not recant their former belief that the spirit phenomena had been genuine.

In 1863, William Howitt gave an example provided by a German missionary who had lived among the Native Americans. Years earlier, he had been baffled by the phenomena he had observed during a séance with a medicine man. Historian Brian Inglis writes:

Hearing thirty years later that the medicine man had become a Christian, the missionary thought that at last he would be able to find out how the trick had been done; but no. "Believe me," the medicine man told him, with evident sincerity, "I did not deceive you; I did not shake the lodge; it was shaken by the power of the spirits." Nor, he insisted, had he employed a "double tongue"— ventriloquism. "I only repeated what the spirits said to me. I heard their voices. The top of the lodge was full of them, and before me the sky and wide lands lay expanded; I could see great distances around me; and I believed I could recognize the most distant objects."[1]

Similar accounts of mediumship and spirit possession have been gathered from traditional cultures around the world, including not only Native American but also African, Chinese, and Nepalese.[2] It is sometimes said that communication with the dead via mediums was rarely reported prior to the start of the modern Spiritualist movement in 1848; but this remark holds true primarily for Western Europe, where atypical constraints have operated. There seems to be every reason to believe that mediumistic communication with the dead has been practiced for centuries in non-European cultures. In his comprehensive 1933 work *Life Beyond Death in the Beliefs of Mankind,* Professor James Thayer Addison surveyed several ancient cultures, and wrote:

In records of ancient Babylonia which cite the various orders of priests are listed "the inquirer of the dead" and "he who raises the spirits of the dead." In Gabun today the fetish doctor calls up the spirits by the sound of his little bell, interprets to them the requests of the living, and returns with the revelation of their consent or refusal. A similar type of medicine-man now serves among the Maoris of New Zealand and the Pelew Islanders, for when he goes into a trance the ghosts can speak through him. Wang Ch'uang, the clever skeptic of first-century China, had been watching just such a ceremony when he wrote "Among men the dead speak through living persons whom they throw into a trance, and the wizards thrumming their black chords, call down souls of the dead, who can then speak through the mouths of the wizards."

But the most famous of all the characters who have talked with the dead are King Saul and Odysseus.[3]

However, even with the threat of being burned alive for necromancy, communication with the dead was still sometimes reported in medieval Europe. Here is an example from sixteenth-century France.

The Case of Sister Alis

This case was published in Paris in 1528, in a pamphlet by Adrian de Montalembert, almoner and preacher for Francis I. It concerns some strange events that occurred at the Abbey of St. Pierre in 1526. Prior to 1516, when some reforms were instituted, the nuns came and went as they wished. In this year a young woman named Alis de Telieux took advantage of her position as sacristan (keeper of sacred objects) to depart for the city with some of the valuables in her protection. In 1524, having fallen on hard times and suffering from disease, she died praying for forgiveness, outside of a small village. Instead of being buried in the abbey as she had wished, she was given a pauper's burial.

In the abbey at this time, there lived a young nun named Anthoinette de Grollee, about eighteen years old, described as wise for her age and of good family. She had come to the abbey before 1516, and when Sister Alis lay dying, she had continually talked of her and called her name.

One night early in 1526, as Anthoinette lay half asleep in bed, she reported that someone lifted her veil, made the sign of the cross on her forehead, and kissed her tenderly. She woke up astonished, saw no one, and dismissed the experience as a dream. However, a few days later she began to hear little raps beneath her feet, as though someone were rapping with a stick underneath the tiles. "I have often heard it," de Montalembert wrote, "and at my request it would rap as many blows as I demanded." The sounds followed her everywhere, and were never heard when she was not present.

The astonished nuns asked Anthoinette what she thought was the source of the sounds. Anthoinette replied that she did not know, but thought that it might be Sister Alis the sacristan, because since the latter's death she had often dreamed of her. The rapping entity was itself questioned, and through a code it confirmed that it was indeed the spirit of Sister Alis. The spirit was asked if it wished the body of Alis to be buried in the abbey. It responded that it did; and so the remains were located, disinterred, and reburied in the abbey.

Much of the rest of the pamphlet deals in tedious detail with the ecclesiastical activities that were set in motion for the benefit of Sister Alis. However, at one point the deceased sister seemed to directly use the voice of Anthoinette to beg for forgiveness, and Gauld writes, "Some of the events narrated could almost have taken place at a modern spiritualist séance; were it not, indeed, that a Catholic bishop had charge of them!" At any rate, the drama came to an end in March 1526, when it seemed as though the spirit of Alis was finally at peace.

Comments on the Case of Sister Alis

At the end of his excellent review of this case, Alan Gauld concludes:

> No purpose would be served by speculating about the phenomena reported in this case. De Montalembert does not go into sufficient detail about the rappings to enable one to form an opinion at this distance of time about whether or not they could have been fraudulently produced. The case is of interest chiefly as a precursor to, and early parallel for, later poltergeist cases in which communication has been held with a purported spirit by means of raps. Such cases have been surprisingly numerous, and it was through one of them—at Hydesville in 1848—that the modern Spiritualist movement began. At Hydesville the two young girls round whom the poltergeist phenomena centred became the first Spiritualist mediums. Had Anthoinette de Grollee lived at a later date and in a different setting she too might have become such another.[4]

The Swedenborg Case

Here is another European story from two centuries later, involving the famous scientist and mystic Emmanuel Swedenborg.

> In 1761 the Countess de Marteville came to Swedenborg to explain that her husband, who had been ambassador to the Netherlands, had given her a valuable silver [necklace] before his death. The silversmith was now demanding an exorbitant payment, even though she was sure that her husband had paid for it already; but the receipt was nowhere to be found. The countess asked Swedenborg to contact her husband to ask about the receipt. Three days later he told her that he had spoken to her husband, who had informed him that the vital document was in a bureau upstairs. The woman replied that the bureau had already been searched, but Swedenborg insisted that she should remove a certain drawer and pull off its false back. The papers were duly found in the secret place, whose existence was only known to the dead count. The story is related by eleven different sources and vouched for by Swedenborg himself when he was later questioned about it.[5]

It was not until the last quarter of the nineteenth century that a large-scale effort was mounted to gather and critically assess reports of communication from the dead. This effort began with the founding of the British Society for Psychical Research in 1882, and with its American counterpart in 1884.

There can be little doubt that some of the founding members of the British and American Society for Psychical Research (SPR) hoped to find impartial evidence in support of survival. The 1870s had been a decade that witnessed the rapid rise of materialism. Inspired by the ongoing success of Newtonian physics and by Darwin's new theory of evolution, writers such as Huxley and Tyndall popularized a version of "scientific" materialism that had shaken the faith of Victorian society. Many of the founders of the SPR, disillusioned with the simple faith of their fathers, longed to take on the materialists at their own game. Using the methods of empirical science, these dissident thinkers hoped to discover sound scientific evidence that would refute the doctrine of materialism. However, by no means did the early members all share the same outlook and attitude. Several of the early investigators were extremely skeptical of survival, and some were even dedicated to demolishing the evidence. But regardless of the hopes of individual members, the SPR was formally committed to investigating the phenomena "without prejudice or prepossession, and in a scientific spirit."

The first president of the SPR, the Cambridge philosopher Henry Sidgwick, expressed the sentiments of several of his cofounders with the following words in his inaugural presidential address:

> We believed unreservedly in the methods of modern science, and were prepared to accept submissively her reasoned conclusions, when sustained by the agreement of experts; but we were not prepared to submit with equal docility to the mere prejudices of scientific men. And it appeared to us that there was an important body of evidence—tending prima facie to establish the independence of soul or spirit—which modern science had simply left on one side with ignorant contempt; and that in so leaving it she had been untrue to her professed method and had arrived prematurely at her negative conclusions. Observe that we did not affirm that these negative conclusions were scientifically erroneous. To have said that would have been to fall into the very error we were trying to avoid. We only said that they had been arrived at prematurely.[6]

Clearly, the work of the SPR filled a large contemporary need. Many of the most capable individuals of the period devoted an enormous amount of time, effort, and money to carrying out the very extensive investigations that were reported in its publications. Some of the early members who were particularly devoted to investigating the survival issue were Frederic Myers, Edmund Gurney, physicists Sir Oliver Lodge and Sir William Crookes, and philosopher Richard Hodgson and writer Frank Podmore. Myers and Gurney seemed favorably disposed toward the idea of survival from early on; Lodge and Crookes were cautious but open-minded; Hodgson and Podmore shared the reputation of being ruthlessly skeptical.

ELEVEN

The SPR Investigates

A medium is a person—usually a woman—who apparently acts as a transmitter between our world and the world of the deceased. The early investigators began by examining mediums that fall into two broad categories: physical and mental mediums.

In physical mediumship, communication with the deceased is alleged to occur through various forms of physical phenomena that occur near the body of the medium. These phenomena would include raps, object movements, and even materializations of deceased individuals. The medium Daniel Douglas Home provided some such evidence for communication with the deceased, and was never exposed as a fraud. But unlike Home, many physical mediums insisted on performing their feats in complete darkness, which, of course, offered endless possibilities for fraud. Seeking to exploit the vulnerability of the grieving, many unscrupulous individuals were to be found among the ranks of professional physical mediums. Several of these were duly exposed as frauds, sometimes by members of the SPR. As a result, the quasireligious movement known as Spiritualism—based in part on physical mediumship—acquired a reputation for being riddled with malpractice. Even Home himself complained bitterly that fraudulent practitioners had brought the entire movement into disrepute and made a mockery of its mission.[1]

This scandalous aspect of physical mediumship persuaded the

founders of the SPR to concentrate instead on the phenomena of mental mediumship. This generally takes two forms. The most frequently seen is that of clairvoyant mediumship. The medium may be in a slightly dissociated state, but is usually not in a trance. He or she claims to "hear" or "see" deceased friends and relatives of people present, and to transmit messages from them. Sometimes the information is presented in the form of symbolic images, which the medium must learn to interpret.

The most advanced form of mental mediumship is what is known as trance mediumship. In this form the normal personality seems to be completely dispossessed by an intruding intelligence, which assumes a varying degree of control over the speech, writing, and behavior of the medium. Usually there is just one entity (the "control") that appears to communicate directly through the medium, and serves to relay messages from deceased acquaintances (the "communicators") to those present at the séance (the "sitters"). Sometimes, however, it appears that a succession of deceased individuals will "drop in" and communicate directly through the medium. In the most extreme cases, known as possession mediumship, the medium's body appears to be completely possessed by the intruding agent, and the medium's personality seems to be replaced entirely by that of a deceased individual.

Trance mediumship—especially in its most extreme form of possession—is by far the rarest form of mental mediumship. But it is this form that received the most attention from members of the SPR. The investigators realized early on that evidence obtained from physical mediumship is notoriously unreliable, and can be easily dismissed on grounds of fraud or mistaken eyewitness testimony. But with trance mediumship, the situation is very different. In these cases, we usually have complete contemporary records of what the mediums say or write, so the question of mistaken eyewitness testimony usually does not arise.

Let us now consider some of the evidence gathered from two of the most impressive trance mediums ever studied by the SPR.

The Mediumship of Mrs. Piper

One of the very first trance mediums to be studied in great depth by members of the SPR was Mrs. Leonora Piper of Boston. Her career as a medium began in 1884 when she consulted a healing medium named J. R. Cocke. During her second visit, she passed into a trance and wrote down a message for one of the other sitters, Judge Frost of Cambridge. The message purported to come from Frost's deceased son, and its evidential value impressed him more than any other he had received during his extensive investigation into mediumship.

Mrs. Piper then set up her own circle, and a series of spirit guides took turns acting as her control. These soon retired from the scene with the arrival of a new control who gave the name "Dr. Phinuit," and claimed to be a deceased French physician. However, no trace of him could be found in French medical records, and his knowledge of French was very scanty. As such, researchers came to believe he was merely a fictitious character invented by Mrs. Piper's subconscious mind. But whatever his ultimate status, Mrs. Piper's trance state certainly did seem genuine. She could be cut, pricked, and even have a bottle of ammonia held under her nose without being disturbed. Within a few minutes of entering a trance, Mrs. Piper would begin to speak with the voice of Phinuit, which was gruff and masculine. When Phinuit was in top form, he would give sitters accounts of the appearances of deceased friends and relatives and would transmit messages from them, often with the appropriate gestures. Copious communications from deceased friends and relatives of sitters would be relayed, and the information would often turn out to be accurate in even the tiniest of details.

On off days, Phinuit would ramble and fish for information, providing valuable ammunition for hostile critics. But even at his most banal, he was capable of springing a surprise. At a sitting on June 3, 1889, Mr. J. Rich gave Phinuit a dog collar. Shortly after, Phinuit said he saw the dog coming, and exclaimed: "Here he comes! Oh, how he jumps! There he is now, jumping upon and around you. So glad to see you! Rover! Rover! No—G-rover, Grover! That's his name!" The dog had once been called Rover, but his name was changed to Grover in 1884, in honor of the election of the U.S. president Grover Cleveland.[2]

Mrs. Piper was discovered for the SPR by William James, who first attended one of her séances with his wife back in 1885. James and his wife gave no information about themselves and said nothing while Mrs. Piper was in trance. Nevertheless, Phinuit spoke to them about matters that James and his wife felt certain nobody but they could have known. James was so impressed that he subsequently sent twenty-five other persons to sit with her under pseudonyms. In a report on her mediumship, written in the spring of 1886, James wrote, "I am persuaded of the medium's honesty, and of the genuineness of her trance; and although at first disposed to think that the 'hits' she made were either lucky coincidence, or the result of knowledge on her part of who the sitter was, and of his or her family affairs, I now believe her to be in possession of a power as yet unexplained."[3]

As a result of James's report, the leaders of the SPR in London engaged Mrs. Piper on a permanent basis by paying her a retaining fee, in order that she would devote herself exclusively to research. In 1887, Richard Hodgson was sent to Boston by the SPR in London to take charge of the investigation. As mentioned earlier, he had the reputation of being a ruthless skeptic, and was also considered an expert in the unmasking of fraud.

Hodgson first had several sittings himself with Mrs. Piper, at which much intimate knowledge, some of it very personal, was shown of deceased friends and relatives of Hodgson. He then arranged for sittings with at least fifty people whom he believed to be complete strangers to Mrs. Piper, and the utmost precautions were taken to prevent her from obtaining any information on the sitters beforehand. Sitters were introduced anonymously or under a pseudonym; they often entered the room only after Mrs. Piper had gone into a trance, and then sat behind rather that facing her. In most of these cases, the results were the same as with Hodgson: most sitters were given facts that they were sure Mrs. Piper could not have known about through ordinary means. For several weeks, Hodgson even had her trailed by detectives, to ascertain whether there were any indications that Mrs. Piper or her husband, or others connected with her, tried to ascertain facts about possible sitters, or employed confederates to do so. But as Hodgson tells us, "not the smallest indication of any such procedure was discovered."[4] William James concurred:

> Dr Hodgson considers that the hypothesis of fraud cannot be seriously maintained. I agree with him absolutely. The medium has been under observation, much of the time under close observation, as to most of the conditions of her life, by a large number of persons, eager, many of them, to pounce upon any suspicious circumstances for [nearly] fifteen years. During that time, not only has there not been one single suspicious circumstance remarked, but not one suggestion has ever been made, from any quarter which might tend positively to explain how the medium, living the apparent life she leads, could possibly collect information about so many sitters by natural means.[5]

Mrs. Piper was even brought to England to be tested, where she knew no one and could have no agents. As in America, sitters were usually introduced anonymously; and Mrs. Piper continued to get impressive results. However, the investigators could not decide if Mrs. Piper was really in touch with deceased individuals or if she were merely gaining the information telepathically from the minds of the sitters.

What proved the turning point for Hodgson were the so-called GP communications. George "Pelham" (a pseudonym for Pellew) was a young Boston lawyer, intensely interested in literature and philosophy. As a friend of Hodgson, the two had discussed the possibility of an afterlife; although GP (Pellew) was extremely skeptical of even the possibility, he did promise Hodgson that if he should die first and find himself still living, he would try his best to communicate.

Two years later, GP met his death accidentally at the age of thirty-two, by a fall in New York in February 1892. About four weeks later, Hodgson accompanied a close friend of GP's to a sitting with Mrs. Piper, with the friend sitting under the assumed name of "John Hart." With Phinuit acting as an intermediary, messages purporting to come from GP were relayed to Hart. It should be remembered that GP had attended a sitting with Mrs. Piper about five years earlier, also under an assumed name, and that Hodgson did not think that Mrs. Piper ever remembered seeing him. But, at any rate, at the sitting George Pellew's name was given in full, the sitter was recognized by his real name, and the communications referred to incidents that were unknown to both the sitter and Hodgson.

One of these unknown incidents concerned James and Mary Howard, who were mentioned by name, along with that of their daughter, Katherine. The message was "Tell her, she'll know. I will solve the problems, Katharine." These words meant nothing to Hodgson or the sitter, but when "Hart" gave James Howard an account of the sitting the next day, these words impressed him more than anything else. GP, when he had last stayed with the Howards, had talked frequently with Katherine (a girl of fifteen) about certain philosophical problems. It turned out that GP had told the girl that he would solve the problems and let her know, using almost the exact same words communicated at the sitting.

Three weeks later a sitting was arranged with the Howards, without their names being given. Phinuit first said a few words; then, suddenly, GP appeared to control Mrs. Piper's voice directly. This new control lasted almost the duration of the séance, the nature of which Hodgson describes.

The statements made were intimately personal and characteristic. Common friends were referred to by name, inquiries were made about private matters, and the Howards, who were not predisposed to take any interest in psychical research, but who had been induced by the account of Mr. Hart to have a sitting with Mrs. Piper, were

profoundly impressed with the feeling that they were in truth holding a conversation with the personality of the friend whom they had
known so many years.[6]

The following passages are from notes taken during that séance, and
may serve to suggest the freedom with which the conversation was carried on. The remarks in parentheses are those made during the séance
by James Howard.

GP: Jim, is that you? Speak to me quick. I am not dead. Don't think
me dead. I'm awfully glad to see you. Can't you see me? Don't you
hear me? Give my love to my father and tell him I want to see him.
I am happy here, and more so since I find I can communicate with
you. I pity those people who can't speak . . .

(What do you do, George? Where are you?)

I am scarcely able to do anything yet. I am just awakened to the reality of life after death. It was like darkness, I could not distinguish
anything at first. Darkest hours just before dawn, you know that,
Jim. I was puzzled, confused. Shall have an occupation soon. Now I
can see you, my friends. I can hear you speak. Your voice, Jim, I can
distinguish with your accent and articulation, but it sounds like a
big bass drum. Mine would sound to you like the faintest whisper.

(Our conversation then is something like telephoning?)

Yes.

(By long distance telephone.)

[GP laughs.]

(Were you not surprised to find yourself living?)

Perfectly so. Greatly surprised. I did not believe in a future life.[7]

In séances from this time on, GP sometimes communicated directly through Mrs. Piper's voice, and sometimes through automatic writing, with the latter becoming more common as time passed. GP's career as a "drop-in" communicator persisted until 1897, and out of 150 sitters who were introduced to GP during that time, he recognized by name twenty-nine of the thirty that George Pellew had known in life (the sole exception was a young woman who had been a child when the living Pellew had last seen her). He conversed with each of these individuals in the appropriate manner, and showed an intimate knowledge of his supposed past relationships with them. As Hodgson writes, in each case "the recognition was clear and full, and accompanied by an appreciation of the relations which subsisted between GP living and the sitters."[8] And there was not a single case of false recognition; that is, GP never once greeted anyone of the 120 that the living Pellew had not known.

Hodgson adds:

> The continual manifestation of this personality—so different from Phinuit or other communicators—with its own reservoir of memories, with its swift appreciation of any reference to friends of GP, with its "give and take" in little incidental conversations with myself, has helped largely in producing a conviction of the actual presence of the GP personality, which it would be quite impossible to impart by any mere enumeration of verifiable statements.[9]

By 1898, when he published his report on Mrs. Piper's mediumship for the SPR, Hodgson had become a firm believer in survival. In large part, his conversion seems to be due to the clear expression of the personality and memories of the deceased George Pellew. Hodgson was convinced that Mrs. Piper had no knowledge of the living Pellew. So how could she have succeeded in dramatically impersonating somebody she had barely met more than four years earlier in a way that convinced thirty people who were intimate with Pellew before he died? Near the end of his report, Hodgson states that, although further experimental evidence may lead him to change his mind, "at the present I cannot profess to have any doubt but that the chief 'communicators' to whom I have referred in the foregoing pages are veritably the personalities that they claim to be, that they have survived the change we call death, and that they have directly communicated with us whom we call living, through Mrs. Piper's entranced organism."[10]

In December 1905, Hodgson died unexpectedly, at the age of fifty, following a game of handball at his club. A week later, messages purporting to come from the deceased Hodgson began to be relayed by Mrs. Piper. Reports of the messages from Hodgson reached his old friend William James. Intrigued, James once again investigated Mrs. Piper's mediumship. His report to the SPR in 1909 covered some seventy-five sittings in which Hodgson was said to be in control. James found much of the material impressive as evidence of supernormal knowledge; and everyone admitted that the Hodgson control showed many of the personal traits of Hodgson. However, James stopped short of committing himself to the view that the messages were indeed from his deceased friend. After all, Mrs. Piper had known the living Hodgson very well, so James felt that Mrs. Piper could be subconsciously dramatizing his personality and furnishing it with information acquired by ESP. At any rate, James's reservations were shared by Mrs. Sidgwick, Sir Oliver Lodge, and J. G. Piddington, all of whom were to go further than James in their commitment to the survival hypothesis.

Comments on the Mediumship of Mrs. Piper

Mrs. Piper's trance mediumship continued until 1911, and she was to play a part in the famous "cross correspondences," which are discussed in chapter 14. The discovery of Mrs. Piper inaugurated an era in which several outstanding mediums—many of them amateurs—put their services at the disposal of researchers, often instead of cultivating a clientele. During this period, most of the leading figures of the SPR, both in America and in England, gave high priority to survival as a research problem.

Next, we will briefly consider another gifted medium studied extensively by the SPR.

The Mediumship of Mrs. Leonard

As a child, Mrs. Gladys Osborne Leonard (1882–1968) would have beautiful visions, of which her conventional parents disapproved. Much later, while married, she held an experimental séance with some friends, and discovered her gifts as a medium. She had passed into a trance and, after recovering, was told that her mother and a young girl named Feda had spoken through her. Feda claimed to be the spirit of an Indian girl whom an ancestor of Mrs. Leonard had married in the early nineteenth century. Although the statements could not be verified, there was a family tradition of such a girl, the story being that she had died in childbirth at an early age. But, whatever her true status, Feda became Mrs. Leonard's chief control and, from that point on, treated her with a mix of tolerance and amused contempt.

As the First World War approached, Feda began to speak of a coming catastrophe, and urged Mrs. Leonard to do her duty to help as many bereaved people as possible with her talents as a medium. When the war started, Mrs. Leonard became a professional medium, and devoted herself to helping the bereaved. Yet, at the same time, she submitted to critical investigation by members of the SPR, and for a time she was also shadowed by detectives to ensure that she did not make inquiries about sitters, or employ agents to do so. The first member of the SPR to study her in detail was Sir Oliver Lodge, who was greatly impressed by communications purporting to come from a son killed in the war. Lodge's book about these communications, *Raymond* (1916), made Mrs. Leonard famous. From then until the early years of the Second World War she was regularly studied by SPR investigators. Feda remained her principal guide throughout the entire period. Most communications were given by speech, with Feda acting as intermediary. Occasionally, other communicators would take control of Mrs. Leonard's voice, and on rare occasions, messages were received in writing.

In many ways the mediumship of Mrs. Leonard resembled that of Mrs. Piper, and there is no need to cover the same ground twice. We saw earlier how Mrs. Piper occasionally produced information that was unknown to any of the sitters, yet later turned out to be accurate. Mrs. Leonard's mediumship is primarily of interest because of the many instances in which she produced such information, which would apparently rule out telepathy with the sitters as the source. The most impressive of these instances took the form of "book tests" and proxy sittings. The latter will be considered in depth in a later section. Here we will examine one of the more unusual of the former.

The origin of the book test is obscure, but at least one writer thinks it quite likely that book tests were first proposed by Feda.[11] Essentially, the principle is that the communicator has to specify the location of a book in a house to which the medium has no access but which was well-known to the communicator while living. The communicator must also specify a page number of that book, on which will be found a passage that conveys some appropriate message.

The following is one of the earliest book tests of which we have a record. On March 19, 1917, Mrs. Leonard gave a sitting to a widow, Mrs. Hugh Talbot. According to Mrs. Talbot, "Mrs. Leonard at this time knew neither my name nor address, nor had I ever been to her or any other medium, before, in my life."[12]

During the first part of the séance, nothing remarkable happened. There was only a "medley of descriptions" of various people. But then suddenly, according to Mrs. Talbot:

> Feda gave a very correct description of my husband's personal appearance, and from then on he alone seemed to speak (through her of course) and a most extraordinary conversation followed. Evidently

he was trying by every means in his power to prove to me his identity and to show me it really was himself . . . All he said, or rather
Feda for him, was clear and lucid. Incidents of the past, known only
to him and to me were spoken of, belongings trivial in themselves
but possessing for him a particular personal interest of which I was
aware, were minutely and correctly described, and I was asked if I
still had them.[13]

Mrs. Talbot was also asked repeatedly if she believed that it was the
deceased Mr. Talbot who was communicating.

Feda kept on saying: "Do you believe, he *does* want you to know it
is really himself." I said I could not be sure but I thought it must be
true. . . .

Suddenly Feda began a tiresome description of a book, she said it
was leather and dark, and tried to show me the size. Mrs. Leonard
showed a length of eight to ten inches long with her hands, and
four or five wide. She [Feda] said, "It is not exactly a *book*, it is not
printed, Feda wouldn't call it a book, it has writing in."

It was long before I could connect this description with anything
at all, but at last I remembered a red leather note book of my husband's, which I think he called a log book, and I asked: "Is it a log
book?" Feda seemed puzzled at this and not to know what a log
book was, and repeated the word once or twice then said, "Yes, yes,
he says it might be a log book." I then said, "Is it a red book?" On
this point there was hesitation, they thought possibly it was, though
he thought it was darker.

The answer was undecided, and Feda began a wearisome description all over again, adding that I was to look on page twelve, for
something written there, that it would be so interesting after the
conversation. Then she said, "He is not sure it is page twelve, it
might be thirteen, it is so long, but he does want you to look and try
and find it. It would interest him to know if this extract is there."[14]

None of this interested Mrs. Talbot. Although she thought she remembered the book, she was not even sure if she still had it, and at any rate, the whole business sounded purposeless to her. She replied "rather indefinitely" that she would see if she could find the book, but this did not satisfy the communicator who was apparently passing messages through Feda.

> She started all over again, becoming more and more insistent and went on to say, "He is not sure of the colour, he does not know. There are two books, you will know the one he means by a diagram of languages in the front . . . Indo-European, Aryan, Semitic languages and others." . . . It sounded absolute rubbish to me.[15]

Thinking that the medium was tired and talking nonsense, Mrs. Talbot was glad when the sitting came to an end. Over dinner that evening, she mentioned the séance to her sister and niece, and "after telling my sister and niece all that I considered the interesting things said in the beginning, I did mention that in the end the medium began talking a lot of rubbish about a book, and asking me to look on page twelve or thirteen to find something interesting." After dinner, her sister and niece begged her to look for the book at once. Although Mrs. Talbot wanted to wait until the next day, she finally gave in, and after a bit of searching found two of her husband's old notebooks at the back of a top bookshelf.

Mrs. Talbot tells us that in her written testimony that she had never opened either one of the notebooks.

> One, a shabby black leather, corresponded in size to the description given, and I absent-mindedly opened it, wondering in my mind whether the one I was looking for had been destroyed or only sent away. To my utter astonishment, my eyes fell on the words, "Table of Semitic or Syro-Arabian Languages."[16]

Even more astonishing was what she found on page thirteen. On this page Mr. Talbot had transcribed, some time in his life, the following passage from a book called *Post Mortem,* published anonymously in 1881:

> I discovered by certain whispers which it was supposed I was unable to hear and from certain glances of curiosity or commiseration which it was supposed I was unable to see, that I was near death. . . .
>
> Presently my mind began to dwell not only on happiness which was to come, but upon happiness that I was actually enjoying. I saw long forgotten forms, playmates, school-fellows, companions of my youth and of my old age, who one and all, smiled upon me. They did not smile with any compassion, that I no longer felt that I needed, but with that sort of kindness which is exchanged by people who are equally happy. I saw my mother, father, and sisters, all of whom I had survived. They did not speak, yet they communicated to me their unaltered and unalterable affection. At about the time they appeared, I made an effort to realize my bodily situation . . . that is, I endeavored to connect my soul with the body which lay on the bed in my house . . . the endeavor failed. I was dead.[17]

There was also "a diagram of languages" in the front, matching the description given through Feda. Mrs. Talbot's sister and niece corroborated Mrs. Talbot's account, and also provided written and signed testimony for the records of the SPR.[18]

Comments on the Mediumship of Mrs. Leonard

Was Mr. Talbot trying to prove his continued existence to his wife by directing her to a relevant passage he had written in a notebook while alive, the existence of which only he was aware? In the next section we consider the other possibilities for this and for other cases of apparent communication with the deceased, and evaluate them in terms of the evidence.

TWELVE

Alternative Explanations

In addition to the hypothesis of genuine communication with the deceased, there appear to be three alternative explanations.

CONSCIOUS FRAUD

Although there have certainly been fraudulent mediums—some of which were exposed by members of the SPR—in the best cases of mental mediums, this does not seem even remotely plausible. Both Mrs. Piper and Mrs. Leonard were investigated in minute detail, and even archskeptic Frank Podmore agreed that not the slightest suspicion of fraud was justified.* Both women were trailed by detectives at certain times; Mrs. Piper was even brought to England where she knew no one, and yet she continued to provide impressive results. In order for fraud to account for the messages, it seems that any conspiracy of fraud would have had to include the investigators and witnesses themselves! Hodgson felt it was necessary to briefly deal with this wild accusation:

It has been suggested that the important witnesses in connection with the GP evidence may have been in collusion with Mrs Piper. The absurdity of this suggestion would be at once apparent if their

---

*Podmore summarized the case against fraud by Mrs. Leonard in his 1898–99 article, titled "Discussion of the Trance Phenomena of Mrs Piper."

real names were given, but since the only real full names given of actual sitters with GP are those of Professor C. Eliot Norton and James M. Peirce, of Harvard University, who are referred to chiefly as cases of being recognized by the communicating GP as personally known to him, I state concerning the others that I know personally all but two of the GP sitters, and most of them intimately, that they belong to the most cultivated and responsible class in the Unites States, and that it would be as absurd to suppose any collusion between them and Mrs Piper as to suppose that the members of the Council of the SPR were in collusion with her.[1]

In the case of Mrs. Leonard's book tests, fraud also seems unlikely. Of course, it is possible that Mrs. Talbot, along with her sister and niece, colluded with Mrs. Leonard—but for what conceivable purpose? It could be argued that Mrs. Talbot and her relatives were paid by Mrs. Leonard to provide written and signed testimony for the records of the SPR, in order to enhance Mrs. Leonard's reputation as a medium. But again, for what purpose? Mrs. Leonard was already growing famous because of Lodge's popular book about her. To bring in three confederates would be very risky, especially if the case were to be scrutinized by the dedicated and critical researchers of the SPR. On the other hand, if Mrs. Leonard acted alone, how would she have gathered the information ahead of time? While there had been another séance two days earlier, confederates would have had to break in to the Talbot place before the second séance, find the book with its passage, and also discover many small details about Mr. Talbot's personal life, all without arousing the suspicion of Mrs. Talbot or her relatives. Then, the information would have had to be presented in a convincing manner on the night of the séance. Recall how Mrs. Talbot described the messages:

Incidents of the past, known only to him and to me were spoken of, belongings trivial in themselves but possessing for him a particular personal interest of which I was aware, were minutely and correctly described, and I was asked if I still had them.

Finally, Mrs. Talbot's niece testified that the notebooks were dusty when found on the shelf. Conscious fraud seems completely out of the question in the most carefully documented cases. For all but the most paranoid conspiracy theorists, this explanation will seem completely inadequate.

SUBCONSCIOUS FRAUD

A somewhat less sinister explanation that has been proposed is that the medium is not consciously deceiving the sitters, but is rather subconsciously dramatizing the communications. The idea is that the medium, in her trance state—similar to a hypnotic trance—is essentially telling the grief-stricken sitters what they want to hear, but may not even be aware of the charade herself. The sitters simply ignore and forget the mistakes made by the medium, but remember and celebrate any correct guesses she stumbles on.

However, this explanation will not get us very far. During the SPR's research into the mediumship of Mrs. Piper and Mrs. Leonard, careful records were made of *everything* the medium said or wrote while in trance. It is clear that, in many cases in which the medium did not know the sitters, the amount of accurate, highly detailed information received far exceeded what could be expected from sheer guesswork. H. J. Saltmarsh, a member of the SPR who did a great deal of investigation into mediumship, devised a method of testing the explanation of chance coincidence. He sent a transcript of two sittings that had been held with the medium Mrs. Warren Elliot to six people who had not visited her, but who had a similar experience to the sitter: each had been affected by the death of a young pilot in the war. The statements were marked for accuracy, and the results for the sitter were then compared with the results from the control group. In the first sitting, out of a total of 5,642 statements, 73 percent of the statements were marked accurate for the sitter, but only 8 percent of the statements were marked accurate for the control group. In the second sitting, out of 5,554 statements, 58 percent were marked accurate for the sitter, but only 9 percent for the control group.

	Total Statements	Actual Marks	Control's Marks
1st sitting	5,642	4,107 (73%)	452 (8%)
2nd sitting	5,554	3,226 (58%)	487 (9%)

Adapted from: Inglis, *Science and Parascience*, 330.

Statistician R. A. Fisher calculated that the odds against the medium obtaining her results by chance were approximately one billion to one. Much more than lucky guesswork is required.

Some critics have maintained that mediums "fish" for information as they go along, in order to pick up hints from the sitters that they are on the right track. These hints could be in the form of explicit verbal agreement, or in more subtle forms, such as facial expressions and body language. It is argued that the medium picks up on these cues to quickly drop any clear misses, and to home in on any correct guesses. However, this criticism became hard to sustain after the invention of proxy sittings—sittings in which a sitter will visit the medium on behalf of a third person who is not present. In several of these cases the sitter did not even know the person for whom information was sought, and so could not possibly have provided any clues. Yet, as we will see later, the successes continued.*

---

*Note that "fishing for information" based on clues provided by sitters also cannot explain cases in which the medium produces correct information not known to any of the sitters present. We have already explored two such cases, and several more will be discussed in the pages that follow.

ESP AND SUBCONSCIOUS FRAUD

The most sophisticated objection to mediumship as evidence of survival combines the extrasensory capabilities of the medium with the drama-tizing powers of her subconscious mind. It is alleged that the medium picks up information telepathically or clairvoyantly and then "dresses it up" in the form of an imitation of a personality. It is asserted that this is a more economical explanation of the communications: we already have independent evidence that telepathy and clairvoyance exist, and so—it is argued—an explanation in terms of ESP is "simpler" than the hypothesis that further assumes discarnate survival.

Curt Ducasse discussed this and made a very insightful comment:

It [has been] urged that possession of such powers by the medium is a more economical explanation of the contents and style of the communications; for the medium is anyway known to exist and so is extrasensory perception; whereas the spirit survival explanation requires one to assume gratuitously (1) that spirits exist; (2) that they are capable of remembering; (3) that they are capable of tempo-rarily "possessing" the body of some living persons; and (4) that they are capable of telepathic communication with some living persons.

The first comment these criticisms invite is that, in discussions of the question of survival, clarity of thought is promoted if, for one thing, one leaves out altogether the weasel word "spirits," and uses instead the word "minds"; the question then being whether there is any evidence that minds that were incarnate continue to exist and to function discarnate, thus surviving their body's death.

When the question of survival is formulated thus in terms not of "spirits" but of *minds,* then the allegation that the survival expla-nation makes gratuitously the four assumptions mentioned above is seen to be erroneous. For (1) that there is minds is not an assump-tion but a known fact; (2) that minds are capable of remembering is likewise not an assumption but is known; (3) that minds are capable of "possessing" living human bodies is also a known fact, for "possession" is but the name of the *normal* relation of a mind to its living body. *Paranormal* "possession" would be a possession in the very same sense, but only temporary, and of a living body by a mind other than its own—that other mind being one which had been that of a body now dead; and (4) that telepathic communication between minds is possible and also a known fact.[2]

As evidence that ESP between the living can explain communications, critics have pointed out that fictitious personalities have played a role in communications from mediums. We have seen how William James and others thought that Dr. Phinuit was a creation of Mrs. Piper's subconscious mind. Chapter 7 of my first book, Science and Psychic Phenomena, presented evidence that altered states of consciousness seem to enhance telepathic abilities. And there is evidence that telepathy between medium and sitter does at least sometimes seem to occur, and is then incorporated into the medium's portrayal of communication from the "deceased." For instance, one day Hodgson had been reading John Lockhart's Life of Scott with great interest. At a sitting with Mrs. Piper the next day, a ludicrous Sir Walter Scott announced himself, and proceeded to give a guided tour of the solar system, even stating that there are monkeys in the sun![3] Stanley Hall once received communications through Mrs. Piper from a young woman named Bessie Beals, a totally fictitious personality invented by him for the purpose of testing the medium.

Finally, as evidence in favor of ESP as an explanation, critics have pointed out that reports of communications have been received through mediums from people presumed dead, but, in fact, very much alive. Such cases are exceptionally rare, but there are a few examples in the literature.

The Gordon Davis Case

By far the most famous case of this sort is the "Gordon Davis" case, recorded by S. G. Soal during his sittings with Mrs. Blanche Cooper, a direct voice medium. Gordon Davis was one of Soal's boyhood acquaintances whom Soal believed had been killed in the First World War. According to Soal, on January 4, 1922, a communicator calling himself "Gordon Davis" appeared to control the speech organs of the medium and spoke in a manner characteristic of Gordon Davis. The communicator seemed to believe that he had been killed, and spoke of two experiences that Davis and Soal had shared—one from boyhood and one from a chance encounter they had at a train station during the war. At a later sitting on January 9, Nada, a regular control of Mrs. Cooper's, purported to speak on behalf of Gordon Davis and described the house the Davis family lived in, referring to several external features, and some furniture and pictures inside it. Finally, Soal reported that on January 30, 1922, Nada spoke briefly about a "black dickie bird" on a piano, and that was the last time anything regarding Gordon Davis was communicated. However, in 1925, Soal was surprised to learn that Davis was very much alive, and went to see him. He found that much of what Nada had said about the house and its contents was correct, but that Davis and his family had not moved into the house until some time *after* Soal's sitting with the medium (although Davis had inspected the house on January 6, 1922, with the intention of purchasing it).[4]

Comments on the Gordon Davis Case

This appears to be a case in which the medium, or her trance personality, acquired the information about Davis and the belief that he was dead telepathically from the mind of Soal, and then presented the information with Davis's characteristic tone of voice and accent. The information about the house may suggest some sort of precognition, although it could be argued that it was received telepathically from the mind of Gordon Davis, given his intentions of moving in.

When Soal published this case in 1926, it received enormous publicity, and made Soal famous both among the public and among psychic researchers. It seems to be an example of a medium exercising an extraordinary amount of ESP in order to unconsciously deceive a sitter into thinking that she was receiving genuine communication from the deceased. The case has been without parallel since then. But what are we to think of it today?

The case is far less impressive today than it was in 1926, as we now have good reason to suspect that Soal "improved" the case. First, in 1978 statistician Betty Markwick demonstrated how Soal fraudulently manipulated the results of his famous card-guessing experiments, and thereby completely discredited Soal's research into ESP.[5] In 1982, Alan Gauld reviewed the Gordon Davis case, and noted that "certain features of it raise doubts—for example, Soal's claim that he was able to record the medium's statements in detail in the dark using only his left hand, and the fact that his brother signed a statement that he had read the communications, which allegedly took place in January 1922, in the Christmas vacation of 1921."[6]

Then, in 1986, BBC writer Melvin Harris examined the primary sources of the Gordon Davis case and uncovered suspicious evidence bearing directly on it. Harris points out that Soal had ample opportunity to commit fraud. In mid-February 1925, he is told that Gordon Davis is alive, and his records from the séances now assume a new importance. Yet no one is allowed to examine and witness them. No copies are sent to the SPR. Instead, Soal keeps these potentially exciting documents to himself for several weeks—until *after* his visit to see Gordon Davis.

And what could possibly account for this extraordinary delay in visiting Davis? Harris quotes Soal's criticisms of another researcher's book, showing that Soal clearly understood the crucial importance of timely corroboration of evidence. So, simple naiveté cannot explain the delay.

What about difficulty in traveling? To account for his continued belief that Gordon Davis was dead, Soal explains that Davis "had started business in Southend and was becoming very well known in the district. I live, however, in Prittlewell and do not very frequently visit either Southend or Rochford." But Harris noted that Soal could have been with Davis in less than ten minutes any time he chose. For

Prittlewell is, in fact, part of Southend! Gordon Davis's offices were only a mile down a straight main road from Soal's house.

Harris proposes another reason for the six-week delay:

> Mr. Soal was a devious character. And it's clear that in the six weeks at his disposal he had plenty of chance to find out things about number 54. I've visited the house myself and noted that all Soal had to do was walk past the place, then ride past on the double-decker bus and record everything that could be spotted through the plain glass windows.
>
> Let's not mince words. I'm asserting that the house forecasts were faked. The original exercise books he used to record his sittings were easily falsified. The metal staples only had to be sprung and the pages would lift out, allowing newly written accounts to be inserted. In that [manner] he was able to create a cunning enigma.
>
> Here I should emphasize that there were genuine "messages" in the accounts that needed no doctoring, but these did not exhibit precognition or anything vaguely startling, and Soal could have learned of all the bits and pieces by quite normal means. Only the house forecasts were destined to make this affair noteworthy and extraordinary. So only those passages needed to be re-jigged or invented.[7]

This, as Harris notes, would only be a "wild, spiteful theory" if he did not have evidence that Soal faked the records. What made Harris suspicious was Soal's account of his visit to see Davis. On that night he took with him a typed copy of the handwritten accounts of the relevant sessions with Blanche Cooper. The typed and handwritten accounts had to be identical, because Soal wanted Davis to comment on each item and sign a statement regarding their degree of accuracy.

After leaving Davis's house at number 54 on the night of his visit, both men walked up to the Davis & Hollins Agency offices, some five minutes away. On reaching the office, Soal suddenly "remembered" to mention something that was not in the typed records he had brought with him, which he called "a curious oversight."

> On my first visit to Mr. Davis' house on April 8, by a curious over-sight I entirely overlooked the statement concerning 'black dicky bird on piano,' and it was not until I reached his office later in the evening that I remembered to mention it. Mr. Davis then informed me that he had in his possession a small ornament in the form of a kingfisher which stood on a black china pedestal. At the time of my visit it was actually standing in a plant pot on the piano and, owing to its being almost hidden inside the plant pot, had escaped my notice.[8]

When Soal wrote his article, he claimed that a brief message about "black dickie bird—think it's on piano" had been communicated on behalf of "Gordon Davis" in the middle of the sitting on January 30, 1922. In his article, Soal even included a sample of the transcript that contains the message. But, as Harris writes:

> This is pure fiction. His knowledge of the bird came from his obser-vation of Davis's kingfisher ornament—not from any séance. When he spontaneously invented this morsel, he'd forgotten one vital fac-tor. He'd forgotten that a complete record of the essential sitting had been in private hands for the past three years.[9]

The Reverend A. T. Fryer had helped Soal investigate some of the messages received via Blanche Cooper concerning James Miles, a young boy who had drowned. According to Harris, Reverend Fryer had been sent copies of all the sittings, and a copy of the sitting with Mrs. Cooper on January 30, 1922, still survives.

> This copy is in Soal's own handwriting. It lists, stage by stage, every statement made that day and it even lists every pause during the sit-

ting. Nothing is omitted—even when the message is as slight as a single letter. Yet there is no mention of Gordon Davis on any page of this record. The dicky-bird message simply *does not exist*.[10]

So, it appears that once again Soal doctored his own records in order to make the evidence more impressive than it really was. Both the Gordon Davis case and his card-guessing experiments brought Soal fame and recognition, and his bizarre personality may have contributed to his behavior. In her exposé of his card-guessing fraud, Betty Markwick wrote, "It is clear from the literature, and from the comments of those who knew Soal personally, that his was indeed a strange personality: obsessive, absorbed, secretive, and subject to bouts of dissociation."[11]

Harris adds that "as well as this, he was dogged by involuntary whispering." He speculates that Soal may have muttered away to himself while sitting with Blanche Cooper, and ended up making records of his own voice!

The six-week delay in contacting Davis, combined with Soal's untruthful remarks about the difficulty in contacting Davis; the ease with which all the major details of the case could have been gathered by fraudulent means during this six-week period; the ease by which the records could have been doctored; Soal's history of fraud; the evidence of fraud in this case; and Soal's strange personality—all these factors combine to render the Gordon Davis case completely worthless as evidence.

As mentioned earlier, genuine cases in which communication is received from someone presumed dead but actually alive are very rare. However, we do have a somewhat more recent example.

The Rosalind Heywood Case

Rosalind Heywood, a respected psychic researcher, has described her own experience in which a medium was obviously acquiring information from the sitter. She writes:

Soon after the Second World War I decided to test a medium by having an anonymous sitting with her and mentally asking the fate of a German friend, of whom I heard nothing since 1938. He was a prominent man of great integrity, and I feared he must have been killed, either by the Nazis or the Russians. He soon appeared to turn up at the sitting, gave his Christian name, spoke through the medium in character and reminded me of various pleasant experiences which he had shared with my family in America, and I had forgotten. He then said he had been killed in grim circumstances which he did not want to talk about. After the sitting I made enquiries as to his fate. He was eventually traced by the Swiss Foreign Office to a neutral country, and in reply to a letter from me he said that he had escaped both Nazis and Russians, had married, was living in two rooms and had never been so happy in his life. Here, then, it looks as if the medium, unknown to herself, was building a picture of the German from my subconscious memories and fears as to his fate.[12]

Comments on the Rosalind Heywood Case

Perhaps this more modest case is a genuine example of convincing yet false mediumistic communication, based entirely on telepathy with the sitter. However, we have also seen cases described above in which more than telepathy between medium and sitters would be required to explain the communications—cases in which *correct* information was sometimes conveyed that was unknown to anyone present. According to the hypothesis of ESP and subconscious fraud, some of the GP communications, for instance, would also require telepathy with persons not present at the séance, regardless of what those people were doing or thinking of at the time.

The book tests described above also require more than simple telepathy as an explanation. The case we considered would involve Mrs. Leonard telepathically reading Mrs. Talbot's mind, finding out small details about her husband, "trivial in themselves but possessing for him a particular personal interest." Then, with Mrs. Leonard pretending "Mr. Talbot" was anxious to prove his identity, she would have had to clairvoyantly scan the bookshelves in Mrs. Talbot's house until an appropriate passage was located in one of Mr. Talbot's old notebooks. And this explanation requires that all of this was done subconsciously by Mrs. Leonard. Again, even assuming that we have any evidence that such a degree of telepathy and clairvoyance ever occurs, the question remains: For what purpose? To subconsciously perpetrate a fraud? Since Mrs. Leonard was presumably paid by Mrs. Talbot, and since Mrs. Talbot presumably thought she received more than her money's worth, we at least have some sort of plausible motive for subconscious deception. The question is: Do we also have any plausible *means* of carrying it out?

Note that not a single individual who has carefully studied the evidence for communication from the deceased via mental mediums has ever proposed any viable alternative to the hypothesis of genuine communication, other than that of ESP combined with subconscious fraud. Let us now examine how this proposed explanation stands up to the facts.

DIFFICULTIES WITH
ESP AS AN EXPLANATION

We have seen that some cases of apparent communication with the deceased are best explained by telepathy between the medium and the sitter. We have also seen that other cases might possibly be explained in terms of telepathy involving not just the sitters, but perhaps other living people as well; and that clairvoyant perception of distant objects might also be involved in some cases.

But there are a number of difficulties with ESP as an explanation of all cases which are not simply fraudulent.

Degree of ESP Required
The most obvious objection to the idea that the best cases are due to telepathy can be illustrated with an extract from the first of two

sittings Mrs. Piper had with the Reverend S. W. Sutton and his wife on December 8, 1893. Hodgson first introduced the sitters under the pseudonym of "Smith," and then Phinuit spoke *on behalf* of the Suttons' deceased daughter, who had died six weeks earlier. A practiced note taker acted as recorder, and the annotations in square brackets are by Mrs. Sutton.

Phinuit said . . . A little child is coming to you . . . He reaches out his hands as to a child, and says coaxingly: Come here, dear. Don't be afraid. Come, darling, here is your mother. He describes the child and her "lovely curls." Where is Papa? Want Papa. [He (Phinuit) takes from the table a silver medal.] I want this—want to bite it. [She used to bite it.] [Reaches for a string of buttons.] Quick! I want to put them in my mouth. [The buttons also. To bite the buttons was forbidden. He exactly imitated her arch manner.] . . . Who is Dodo? [Her name for her brother George.] . . . I want you to call Dodo. Tell Dodo I am happy. Cry for me no more. [Puts hands to throat.] No sore throat any more. [She had pain and distress of the throat and tongue.] Papa, speak to me. Can you not see me? I am not dead, I am living. I am happy with Grandma. [My mother had been dead many years.] Phinuit says: Here are two more. One, two, three, here,—one older and one younger than Kakie. [Correct.] . . .

Was this little one's tongue very dry? She keeps showing me her tongue. [Her tongue was paralyzed, and she suffered much with it to the end.] Her name is Katherine. [Correct.] She calls herself Kakie. She passed out last. [Correct.] Where is horsey? [I gave him a little horse.] Big horsey, not this little one. [Probably refers to a toy cart-horse she used to like.] Papa, want to go wide [ride] horsey. [She plead this all through her illness.] . . .

[I asked if she remembered anything after she was brought down-stairs.] I was so hot, my head was so hot. [Correct.] . . . [I asked if she suffered in dying.] I saw the light and followed it to this pretty lady

. . . Do not cry for me—that makes me sad. Eleanor. I want Eleanor. [Her little sister. She called her much during her last illness.] I want my buttons. Row, row,—my song,—sing it now. I sing with you. [We sing, and a soft child voice sings with us.]

> *Lightly row, lightly row,*
> *O'er the merry waves we go,*
> *Smoothly glide, smoothly glide,*
> *With the ebbing tide.*

[Phinuit hushes us, and Kakie finishes alone.]

> *Let the wind and waters be*
> *Mingled with our melody,*
> *Sing and float, sing and float*
> *In our little boat*

. . . Kakie sings: Bye, bye, ba bye, bye, bye, O baby bye. Sing that with me, Papa. [Papa and Kakie sing. These two were the songs she used to sing.] Where is Dinah? I want Dinah. [Dinah was an old black rag-doll, not with us.] I want Bagie [Her name for her sister Margaret.] I want Bagie to bring me my Dinah . . . Tell Dodo when you see him that I love him. Dear Dodo. He used to march with me, he put me way up. [Correct.][13]

Throughout the two sittings, no information was communicated that lay outside the knowledge of the sitters. Does this mean that we can attribute all of Mrs. Piper's "hits" to telepathy with the sitters? In his review of this case, Gauld writes, "I know of no instance of undeniable telepathy between living persons, or for that matter of any other variety of ESP, in which the flow of paranormally acquired information has been so quick, so copious, and so free from error."[14]

The amount of detailed information conveyed quickly and

accurately certainly far exceeds anything seen in both the anecdotal and experimental evidence.

We have also seen examples in both Mrs. Piper's and Mrs. Leonard's mediumship in which the medium displays knowledge not known to her or to the sitters. But in order to *conclusively* eliminate telepathy between medium and sitters as an explanation (as well as the technique of "fishing" for information), the technique of proxy sittings was developed. As the name suggests, a proxy sitting is one in which a sitter will visit the medium on behalf of a third person who is not present. The best known of all proxy sittings are the numerous sittings with Mrs. Leonard at which the Reverend Drayton Thomas acted as proxy, usually on behalf of bereaved parents and spouses who had contacted Thomas by mail. If the proxy sitter does not even know the person he is representing, then telepathy with the sitter is obviously ruled out as the source of information.

One of the best known proxy sittings was arranged by Professor E. R. Dodds, a well-known critic of the evidence for survival. Dodds asked Thomas to do a proxy sitting with Mrs. Leonard, but not on his behalf. It was for a Mrs. Lewis, who wanted to contact her deceased father, a Mr. Macaulay. Thus, the sitting was not even secondhand, on behalf of Dodds, but thirdhand. Both Mrs. Lewis and Mr. Macaulay, who in life had been a hydraulic engineer, were completely unknown to both Thomas and Mrs. Leonard. The only facts that Thomas was told about Mr. Macaulay were his name, his hometown, and his date of death. Yet Feda seemed to get in touch with him right away. She described instruments he worked with, mathematical formulas he used, and more personal matters, such as his pet name for his daughter. She also gave the names of three people who had shared with him an especially happy period of his life. However, one name puzzled her, and she said, "It might be Reece but sounds like Riss."

None of this meant anything to Thomas. He sent the information to Dodds, who in turn passed it on to Mrs. Lewis. She was impressed by the information, and stated that the names and nickname given were correct, but found the reference to "Reece" particularly interesting. During the happy period referred to, her elder brother had hero-worshipped an older schoolboy whose name was Rees. Her brother had stated that his name was spelled "Rees" and not "Reece" so many times that his younger sisters would tease him by singing "Not Reece but Riss" until their father stopped them.

Over five sittings, 124 items of information were given, of which 51 were classified as correct, 12 as good, 32 as fair, 2 as poor, 22 as doubtful, and 5 as wrong.

Dodds, the skeptical investigator behind this experiment, remarked:

It appears to me that the hypothesis of fraud, rational influence from disclosed facts, telepathy from the actual sitter, and coincidence cannot either singly or in combination account for the results obtained. Only the barest information was supplied to sitter and medium, and that through an indirect channel.[15]

In order for telepathy to explain this case, it would be necessary for Mrs. Leonard's trance personality to have telepathically tapped into the mind of Mrs. Lewis, two removes away. There is certainly no experimental evidence for such an indirect form of telepathy; and the anecdotal evidence strongly suggests that telepathy usually operates between people who are emotionally linked or, at least, associated in some way.

In the proxy case just considered, all the information was known to one person—Mrs. Lewis. But in the final proxy case we will consider, no single person knew all the required information.

The case began when Drayton Thomas received a letter from a Mr. Hatch, whose ten-year-old stepson had recently died of diphtheria. Neither Thomas nor Mrs. Leonard had ever met Mr. Hatch or any of his family, and so knew next to nothing about them. Over a series of eleven sittings "Bobbie," speaking through Feda, made unmistakable references to matters such as a "Jack of Hearts" costume he had once worn, some gymnastics equipment set up in his room, and a girl skater of whom he was fond. Most curious of all were references to some "pipes," and through Feda the opinion was repeatedly expressed that Bobbie's illness could be traced to something poisonous connected with these pipes. It was said that the pipes were not at the boy's home; that animals would be a guide to their location; that Bobbie's family did not know of the place, but that he went there with another boy.

When Mr. Hatch and Bobbie's mother read the scripts, they were utterly puzzled by these references. But finally, the communicator gave directions to the location of the pipes, and following these directions the investigators found two pipes through which spring water issued into pools and from which animals would drink. A medical officer testified in writing that the water was not fit for drinking purposes, and that a person who drank it might develop an acute infection. Bobbie's friend Jack admitted that he and Bobbie had "played with the water" in the weeks shortly before Bobbie fell ill.

The difficulty with telepathy as an explanation is not only that Bobbie's family and friends were unknown to Thomas and Mrs. Leonard. In this case we have the further difficulty that no *one* person had all the required information. Bobbie's family did not know of the existence of the pipes; his friends would, of course, but would have had no idea that Bobbie's illness was due to his playing with the water. If the information conveyed was due to telepathy among the living, then Mrs. Leonard's trance-consciousness pieced together fragmentary bits of information from people she did not even know in order to fabricate convincing messages from a deceased person she had never met.

Thomas commented on this case as follows:

Critics who wish to apply the telepathic hypothesis to this case will need to assume, without any justification for such an assumption, that thoughts pass between people who have not heard of each other and between whom there is no link save that they were interested in a person who died. And further, the selection must be assumed to act with unerring discretion, so that no facts are allowed to pass that do not relate to the inquiry at hand. In short, *everything must happen exactly as if* an intelligent supervisor were obtaining information from the deceased for the purposes of the inquiry.[16]

These proxy cases may be difficult to explain as a result of ESP, but the so-called "drop-in" cases are even more difficult. These are cases in which a deceased personality, unknown to anyone present, simply "drops in" to a séance, and begins passing messages through to the sitters. In such cases there is no apparent link, however tenuous, to any living person or persons who have the required information. The facts about the great majority of drop-in communicators are not particularly eye-catching, and mediums and sitters do not seem to have any special motive for desiring information about the deceased person. However, as Stevenson writes, "Some 'drop in' communicators have explained their presence very well and their motivation to communicate is an important part of the whole case which has to be explained."[17] These communicators may explain that they wish to relieve the grief of living friends; that they are lost in a kind of limbo where the medium is their only means of contact with others; that they are linked through common interest to persons present; or that they are altruistically trying to help.

Of course, cases of this kind are easy to fake. A fraudulent medium can easily "bring through" alleged communications from an unknown communicator and set the sitters off on a trail of research for a person whose existence was already well known to the medium. Stevenson lists several fraudulent cases, including one he probed himself, but also maintains that "in the better cases of this type, the communicated information includes facts never in print, or never in print in any one source, and known only to one or a small circle of family members."[18] In such cases fraud can be ruled out as an explanation.

An early example of such a case occurred at a séance held November 17, 1887, at the home of a nobleman, M. Nartzeff, in Tambof, Russia.

The other three persons present were his aunt, his housekeeper, and the official physician of Tambof.

The séance began at 10 p.m. at a table placed in the middle of the room, by the light of a nightlight placed on the mantelpiece. The left hand of each person was placed on the right hand of their neighbor, and the foot of each person touched their neighbor's foot. Sharp raps were suddenly heard in the floor, then in the wall and ceiling, and then in the center of the table, with such violence and so often that the table trembled the whole time.

The report of the séance reads, in part:

M. Nartzeff asked: "Can you answer rationally, giving three raps for yes, one for no?" "Yes." "Do you wish to answer by using the alphabet?" "Yes." "Spell your name." The alphabet was repeated, and the letters indicated by three raps—"Anastasie Pereliguine." "I beg you to say now why you have come and what you desire." "I am a wretched woman. Pray for me. Yesterday, during the day, I died at the hospital. The day before yesterday I poisoned myself with matches." "Give us some details about yourself. How old were you? Give a rap for each year." Seventeen raps. "Who were you?" "I was a housemaid. I poisoned myself with matches." "Why did you poison yourself?" "I will not say. I will say nothing more."[19]

The report was signed by all four persons present, along with a document in which they all swore that they had no previous knowledge of the existence or death of Anastasie Pereliguine, and that they heard her name for the first time in the séance.

The physician present, Dr. Touloucheff, did not at first consider the communication genuine, as the police usually informed him at once of all cases of suicide. But he sent a letter to his colleague at the local hospital, simply asking if there had been any recent case of suicide at the hospital and if so, for the name and particulars. A certified copy of the letter of his reply reads, in part:

On the 16th of this month I was on duty; and on that day two patients were admitted to the hospital, who had poisoned themselves with phosphorous . . . the second, a servant in the insane ward [a part of the hospital], Anastasie Pereliguine, aged seventeen, was taken in at 10 p.m. This second patient had swallowed, besides an infusion of boxes of matches, a glass of kerosene, and at the time of her admission was already very ill. She died at 1 p.m. on the 17th.[20]

We can see from the letter that the information did exist in the mind of at least one living person, but it is difficult to determine any link at all between the information regarding Anastasie's suicide and the séance. None of the participants knew of her, and the hospital physician presumably did not know anything about the séance—so it is difficult to see how telepathy from the living could account for the message (ignoring the question of how the raps were produced). On the other hand, the survival of Anastasie and her memories would account both for the motive and the information.

The Case of Runolfur Runuolfsson

There is in the literature at least one carefully investigated case in which a drop-in communicator made a series of correct statements that could not have been obtained—normally, telepathically, or clairvoyantly— from any single living person or written document. It was received through a well-known Icelandic trance medium, Hafsteinn Bjornsson. Hafsteinn* did not earn his living as a professional medium, although he did accept fees from sitters. His regular control, "Finna," would relay messages from other communicators, but sometimes these other personalities would directly communicate through Hafsteinn.

In the winter of 1937–38 Hafsteinn began to conduct regular

---

*It is customary in Iceland to identify persons (e.g., in the phone book) primarily by their first names. This custom will be followed here.

séances with a home circle in Reykjavik. One of the earliest communicators dropped in intermittently, refused to give his name, and kept repeating that he was looking for his leg. This quickly became both irritating and boring.

In January 1939, the circle was joined by Ludvik Gudmundsson, who owned a house in the village of Sandgerdi, about forty miles from Reykjavik. Much to Ludvik's surprise, the anonymous communicator was delighted to see him. When Ludvik asked the mysterious communicator who he was, he again refused to reveal his identity. However, he did say that his missing leg was in Ludvik's house at Sandgerdi! After this ridiculous claim, the members of the circle ran out of patience and told the interloper that if he did not tell them who he was, they would no longer speak to him. Refusing to do so, he left. But he returned a few weeks later in a conciliatory mood, and gave the following statement:

My name is Runolfur Runuolfsson, and I was 52 years old when I died. I lived with my wife at Kolga or Klappakot, near Sandgerdi. I was on a journey from Keflavik [about six miles from Sandgerdi] in the latter part of the day and I was drunk. I stopped at the house of Sveinbjorn Thordarson in Sandgerdi and accepted some refreshments there. When I went to go, the weather was so bad that they did not wish me to leave unless accompanied by someone else. I became angry and said I would not go at all if I could not go alone. My house was only about 15 minutes' walk away. So I left by myself, but I was wet and tired. I walked over the kambuin [pebbles] and reached the rock known as Flankastadaklettur which has almost disappeared now. There I sat down, took my bottle, and drank some more. Then I fell asleep. The tide came in and carried me away. This happened in October, 1879. I was not found until January, 1880. I was carried in by the tide, but then dogs and ravens came and tore me to pieces. The remnants [of my body] were found and buried in Utskalar graveyard [about four miles from Sandgerdi]. But then the thigh bone was missing. It was carried out again to sea, but was later washed up again at Sandgerdi. There it was passed around and now it is in Ludvik's house.[21]

He said proof of his story could be found in the Utskalar church book. Intrigued, the members of the circle examined the church book, and found the following entry:

> On October 16, 1879, Runolfur Runolfsson, living in Klappakot, was missing on account of some accidental or unnatural occurrence on his way home during a storm . . . in the middle of the night . . . the sea carried him away . . . his bones were found dismembered much later.

A later entry indicated that he had been buried on January 8, 1880, but said nothing about a missing thigh bone.

Ludvik knew nothing about a thigh bone in his house, but after questioning some of the older men in the village, he learned that years earlier a human thigh bone had been found and passed around. One of the men thought that it had finally been interred in an interior wall of Ludvik's house. After locating one of the carpenters who had built the house, Ludvik learned that this was indeed true, and the carpenter was able to point out the spot. When the wall was opened the femur of a very tall man was found and recovered, supporting an earlier statement of Runolfur that he had been an unusually tall man.

Most of the remaining statements were verified from entries distributed between two manuscripts, the Utskalar church book and the Reverend Sigirdur Sivertsen's *Annals of Sudurnes,* which at the time was unpublished and sitting in the National Library at Reykjavik. His grandson confirmed that Runolfur had been tall, although he had not known him, and did not know about the bone. Haraldsson and Stevenson carefully investigated this case, and concluded, "It does not seem feasible to attribute all of this information to any single person or any single written source. And this would be true, we believe, whether the medium acquired the information normally or by extrasensory perception."[22]

As a coda to this case, the following may be of interest. Sixty years after Runolfur's death, and three years after the first communications that apparently came from him, the femur was buried in a traditional Icelandic ceremony. The clergyman gave a sermon eulogizing the dead man, a choir sang, and afterward there was a reception at the clergyman's home. Several of the regular sitter's at Hafsteinn's séances attended the burial ceremony and party, but the medium was not present.

At a séance held immediately after the burial ceremony Runolfur expressed gratitude, saying he had been present at the ceremony and reception, and described both in detail. To Ludvik he was particularly grateful, as he and his wife had arranged the ceremony. But Runolfur's story did not end with the burial of the thigh bone. He continued to communicate through Hafsteinn, becoming gentler and increasingly helpful to other communicators. Eventually, he became the medium's main control, and was still functioning in this capacity when Haraldsson and Stevenson investigated the case.

ALTERNATIVE EXPLANATIONS: CONCLUSION

If the cases described above, and other similar cases, are indeed examples of ESP on the part of the medium, then they are examples of ESP of a degree that is seldom if ever seen, apart from such cases of alleged communication with the deceased.

First of all, in the most impressive cases, the sheer speed, quantity, and level of accuracy and detail of the information conveyed through mediums greatly exceeds that of virtually all reported instances of ESP, whether experimental or anecdotal. In the best cases the flow of knowledge is comparable to that which might occur in an ordinary conversation. By contrast, the very best subjects in a Ganzfeld experiment might guess (at most) 50 percent of the pictures correctly, when 25 percent would be expected by chance. Nothing in their performance would suggest that "messages" could be communicated to them.

Secondly, we have seen that, in some cases, the information, if conveyed via ESP, must have come from multiple sources, some of them completely unknown to both medium and sitters. There is very little evidence that ESP can provide detailed, copious, and correct information about a person when the required information is scattered among multiple, distant sources.* This raises the question of just how ESP was able to locate and collate the information—information that the alleged communicator, if still living, might be expected to remember. On the other hand, this question does not arise with the hypothesis that the communications are what they claim to be, because then only a single source of information would be required: the memory of the deceased.

---

*The only exceptions appear to be the result of experiments in psychometry—in which a sensitive is given an object belonging to a person and then describes that person. Even here, however, the performance of the sensitive does not seem to quite match up to the best cases of mediumship in terms of rapidity of information flow and level of detail. The most impressive evidence of psychometry comes from the work of French physician E. Osty, but, as Gauld remarks, "Unfortunately, Osty's standards of evidence and presentation leave a great deal to be desired" (see Gauld, *Mediumship and Survival,* chapter 10).

THIRTEEN

Super-ESP as an Explanation?

The difficulties of using ESP as an explanation for the most impressive cases of mediumship have resulted in the hypothesis of super-ESP—that is, ESP of a range and power rarely if ever found in experiments or anecdotal reports. Defenders of the super-ESP hypothesis point out that the limitations of ESP are not currently known, and so argue that we have no right to exclude ESP as a possible explanation of alleged communication from the deceased.*

But evidence for the existence of ESP of the required power and range is practically nonexistent. Defenders of the super-ESP hypothesis are hard-pressed to find any such examples—outside of cases of apparent communication from the deceased.

We have also noted that ESP usually operates between people who share some emotional connection, or who are otherwise linked in some way. But in the proxy cases discussed, the link was extremely tenuous; in the drop-in cases, there was apparently no link at all. Yet it is maintained that an enormous amount of telepathy occurred between individuals with whom there was little or no association or connection.

---

*Note that I use the term super-ESP and not super-psi. The term *psi* refers to extrasensory perception (ESP) plus psychokinesis. The latter is simply not relevant here, as I deal only with mental mediumship, as opposed to the much more controversial physical mediumship.

This final point has a more subtle implication. In order to account for cases in which there was an absence of any sort of emotional link between medium, sitters, and the deceased, we are beginning to require the operation of something not only different in degree from telepathy as found in experiments and anecdotal reports; in these cases we are beginning to require the operation of something different *in kind*. This difference in kind will become even more apparent when we consider the other difficulties facing the super-ESP hypothesis.

PURPOSE CONTRARY TO THAT OF THE MEDIUM OR SITTERS

The evidence for survival discussed so far is mostly evidence for the existence of memories of the deceased. We have examined evidence for the communication of facts that were not possessed by any single living person or on any single document, but which the alleged communicator, if alive, would be expected to remember. Memories are invaluable as indicators of identity: not even fingerprints so uniquely identify each one of us as our own set of memories.

But more than the existence of mere memories would be required to constitute the survival of a person. Living people have purposes, points of view, personalities, knowledge and skills, in addition to a storehouse of memories. It is to evidence for the persistence of these additional traits of the deceased that we now turn, starting in this section with evidence of purpose.

One such purpose, which is frequently expressed by communicators, is that of proving their own survival, in order to bring consolation to grieving relatives. This is a purpose that a large number of the deceased might be expected to show, if they do survive; so the fact that any one communicator seems to show this purpose is not in itself evidence for survival. However, in our review of Mrs. Leonard's mediumship, we have seen one case in which an alleged communicator seemed to insist on delivering a message that his wife did not wish to hear.

According to Mrs. Talbot's notes, the communicator was trying by every means in his power to prove his identity. Clearly and
lucidly, he recited many incidents from the past, and talked of trivial
belongings that possessed some personal significance for the living
Mr. Talbot. Repeatedly, Mrs. Talbot was asked if she believed it
really was her husband; when she said she thought so, "but could
not be sure," the communicator began "a tiresome description of a
book." When the exact color of the book could not be established,
"Feda began a wearisome description all over again." Reading her
account, one can almost feel Mrs. Talbot's sense of boredom and
bewilderment.

> I was rather half-hearted in responding to all this, there was so much
> of it, and it sounded so purposeless . . . But the chief reason I was
> anxious to get off the subject was that I felt sure the book would not
> be forthcoming; either I had thrown it away, or it had gone with a
> lot of other things to a luggage room in the opposite block of flats
> where it would hardly be possible to get at it. However, I did not
> quite like to say this, and not attaching any importance to it, replied
> rather indefinitely that I would see if I could find it. But this did
> not satisfy Feda. She started all over again, becoming more and more
> insistent . . .[1]

Thinking the medium was talking nonsense, Mrs. Talbot pacified
her by promising to look for the book, and was glad when the séance
ended. It was only after Mrs. Talbot told her relatives that night that
"in the end the medium began talking a lot of rubbish about a book"
that she was pressured into locating the striking passage. In "real life,"
ESP seems to operate according to the desires and emotions of the parties involved. If the only parties involved in this case were the medium
and Mrs. Talbot, then it is difficult to see whose desires were being
met during the lengthy exchange the sitter found so "tiresome" and
"purposeless."

The Case of Schura's Warning

The following case is highly unusual, because of the degree to which the purpose of the alleged communicator seems to be contrary to that of the mediums and sitters. This odd case was reported in detail by a Russian corresponding member of the SPR, Alexander Aksakov, imperial councilor to the czar.

In January 1885, Mrs. A. von Wiesler (Aksakov's sister-in-law) and her daughter Sophie began to experiment with a planchette (pointer) and an alphabet written out on a sheet of paper. Mother and daughter lightly placed their fingers on the planchette, and for a few weeks nothing happened, apart from the name of Sophie's deceased father—Andreas—being continually spelled out.

Then, on January 22, the name "Schura" (the pet name for Alexandrine) was spelled out. This new communicator claimed to be the deceased daughter of somewhat distant acquaintances. Schura, who had adopted revolutionary views, had ended her life by poison at the age of seventeen a week earlier, following the imprisonment and death of a like-minded male cousin whom she had loved dearly. Now she was demanding that another cousin, Nikolaus, be brought at once to a sitting. According to Schura, Nikolaus had fallen in with a band of radicals and was in danger of compromising himself politically. However, Sophie and her mother expressed hesitation for reasons of social propriety, as their acquaintance with the family of Nikolaus was far from intimate. "Absurd ideas of propriety!" was "Schura's" indignant reply.

All this was very characteristic of the living Schura, who had been very decisive and forceful, and who had come to despise the conventions of society. However, Sophie and her mother continued to hesitate. "Schura's" demands for them to act became more and more vehement at successive sittings, until finally, on February 26, she wrote, "It is too late . . . expect his arrest." These were "Schura's" last words. The von Wieslers then contacted Nikolaus's parents, who were, however, quite satisfied in regard to their son's conduct.

Two years later Nikolaus was arrested and exiled because of political assemblies he had attended in January and February 1885—the very months in which "Schura" was insisting that steps should be taken *immediately* to dissuade Nikolaus from taking part in such meetings. Aksakov writes:

> Only now were the communications of "Schura" estimated at their true value. The notes which Mrs von Wiesler had made were read again and again by the families both of "Schura" and of Nikolaus. "Schura's" identity in all those manifestations was recognized as incontestably demonstrated, in the first place, by the main fact in relation to Nikolaus, by other intimate particulars, and also by the totality of the features which characterized her personality.[2]

Comments on the Case of Schura's Warning

This case creates several difficulties for the super-ESP hypothesis. First of all, it is an example of a "drop-in" communicator, one who in life was only slightly known to the von Wieslers. They certainly knew nothing of Schura's political secrets, yet these and many other intimate facts were communicated. Secondly, the purpose of the communications received was definitely not that of the operators of the planchette board (who functioned as both mediums *and* sitters). Since they knew the other family only slightly, the thought of contacting them about so intimate a family matter embarrassed them. Yet the purpose shown in the communications would certainly have been that of the living Schura, if she had known of the danger to Nikolaus. Finally, the purpose was carried out in the direct and forceful manner that was characteristic of the living Schura, and with her typical disdain for the social conventions to which the von Wieslers felt so bound.

Manifestations of the personality of the deceased will be discussed in greater detail later. A more subtle problem for the super-ESP hypothesis is the fact that in some cases, communications seem to be unmistakably from the *perspective* of the deceased.

COMMUNICATION FROM THE
PERSPECTIVE OF THE DECEASED

Consider the case of the "Kakie" communicator mentioned earlier, in which the deceased daughter of the Reverend S. W. Sutton appeared to communicate through Mrs. Piper's Phinuit control. All the facts received were known to those present, but the facts were presented from the *child's* point of view. If the facts were obtained telepathically from the minds of the sitters, then it appears that Mrs. Piper must have obtained parent's-eye-view information about Kakie from the sitters, and then, with a great deal of dramatic skill, have played back those facts from Kakie's perspective.

What is even more difficult to explain on the basis of ESP is that at both sittings associations were made that seemed to be in the mind of the child, but not in the minds of the adults. For instance, during the first sitting the Kakie communicator asked at one point for a horse:

Where is horsey? [I gave him a little horse.] Big horsey, not this little one. [Probably refers to a toy cart-horse she used to like.]

And at the second sitting, the same request:

Kakie wants the horse. [I gave him the little horse she played with during her illness.] No, that is not the one. The big horse—so big [Phinuit shows how large]. Eleanor's horse. Eleanor used to put it in Kakie's lap. [This horse was packed, in Trenton, and had not occurred to me in connection with Kakie. What she said of it was true.][3]

At the first sitting Kakie asked twice for "the little book," which Mrs. Sutton thought at the time referred to a linen picture book. At the second sitting Kakie, through Phinuit, asked, more specifically, for "the little bit of a book mama read by her bedside, with the pretty bright things hanging from it—mama put it in her hands—the last thing she remembers."[4] Both requests now seemed to refer to a little prayer book with symbols in silver, read to Kakie as she lay dying, and placed in her hands after her death.

Gauld comments on what these passages seem to imply.

> If we are to say that Mrs Piper could select from the sitters' minds associations conflicting with the ones consciously present and utilize them in order to create the impression that the communicator's thoughts moved along lines distinctively different from the sitter's, we are beginning to attribute to her not just super-ESP but super-artistry as well.[5]

There are also cases on record in which the communicator seems to contradict and correct the medium. The American researcher Walter Franklin Prince and his adopted daughter Theodosia visited the medium Mrs. Soule on several occasions, and during one visit Theodosia's mother appeared to control the medium. At one point it seemed she was trying to remind her daughter of a visit to a neighbor's farm to see a calf (colloquially a "Bossy"), but was experiencing difficulty.

> We went to a neighbor's to see a pet Bunny—pause—pet Bunny BB Bunny—pause—No, it was a pet Bunny BB Bunny B—long pause—(medium moans) Milk—a small cow Bossy.[6]

Prince remarks:

> Who can doubt that someone or something intended "Bossy" . . . from the first? Else why did the communicator stop at Bunny every time and begin again, express dissatisfaction, pause as though pondering what was the matter or how to remedy it, experience emotion which extorted moans from the medium, and finally say "small cow" as though to avoid the word beginning with B? If two minds were engaged in the process, the second receiving from the first, we

can see how this second, call it the "control" or the medium's sub-conscious, would, when the "pet B-" was reached, conceive the picture of a rabbit and cling to the preference for some time despite the efforts of the first mind to dislodge it.[7]

There are also many examples of mistakes and subsequent corrections in the records of sittings with Mrs. Leonard. Insight into what seems to be occurring at times may be gained by considering the various methods the communicators seem to use in order to pass messages through. As mentioned earlier, most of the messages were relayed by Mrs. Leonard's "Feda" control, and the communicators distinguished two ways in which they can give messages to Feda. They can actually speak to her using words; or they can pass to her thoughts or visual images.

Drayton Thomas spent years studying her mediumship, and kept elaborate records of what transpired during sittings. Thomas observed that the medium's body is often in a position of listening when Feda is receiving a message. To the sitters it seemed as though messages were being dictated to Feda, which she would then repeat. Feda also seemed to occasionally make mistakes of the precisely the sort that we would expect if she had indeed misheard a word. Thomas provided the following examples from his notes.

> **FEDA:** Week after week for fears—(long pause as is the misheard word caused a check in the flow and a faltering). Years. Week after week for years.
>
> **FEDA:** I see greatly—What did you call it? Something—I've missed something. I'm sorry. Well, he says, I see great differences.
>
> **FEDA:** We cannot as—as—We cannot, What? Oh, I can't get that word. Well, say it another way, Feda, he says.[8]

Perhaps the most interesting corrections are the ones made by what Thomas called the "direct voice." An odd feature of Mrs. Leonard's mediumship was this: at times when Feda was in control and relaying messages from another communicator, she would be interrupted by a whisper coming apparently from the empty air a foot or two in front of the medium. This "direct voice" seemed to be that of the communicator, and would correct and clarify the statements that Feda was making through Mrs. Leonard. The following are two such examples.

> **FEDA:** Willy—What? Who's he? Willy somebody—I can't get his other name. Willy—somebody is compelling you. Wait a minute, I've mixed that up.
>
> **D.V.:** *It is not that at all.*
>
> **FEDA:** Willy-nilly? Is that right? Willy-nilly you are being compelled . . .
>
> **FEDA:** Stuart thinks he will have more important work later, though he doesn't know quite what it is.
>
> **D.V.:** *At present—*
>
> **FEDA:** Present? He doesn't know at present. What is it then? "NO," he said. "I don't know what it is quite. Full stop." Full stop? But at present I am helping with . . .[9]

Thomas points out how the second example indicates a distinction between speaker and listener. Feda had mistakenly joined the first two words of a new sentence to the end of the previous one. The communicator repeats the end of the first sentence, indicates a full stop, and then continues with the next sentence.

The direct voice sometimes seems to correct Feda's choice of words, even when Feda inserts her own comment.

> **FEDA:** It's just as if things become separate, like the spectrum, he calls it. (Then, adding for herself—) A man once said Feda was a spectrum.
>
> **D.V.:** *Spectre, not spectrum!*
>
> **FEDA:** He says, spectrum; everything gets divided.[10]

And at times the direct voice appears to express frustration with

Feda, as though irritated by the effort of trying to dictate to a rather obtuse secretary.

> **FEDA:** He says that the pheno*meter*—phenomena—He's got a thermometer!
>
> **D.V.:** *I was not talking about thermometers!*
>
> **FEDA:** Oh, he says, phenomena. Is that right? The phenomena referred to.
>
> **FEDA:** Your father says—
>
> **D.V.:** *A few days out!*
>
> **FEDA:** A few days out? What, out of bed?
>
> **D.V.:** *No, no, no no!*
>
> **FEDA:** A few days out? Oh, I'll tell him. He was a few days out in his reckoning about the war.[11]
>
> **ON ANOTHER OCCASION:**
>
> **FEDA:** He says you must have good working—What? Hippopotamuses?
>
> **D.V.:** *Hypotheses.*
>
> **FEDA (MORE LOUDLY):** Hippopotamuses.
>
> **D.V.:** *Hypotheses—and don't shout!*
>
> **FEDA:** I'm not shouting. I'm only speaking plainly.[12]

These examples create an obvious difficulty for the hypothesis of telepathy from the living. For there is no evidence that telepathically received information is ever first received wrongly, and then *corrected*. But the mistakes and subsequent corrections make perfect sense if the messages are, in fact, what they purport to be.

MANIFESTATIONS OF PERSONALITY

We have already seen several examples of mediumship in which the distinctive personality of the deceased appears evident in the communication. The following remarks, fairly typical, were made after séances with Mrs. Piper during which deceased friends of the sitters seemed to speak directly through the entranced medium.

The clearly-marked personality of the friend, whom I will call T., is to me the most convincing proof of Mrs P.'s supernatural power, but it is a proof impossible to present to any one else.[13]

Another sitter remarked:

In a great many little ways he is quite like what my friend used to be when living, so much so that I am afraid it would take a great deal of explanation to make me believe that his identical self had not something to do with it, wholly apart from the medium's powers or from anything that may be in my own mind concerning him.[14]

The Reverend M. A. Bayfield commented in great detail on messages received through the English medium Mrs. Willet, purporting to come from his old friend Dr. A. W. Verrall after his death in 1912. After quoting some typical passages, Bayfield writes:

All this is Verrall's manner to the life in animated conversation. . . . When I first read the words quoted above I received a series of little shocks, for the turns of speech are Verrall's, the high-pitched emphasis is his, and I could hear the very tones in which he would have spoken each sentence.[15]

An intimate friend of Verrall's from his undergraduate days agreed with Bayfield's assessment, as did a niece of Verrall's and his surviving wife. Verrall's characteristic sense of humor and impatience could be found in the scripts, leading Bayfield to write:

We have here an extraordinary faithful representation of Verrall in respect of a peculiar kind of impatience and a habit of emphasis which he had in conversation, and of his playfulness and sense of humour. In what way are these life-like touches of character introduced? How are they worked into the essential matter of the scripts? Have they the air of being inserted by an ingenious forger . . . or do they give us the impression of being spontaneous and genuine?[16]

For Bayfield there was no doubt about the nature of the scripts.

Nowhere is there any slip which would justify the suspicion that in reality we have to do with a cunningly masquerading "sub." Neither the impatience, nor the emphatic utterance, nor the playfulness has anywhere the appearance of being "put on,"—of being *separable from the matter of the scripts.* . . . to me at least it is incredible that even the cleverest could achieve such an unexampled triumph in deceptive impersonation as this would be if the actor is not Verrall himself.[17]

It should be mentioned that Mrs. Willett did meet the living Dr. Verrall three times, although her acquaintance with him seems to have been very slight. None of the investigators felt that she knew him intimately at all. However, in the case of the "GP" communications, the relationship between the living Pellew and the medium Mrs. Piper was even slighter—he was somebody she had barely met more than four years earlier, when he attended a single sitting with her, under an assumed name. Yet when the GP communicator spoke through Mrs. Piper, the reproduction of Pellew's personality was so lifelike that it convinced thirty people who were intimate with Pellew before he died that they were indeed conversing with their deceased friend. Even the skeptical Hodgson became convinced that he was speaking with his old friend.

It should be clear that the Gordon Davis case (assuming it is not *completely* fraudulent) and the case involving the "communication" through a medium of the still-living German friend of Rosalind Heywood, bear only the most superficial resemblance to the GP communications. In the Gordon Davis case, we have the mere reproduction of voice peculiarities and of two memories in the single brief conversation Soal claimed to have had with the purported Gordon Davis. In the second case the details are scanty, but it does not appear to be any more impressive. In both of these cases telepathy with the sitter is enough to account for the vocal peculiarities, the memories mentioned, and the agreement of the "communicator" that he had died.

The GP communications are radically different. Not only was *correct* information given that was unknown to the sitters, but the GP personality appeared and manifested itself in a consistent manner regardless of whether or not the sitter knew the living Pellew.* The GP personality appeared again and again, engaged in lengthy conversations with those who knew the living Pellew very well, and convinced all of them that they were indeed speaking with their old friend. By contrast, the "communications" received by Soal and Heywood involve no more difficulty in execution than the example of an actor impersonating a historical figure in a brief skit.

It seems that, in the best cases in which a whole personality seems to make itself known, something more than extrasensory perception is required. This seems to be the case even if we grant—purely for the sake of argument—that the medium possesses enormously extended powers of ESP. Something more is required, for there is an enormous gap between *knowing mere facts* about a person, and translating those facts into a convincing impersonation of someone either unknown or barely known to the actor. An entirely different skill is required—a skill that cannot be reduced to a mere knowledge of facts. Allan Gauld illustrates the difference with an example from his own research:

---

*Hodgson writes: "The manifestations of this GP communicating have not been of a fitful and spasmodic nature, they have exhibited the marks of a continuous living and persistent personality, manifesting itself through a course of years, and showing the same characteristics of an independent intelligence whether friends of GP were present at the sittings or not. I learned of various cases where in my absence active assistance was rendered by GP to sitters who had never previously heard of him" (Hodgson, "A Further Record of Observations," 330).

Some 10 or 12 years ago I spent a good deal of time studying the papers and diaries or FWH Myers and Henry Sidgwick, thus learning a good many intimate details about their lives, characters, friends, families, and domestic arrangements. Yet I could no more deploy this accumulated knowledge to develop impersonations of them which would have passed muster before their close friends than I could fly. The gap between accumulating such knowledge and deploying it in the construction of a realistic communicator is enormous.[18]

George Pellew had attended one séance with Mrs. Piper as an anonymous sitter four years before his death; yet the GP communicator conversed with the friends and relatives of George Pellew in a completely convincing manner for a period of five years. Since correct information not even known to the sitters was sometimes conveyed, the degree of telepathy required is staggering. The communications would have required *instant* telepathic acquisition of facts about Pellew whenever they were needed in conversation, taken from the minds of his living friends, relatives, and acquaintances—regardless of whether they were known to the medium, and regardless of whatever they happened to have been thinking about at the time. Then, the facts would have to be presented within a lifelike impersonation of someone Mrs. Piper had barely met four years earlier, lifelike enough to convince dozens of witnesses who had intimately known the living Pellew that they were indeed conversing with their old friend or relative. There is simply no evidence that telepathy can be employed to successfully impersonate an individual someone has never knowingly met with anything approaching the level of accurate detail shown in this case. Even super-ESP does not seem to be enough to account for the lifelike manifestation of Pellow's personality through the entranced medium.

There is one final point to be made regarding the GP communications. The reader may recall that the GP communicator never failed to recognize the friends and acquaintances of the living Pellew, with one exception: a young woman who had been a child when the living Pellew had last seen her. At the first sitting Miss Warner had with Mrs. Piper, "Phinuit" was the predominant control and gave Miss Warner a good deal of correct information concerning her family and friends. GP communicated briefly at the end of the sitting, to ask about an old friend of his named Rogers, and to send regards to him. The sitter mentioned that she remembered GP, but that he knew her mother better. At Miss Warner's second sitting, held the next day, GP asked who she was, and Hodgson replied that her mother was a special friend of Mrs. Howard. The following exchange then occurred.

> I do not think I knew you very well. (Very little. You used to come and see my mother.) I heard of you, I suppose. (I saw you several times. You used to come with Mr. Rogers.) Yes, I remembered about Mr. Rogers when I saw you before. (Yes, you spoke of him.) Yes, but I cannot seem to place you. I long to place all of my friends, and could do so before I had been gone so long. You see I am farther away. . . . I do not recall your face. You must have changed. . . . (R.H.: Do you remember Mrs Warner?) Of course, oh, very well. For pity sake are you her little daughter? (Yes.) By Jove, how you have grown. . . . I thought so much of your mother, a charming woman. (She always enjoyed seeing you, I know.) . . . I wish I could have known you better, it would have been so nice to have recalled the past. (I was a little girl.)[19]

These sittings were held five years after the death of George Pellew, and Pellew had not seen Miss Warner for at least three years before his death, when she was only a little girl. Since she had changed a great deal in the eight years, the nonrecognition by George Pellew would have been perfectly natural.

However, on the hypothesis of telepathy, there seems to be no explanation for GP's failure to recognize Miss Warner. Both Miss Warner and Richard Hodgson were aware of the fact that Miss Warner had known Pellew when she was a little girl, so sources for telepathy were at hand. If the personality of GP was only a creation of the subconscious mind of Mrs. Piper patching together telepathic information, it would seem natural for Miss Warner to have been "recognized." GP's nonrecognition of the girl he had known only as a child is therefore evidence of the independent existence of George Pellew, in contrast to being only some secondary personality dependent on the minds of the living.*

MANIFESTATIONS OF SKILLS

The final difficulty for the super-ESP hypothesis that we will consider in this section comes from cases in which the medium demonstrates skills known to be possessed by the deceased, but not known to be possessed by the medium. Such displays of skills not normally acquired are even more difficult to explain in terms of ESP than lifelike impersonations of deceased individuals never knowingly met.

---

*A few years later the reverse happened: GP recognized someone who did *not* remember him. Hodgson describes what happened: "After GP began to write, I asked:——"(Do you know this gentleman, MJ Savage?) [Mr. Savage had had sittings years previously and was known to Mrs Piper.] Yes. I do. How are you sir? Speak to me. This is too delightful. I am so pleased to see your face again. (You remember meeting him in the body?) Oh yes, well, I do well."

I supposed at the time that Mr. Savage had never met GP, and that was Mr. Savage's opinion also, and we both expected the answer "No" to my first question . . . Very soon, however, during the sitting, I recalled what I had temporarily forgotten, viz., that when [the living] GP had his sitting with Mrs Piper on March 7th, 1888, the Rev. MJ Savage was the Committee Officer, who was present officially at the sitting. But GP was not introduced under his real name to Mr. Savage . . . (Hodgson, "A Further Record of Observations," 326 [emphasis added]).

The Mediumship of
Mrs. Willet

The first example comes from the mediumship of Mrs. Willet. Unlike Mrs. Piper and Mrs. Leonard, when the English medium Mrs. Willet went into a trance, she did not lose control of her body as if she were asleep or in a faint. She would sit up and talk in a natural way, and Mrs. Willet had no regular control. Messages usually appeared to be conveyed to her directly, and she would then pass them on to the sitters. However, after regaining her normal consciousness, she usually remembered little or nothing of what had taken place. Clearly, she was no ordinary trance medium.

Her two main communicators claimed to be the surviving spirits of Edmund Gurney, who had died in 1888, and Frederic Myers, who had died in 1901. Both men were classical scholars and founders of the Society for Psychical Research, and both had made sizable contributions to research into mediumship and other psychic phenomena. When alive, Gurney and Myers were avid philosophers, widely read in philosophy and psychology. On several occasions the alleged postmortem personalities of Gurney and Myers communicated through Mrs. Willet the request that one of the sitters be their friend G. W. Balfour, a keen psychic researcher and president of the SPR from 1906 to 1907. On numerous occasions Balfour had engaged in philosophical discussions with Gurney and Myers before they died.

With Balfour and others present, Mrs. Willet would enter a deep trance. Lively philosophical discussions would then ensue, between Balfour and the communicators "Myers" and "Gurney." The philosopher C. D. Broad commented on the content of these discussions, and wrote that all the communications were "plainly the product of a highly intelligent mind or minds, with a keen interest in psychology, psychical research and philosophy, and with a capacity for drawing subtle and significant distinctions."[20] The purported communicators also showed a thorough acquaintance with the views and terminology of books written by the living Myers and Gurney.

At these sittings there was not merely an outpouring of views, which the sitter simply passively recorded and accepted. On the contrary, the sittings provided excellent examples of the conversational give-and-take that by itself stretches the ESP hypothesis nearly to the breaking point. In between sittings Balfour would leisurely examine the record of a previous sitting, and then at the next sitting would make criticisms or suggestions, and would ask for explanations of obscure matters. The communicators would address the issued raised, and would accept, or at times vigorously reject, Balfour's suggestions. The philosopher Robert Almeder wrote that some of the sittings "were purely philosophical and sound like the transcript of an Ivy League graduate seminar on classical philosophy."[21]

Mrs. Willet's mediumship strains the ESP hypothesis in two crucial ways. First, Mrs. Willet had never met Myers or Gurney, yet Balfour and others were convinced that the Myers and Gurney communicators acted and spoke in ways uniquely characteristic of Myers and Gurney. Second—and perhaps even more startling—Mrs. Willet was neither educated nor interested in philosophy, and showed little patience for such discussions. The attitude of her trance personality (as well as her normal personality) toward the communications can best be described as one of boredom and bewilderment. At one point, when the Gurney personality was discussing in detail some philosophical problem, she exclaimed "Oh, Edmund, you do *bore* me so!" At another point she complained, "You see it seems a long time since I was here with them [with Myers and friends] and I want to talk and enjoy myself. And I've all the time, to keep on working, and seeing and listening to such boring old—Oh Ugh!"[22] When the communicators were comparing three conflicting views of the mind-body relationship—interactionism, epiphenomenalism, and parallelism—she seemed to have great problems communicating the word *interaction*. At last she said, "I've got it." And then, "Oh but now I've got to give it out. Oh, I'm all buzzing. I can't think why people talk about such stupid things. Such long stupid words."[*23]

Unlike the Hodgson communications, we cannot attribute these communications as due to ESP, plus the dramatizing powers of the medium's trance personality. First of all, Mrs. Willet never met the living Myers or Gurney, and—given the technology available at the time—almost certainly never had the opportunity of studying audiotapes of their voices. Second, the high-level philosophical discussions reflect an acquired skill—the skill of philosophizing well. There is evidence that ESP can be used to acquire facts—to learn that something is true. But there is a substantial difference between knowledge *that* something is true, and knowledge of *how* to do something. The knowledge of how to do something—such as play an instrument or speak a language—frequently requires a skill that is only developed through years of solid practice. If learning to philosophize well is one such skill, then it is a skill for which there is no evidence that mere perception—extrasensory or otherwise—can be used to instantly acquire.

Comments on the Mediumship of Mrs. Willett
Reflecting on this case, C. D. Broad wrote:

> Suppose we altogether rule out the suggestion that Myers and Gurney in some sense survived bodily death and were the deliberate initiators of these utterances. We shall then have to postulate in some stratum of Mrs Willet's mind rather remarkable powers of acquiring information from unread books or the minds of living persons or both; of clothing it in phraseology characteristic of Myers and Gurney, whom she had never met; and of working it up

---

*Incidentally, the two communicators clearly favor interactionism. When the Gurney personality was passing messages, Mrs. Willet said: "You can't make parallelism square he says with the conclusions to which recent research points. *Pauvre parallelistes!* They're like drowning men clinging to spars. But the epiphenomenalistic bosh, that's simply blown away. It's one of the blind alleys of human thought. Oh! I don't want to hear any more. I'm tired."

and putting it forth in a dramatic form which seemed to their friend Balfour to be natural and convincing.[24]

At any rate, Balfour found the communications so natural and convincing that he came to believe that he was indeed discussing philosophy with the departed spirits of Myers and Gurney, and that no other hypothesis could explain the data as well. The philosophical views expressed by the Myers and Gurney communicators certainly did not seem to come from his mind, since both of the communicators contradicted Balfour's opinions on several occasions. When, for instance, Balfour argued that the conscious and subconscious minds of one person may communicate with each other by telepathy, the Myers personality would have none of that. When, on another occasion, Balfour suggested that the conscious and subconscious selves were as separate as two persons are separate, the Gurney communicator firmly replied, "Bosh! Different aspects of the same thing."

Note also the radical difference between this case, and the cases of Gordon Davis and Rosalind Heywood's German friend. The latter two cases can be compared to an example of an actor impersonating a famous scientist in a brief skit, in which the actor recalls a few known facts about the person with the gestures, tone of voice, and pet phrases he had learned were characteristic of that scientist. Apart from the matter of *how* the information about the character was gathered—via telepathy as opposed to study and observation—no greater difficulty in execution is involved in these two cases. But the case we have just covered, under the ESP hypothesis, would be equivalent to an actor, untrained and uninterested in science, engaging in several lengthy improvisational discussions and debates with an old friend and colleague of a certain scientist over a telephone, in a manner so true and lifelike that it manages to completely convince his old friend that it really *is* that scientist on the other end of the line.

Of course, the skeptic may object at this point that the ability to philosophize well, unlike the ability to discuss science or play a musical instrument, does *not* require a skill that is only developed through years of solid practice. The skeptic may argue that, at some level, Mrs. Willet was indeed capable of philosophizing well, even though her normal personality knew little philosophy and had even less patience for any such talk.* However, this objection most certainly does not apply to the ability to speak a foreign language.

THE LANGUAGE CASES

The Hungarian Case

A 1939 edition of the London paper *Psychic News* carried an account of Dr. Nandor Fodor's first encounter with the medium Arthur Ford.[†] Having arrived unexpectedly the day before the séance, his good friend William Cartheuser introduced him to Ford just before the sitting.

Ford's mediumship was of the possession variety. He would go into a trance, and a control named Fletcher would speak through him. Occasionally, another personality would appear to control Ford's vocal apparatus, and to speak directly through him. On this occasion Fodor asked Fletcher if he would bring forth someone who could speak Hungarian, Fodor's native tongue. Fletcher said he would try, and a period of silence followed. Dr. Fodor's account continues.

> I hear a voice. Cold shivers run down my back. It sounds like a distant cry. It is repeated. Someone is calling my name.
>
> "Who—who is it? Whom do you want?" I ask hoarsely in my native tongue.

---

*The dubious nature of this point will be obvious to anyone who has found an introductory philosophy course difficult.

[†]In his long career as a famous medium, Ford was never shown to be a fraud. Among his many admirers were *Apollo 14* Astronaut Edgar Mitchell, Queen Maud of Norway, Aldous Huxley, Upton Sinclair, and the rigorously skeptical Harvard psychologist and psychic researcher William McDougall. For more information, see Spraggett and Rauscher, *Arthur Ford*.

The call is more explicit: "Fodor—*Journalist!*"

The last word shakes me to the core. It is pronounced in German. It is the only German word my father ever used. He used it only when he spoke about me!

I stammered an answer. Craning my neck in the dark—I listened with strained nerves to tatters of a terrific struggle for expression.

"Edesapa—edesapa—" (Dear father—dear father—)

The voice vibrates with emotion. It makes me hot and burning. I sound unnatural to myself: *"Apam? Apam?"* (Father, dear?)

"Iges. Edes fiam—" (Yes, dear son—)

I cannot describe the minutes that followed. From beyond the Great Divide somebody who says he is my father is making desperate efforts to master some weird instrument of speech, and trembles with anxiety to prove his presence by speaking in his native tongue:

"Budapest—new ertesz? Enekelek—Magyar Kislany vagyok." (Budapest—don't you understand?—I will sing—)

I don't know the song. Two lines rhyming. Have I heard them before? I recognize the pet name of my eldest brother, to whom my father was very attached.

The voice comes from near the ceiling. But it comes nearer at my request. It is still struggling for words.

Fletcher takes pity and explains. "Your father wishes to tell you that he died on January 16. It is for the first time he tries to speak. That makes it very difficult for him."

The interruption brings relief. The voice becomes much clearer. It gives me a message about my mother and sister.

Then: *"Isten aldjon meg, edes fiam."* (God bless you, my son.)

The voice speaks again in Hungarian: *"Esti Ujsag."* (*Evening News.*)

My wife screams.

Esti Ujsag was the newspaper on which her brother was employed before he died.

"Sanyika?"

"Yes."

I feel her voice trembling with excitement.

The voice is youthful and explosive. It speaks as my wife's brother would. He knows all about the family and is always about. He has but one regret: *"Szegeny Vilmis basci!"* (Poor Uncle Vilmos.)

"Why, what is wrong with Uncle Vilmos?"

"He is not well, he will go blind."

We receive the prophecy in dead silence.

My experience was more unusual than that of the majority. I was a foreign daily in New York. I had few friends, they were all new ones. None of them knew about my old country relations. Yet the statements about my family were correct.

The voice spoke in Hungarian. Plain as the words were, my native tongue offers a variety of expressions for the relationship between father and son.

The voice made no mistake. My father was in the habit of using the *very* words. He had forgotten his German years before. It was no more spoken at home. The only word retained was *"journalist."* He was very proud of his boy, the journalist. The Hungarian equivalent of *ujsagiro*. He never used it. He preferred the German term.

The reference to the date of his death was not correct. He did not die on January 16. But he was buried on that day.

Uncle Vilmos, as predicted, went blind—and commited suicide! I know him as Uncle Villy. Vilmos (the proper name) left me uneasy. I had the matter out with my mother-in-law two years later when I revisited Budapest. She opened her eyes wide.

"Why, didn't you know? My boy alone in the family called him Uncle Vilmos. He was Uncle Villy to everybody else!"[25]

Comments on the Hungarian Case

There is no evidence whatsoever that Arthur Ford knew how to speak Hungarian. And because Dr. Fodor arrived unexpectedly from Europe and was invited at the last moment to attend Ford's séance, it is highly unlikely that Ford had an opportunity to learn intimate details about Fodor's family, and to express them in Hungarian. Of course, Ford could have learned the facts about Fodor's family via ESP. But there is not a shred of evidence that anyone can learn to speak an unknown foreign language via ESP.

It is possible that Fodor suffered a highly unusual auditory hallucination—but then we would have to say that his wife suffered the same hallucination at the same time. It may seem more plausible to suggest that the whole episode was a hoax invented by Ford, Cartheuser, and the Fodors. But what would these people have to gain from such a hoax? However, in the next case fraud seems to be completely out of the question.

The Greek Case

In 1855 Judge John Worth Edmonds, president of the New York State Senate and later judge of the Supreme Court of New York, reported a case in which a trance medium spoke in a language of which she was normally entirely ignorant, and used it to convey accurate information that was unknown to anyone present. The medium was Miss Laura Edmonds, daughter of Judge Edmonds. It almost goes without saying that Judge Edmonds was widely regarded as a person of unquestionable integrity and considerable intelligence.

At one time the judge had studied psychic research in order to demonstrate the worthlessness of the activity. One can only imagine what he thought when his own daughter Laura began to shine as a developing medium.

Nevertheless, her abilities became more remarkable over time, and Judge Edmonds eventually became convinced that his daughter's gift was genuine. One of her most impressive gifts was an ability to "speak in many tongues," as he put it.

> She knows no language but her own, and a little smattering of boarding-school French; yet she has spoken in nine or ten different

tongues, sometimes for an hour at a time, with the ease and fluency of a native. It is not unfrequent that foreigners converse with their Spirit friends, through her, in their own language. A recent instance occurred, where a Greek gentleman had several interviews, and for several hours at a time carried on the conversation on his part in Greek, and received his answers sometimes in that language, and sometimes in English. Yet, until then, she had never heard a word of modern Greek spoken.[26]

A few years later Edmonds elaborated on the séance with the Greek gentleman.

The incident with the Greek gentleman was this: One evening, when some twelve or fifteen people were in my parlor, Mr E. D. Green, an artist of the city, was shown in, accompanied by a gentleman whom he introduced as Mr Evangelides. He spoke broken English, and Greek fluently. Ere long, a Spirit spoke to him through Laura, in English, and said so many things to him, that he identified him as a friend who had died at his house a few years before, but of whom none of us had ever heard.

Occasionally, through Laura, the Spirit would speak a word or a sentence in Greek, until Mr E inquired if he could be understood if he spoke in Greek? The residue of the conversation, for more than an hour, was, on his part entirely in Greek, and on hers, sometimes in Greek and sometimes in English.

He was sometimes very much affected, so much so as to attract the attention of the company, some of whom begged to know what is was that caused so much emotion. He declined to tell, but after the conversation ended, he told us that he had never before witnessed any Spirit manifestations, and that he had, during the conversation, tried experiments to test that which was so novel to him. These experiments were in speaking of subjects which he knew Laura must be ignorant of, and in frequently and suddenly changing the topic from domestic to political affairs, from philosophy to theology, and so on. In answer to our inquiries—for none of use knew Greek—he assured us that his Greek must have been understood, and her Greek was correct.[27]

Years after this, Edmonds explained why Evangelides had been so emotionally affected by what Laura had said.

One evening I had a visit from a stranger, a Greek named Evangelides; it was not long before he was speaking to Laura in his own tongue. In the course of the conversation he seemed greatly affected, and even shed tears. Six or seven people were present, and one of them asked the reason for his emotion. The Greek avoided a direct reply, saying that it was a question of family matters.

On the next day he renewed his conversation with Laura, and since there were no strangers in my house this time, he gave us the desired explanation. The invisible personality with whom he was speaking, with Laura as an intermediary, said that he was an intimate friend, who had died in Greece, the brother of the Greek patriot, Marco Bozarris. The friend informed Evangelides of the death of his [Evangelides's] son, who had stayed in Greece and had been in excellent health when his father left for America.

Ten days after his first visit Evangelides informed us that he had just received a letter telling him of the death of his son. The letter must have been on its way at the time of his first interview with Laura.[28]

Comments on the Greek Case

Fraud seems out of the question in this case. What would the participants gain from such a hoax? Would the risk of discovery for a person such as Judge Edmonds be worth whatever entertainment value there could possibly be in perpetrating such a hoax?

One critic has suggested that because Evangelides was the only person present who spoke Greek, we have no independent verification that the medium did, in fact, speak fluent Greek. In other words, Evangelides spoke in Greek to the medium, and hallucinated that the medium replied in Greek (everyone else present testified that the medium was not speaking English). But Evangelides broke down and wept when he learned that his son had died, a fact that was subsequently confirmed. But, as Almeder writes:

> If we were to accept that the sceptic is right here, we would need to suppose what has never occurred in the history of humankind, namely, that two people could have a conversation in two different languages and that one of them could acquire from the other, via this conversation, veridical information about an event that neither could have known about.[29]

Judge Edmonds made the following observations about what happened during the séance:

> To deny the fact is impossible, it was too well known; I could as well deny the light of the sun; nor could I think it an illusion, for it is in no way different from any other reality. It took place before ten educated and intelligent persons. We had never seen Mr. Evangelides before; he was introduced by a friend that same evening. How could Laura tell him of his son? How could she understand and speak Greek which she had never previously heard?[30]

The Mediumship of Carlos Mirabelli

The Brazilian medium Carlos Mirabelli was born in São Paulo in 1889, the son of Italian immigrants. Mirabelli was carefully investigated by many eminent members of Brazilian society and, if reports of his mediumship are to be believed, then he must certainly be considered one of the most impressive mediums ever documented.

Reports of Mirabelli's mediumship were widely reported in Brazil, and eventually came to the attention of European investigators. Before giving the case publicity, the *Zeitschrift fur Parapsychologie* (*Magazine for Parapsychology*) felt it necessary to investigate the possibility of a hoax, and inquired from the Brazilian consul at Munich the reputation of the witnesses to Mirabelli's feats. Eric Dingwall wrote:

> The answer was positive and the Consul added that 14 persons on the submitted list were his personal acquaintances and to whose veracity he would testify, nor had he the right of questioning the statements of other people on the list, known to him not only as scientists but also as men of character.[31]

In 1919 the *Academia de Estudos Psychicos* formed a committee to investigate Mirabelli. According to Dingwall, the *Zeitschrift* described the members as follows:

> Apart from two university professors, 555 people studied the medium, among them 450 Brazilians and 105 foreigners. Their professions were: 72 M.D.s, 18 chemists, 12 engineers, 36 lawyers, 8 translators, 89 statesmen, 128 merchants, 18 journalists (and others of widely divergent professions).[32]

Dingwall brought this case to the attention of the English-speaking world, using translations of the original Portuguese and German documents. Several remarkable abilities were attributed by witnesses to Mirabelli, but those that concern us here relate to his abilities to speak and write in several languages while in a trance.

Although Mirabelli was poorly educated and presumably able to speak only Portuguese (and perhaps some Italian), when in trance states the medium "spoke 26 languages including 7 dialects; it wrote in 28 languages, namely Latin, Chaldaic and Hieroglyphics ... A list of languages in which the talking is done comprises Brazilian dialects as well as all European languages and includes such as Japanese, Chinese, ancient Greek, Hebrew, Syrio-Egyptian and others. His talks concern a wide range of subjects from medicine, law, sociology to astronomy, musical science and literature, all of which, says the medium, are inspired by his 'leaders' such as Galileo, Kepler, Voltaire, or Lenin."[33]

The list of topics covered in the automatic writing is also varied, and also purports to come from the deceased. Dingwall writes:

So we find Johann Huss impressing Mirabelli to write a treatise of 9 pages on 'the independence of Checho-slovakia' in 20 minutes; Flammarion inspiring him to write about the inhabited planets, 14 pages in 19 minutes, in French; Muri Ka Ksi leading him to treat the Russian-Japanese war in Japanese, in 12 minutes to the extent of 5 pages; Moses is his control for a four page dissertation entitled "The Slandering," written in Hebrew; Harun el Raschid makes him write 15 pages in Syrian; and the most odd feature mentioned is an untranslatable writing of three pages in hieroglyphics which took 32 minutes.[34]

The cases described above involve mediums suddenly demonstrating skills that normally require years of practice to acquire: philosophizing at a high level and speaking an unknown foreign language fluently. The next remarkable case involves a medium displaying yet another skill, and at a level very few people normally possess.

Chess Game
with a Deceased Grandmaster

The remarkable story of a chess game played between living and deceased grandmasters began in 1985 when asset-manager and amateur chess player Dr. Wolfgang Eisenbeiss decided to initiate a chess match between living and deceased persons. Eisenbeiss had been acquainted with the automatic-writing medium Robbert Rollans (1914–1993) for eight years, and trusted his assertion that he did not know how to play chess and had no knowledge of chess history. Rollans was not paid for his services, and his stated motive for participation was to provide support for the survival hypothesis.

Eisenbeiss was able to persuade the world-famous chess champion Viktor Korchnoi, then ranked third in the world, to participate. Korchnoi was ranked second in the world for more than a decade, and was described in *Chessbase* (April 4, 2002) as "unquestionably one of the great chess players of all time."

Eisenbeiss gave Rollans a list of deceased grandmasters and asked him to find one who would be willing to participate in a game. On June 15, 1985, a communicator claiming to be the deceased Hungarian grandmaster Geza Maroczy confirmed his willingness to play, and then opened the game by making the first move. Geza Maroczy was ranked third in the world in 1900, and was known for his remarkably strong endgame.

The Maroczy communicator provided his motivation for participating in the game as follows:

> I will be at your disposal in this peculiar game of chess for two reasons. First, because I also want to do something to aid mankind living on earth to become convinced that death does not end everything, but instead the mind is separated from the physical body and comes up to us in a new world, where individual life continues to manifest itself in a new unknown dimension. Second, being a Hungarian patriot I want to guide the eyes of the world into the direction of my beloved Hungary a little bit. Both these items have convinced me to participate in that game with the thought of being at everyone's service.[35]

The Match

For the sake of simplicity, in the following I will refer to "the communicator identifying himself as Maroczy" as simply *Maroczy*.

As mentioned, *Maroczy* opened the match with the first move, which was directly passed by Rollans to Eisenbeiss, who then forwarded the move to Korchnoi. Korchnoi's countermove was relayed back to Rollans via Eisenbiess, and the entire game was played with Eisenbeiss as the intermediary. At no time did Rollans and Korchnoi have direct contact with each other, except for a handshake when they met during a TV show in September 1992, four and a half months before the end of the game.

Thirteen months into the game, at the twenty-seventh move, Korchnoi commented on the quality of his opponent's play.

> During the opening phase Maroczy showed weakness. His play is old-fashioned. But I must confess that my last moves have not been too convincing. I am not sure I will win. He has compensated the faults of the opening by a strong end-game. In the end-game the ability of a player shows up and my opponent plays very well.[36]

The game continued, always with Eisenbeiss as the intermediary, for seven years and eight months, until February 11, 1993, when *Maroczy* resigned at move forty-eight. The long duration was due to Korchnoi's frequent travels (these were the days before widespread e-mail and text messaging), and to Rollans's illness when he was unable to set up communication; in fact, Rollans died at age seventy-nine, just nineteen days after *Maroczy* resigned.

The full match went as shown on the following page.

1. e4	e6	19. Qe4	Qe4+	37. Rf5+	Kxg4
2. d4	d5	20. fxe4	f6	38. h6	b3
3. Nc3	Bb4	21. Radl	e5	39. h7	Ra8
4. e5	c5	22. Rd3	Kf7	40. cxb3	Rh8
5. a3	Bxc3+	23. Rg3	Rg6	41. Rxf6	Rxh7
6. bxc3	Ne7	24. Rhgl	Rag8	42. Rg6+	Kf4
7. Qg4	cxd4	25. a4	Rxg3	43. Rf6+	Kg3
8. Qxg7	Rg8	26. fxg3	b6	44. Rfl	Rh2
9. Qxh7	Qc7	27. h4	a6	45. Rdl	Kf3
10. Kdl	dxc3	28. g4	b5	46. Rfl+	Rf2
11. Nf3	Nbc6	29. axb5	axb5	47. Rfx2+	Kxf2
12. Bb5	Bd7	30. Kd3	Kg6	0 – I	
13. Bxc6	Bxc6	31. Rfl	Rh8	**Maroczy resigns**	
14 Bg5	d4	32. Rhl	Rh7	(48. b4	c2
15. Bxe7	Kxe7	33. Ke2	Ra7	49. Kxc2	Ke2 ·
16. Qh4+	Kxe7	34. Kd3	Ra2	50. b5	d3+
17. Ke2	Bxf3+	35. Rfl	b4	51. Kc3	d2
18. gxf3	Qxe5+	36. h5+	Kg5	52. qb6	dl+Q)*

*Moves 48–52 show how the game would have played out and provide the reason *Maroczy* resigned at move 47.

Comments on Chess Game with a Deceased Grandmaster

Neuropsychiatrist Vernon Neppe, who is also a former South African chess champion, reanalyzed this case in 2007, with the aid of a chess-playing computer program. Specifically, he wanted to answer these three questions:

1. At what level did *Maroczy* play this chess game?
2. Could a chess computer reproduce this game?
3. Was the *Maroczy* style something a computer could replicate?

Regarding the level of play, Neppe concluded:

> In my opinion, *Maroczy* played at least at the Master level, and very debatably and less likely, at a rusty, lowish grandmaster level. This level could not have been achieved by the medium even after great training, assuming the medium was not a chess genius.[37]

Neppe's only criticism of *Maroczy*'s play was his weak opening: like Korchnoi, he found this old-fashioned. Chess theory has made enormous strides in the way games should be opened since the death of Geza Maroczy, and Neppe blames *Maroczy*'s loss on his weak opening. Concerning *Maroczy*'s seventh move, Neppe writes, "It is fitting and supporting the style of Maroczy . . . [but] . . . Modern chess opening theory looks askance at such moves."[38] Concerning *Maroczy*'s tenth move, he writes, "The key move in the game, the tenth, making *Maroczy*'s game difficult, was legitimate at the time of Maroczy's death though very much out of fashion later."[39] However, three moves later, "From that point (move 13) on, *Maroczy,* in my opinion, plays perfect chess and no moves can be seriously criticized."[40]

Like Korchnoi, although Neppe found weakness in *Maroczy*'s opening, he was also very impressed with the skill with which *Maroczy* played from that point on. Knowledge of modern opening theory provides players with an enormous advantage however,* and Neppe points out that "given detailed re-analyses by grandmaster mathematician Dr. John Nunn (1999) of average standards in leading tournaments of a

---

*Neppe writes, "Opening theory is the most time-intensive part of chess competition at very high levels, since inferior players can obtain enormous advantage over the more naturally gifted if they have encyclopedic knowledge of the intricacies of chess openings" ("A Detailed Analysis of an Important Chess Game," 142).

century ago, the legitimate top players of the 1910 era might arguably play only at Master level or lower today."[41]

Neppe then tried to answer the question as to whether a computer could have simulated the game. Accordingly, he set the program Sigma Chess 6.0 to respond to Korchnoi's moves, and then compared the computer's choices with those of *Maroczy*.

> *Maroczy* played human-type moves, and the computer simulation played computer-type moves correcting what it thought were inferior moves (e.g. in moves 23 and 24) despite their illogicality. *Maroczy* clearly played the endgame far better than the computer, which might have been expected. This is not only because of Marcoczy's known endgame versatility, but because the wide number of choices a computer has in a chess endgame give it too many alternatives; humans understand chess strategy better than computers and can thrive on the logic required.[42]*

Neppe noted that the old-fashioned opening style of *Maroczy's* game also makes it unlikely that a computer was used to hoax the game.

> It is significant that the chess computer I was using (and a well-known modern one, Fritz 9) does not even consider *Maroczy's* 12. Bb5 as a legitimate alternative. This fact is important because it

---

*Philosopher and chess enthusiast Tim McGrew of Michigan University has extensively analyzed the ability of computers to play chess, and wrote: "It is chiefly by this characteristic—the readiness of the program to abandon the strategically indicated paths in the dubious pursuit of material gains—that computers can be distinguished from human beings in blind tests. The trouble is not just that humans sometimes make gross mistakes—the machine could be programmed to blunder from time to time as well—but rather that currently programmers have no idea how to enable the machine to select the relevant features of the position or to form and follow plans. Barring a conceptual breakthrough in this direction, computer chess is and will remain detectably inhuman" (McGrew, "The Simulation of Expertise: Deeper Blue and the Riddle of Cognition").

suggests that anyone hoaxing the game is unlikely to have done so with a computer.[43]

Comparing the style of *Maroczy*'s game with the style of a computer's game, Neppe wrote:

> *Maroczy* played in a style reminiscent of the early twentieth century, and demonstrated the endgame expertise he was famous for. . . . In any event, the differences in style between an accomplished chess player (like a grandmaster) and even the most remarkable computer hardware and software are profound.[44]

Considering the possibility of fraud with the use of a computer, Neppe concluded:

> A simulated computer analysis shows that *Maroczy*'s style and many of his moves appear very different from that of the relatively basic chess computer used for the analysis. In short, the alternative hypothesis of fraud by means of a chess computer playing *Maroczy*'s moves is unlikely. More specifically, it is my opinion that a chess computer could not reproduce this game as of the 1980s. Nor is it likely that it could replicate *Maroczy*'s play even today because of the stylistic elements.[45]

In other words, computer technology—both software and hardware—was simply not advanced enough in the 1980s to play at the master or low grandmaster level, and thus was not advanced enough to give a chess grandmaster a challenging game. Furthermore, it is unlikely the software would be programmed to use an old-fashioned opening. Finally, computer programs cannot—at least at the present—simulate a human style of play, and certainly cannot simulate the unique style of play of an accomplished chess player such as Maroczy.

Neppe also rejected the possibility that one or more living chess masters were consulted to play some of *Maroczy*'s moves. Rollans the medium was unfamiliar with the rules of chess, had an impeccable reputation for honesty, and apparently did not know any chess masters.

Commenting on the possibility of fraud, Eisenbeiss and Hassler had earlier written:

> Since 1982 Eisenbeiss had been acquainted with the automatic-writing medium Robert Rollans (29 January 1914–2 March 1993). He knew him and worked with him for 8 years, well enough to trust his assertion that he did not know how to play chess, had no knowledge of chess history, and was not cheating through secret communication with a living chess expert. Rollans was not paid for his services. His motive was to support the survival hypothesis. His widow attests to this judgement (a copy of the letter of confirmation has been lodged with the Editor).[46]

Eisenbeiss and Hassler also testified on behalf of Rollans's honesty.

> To the best of our knowledge, Mr Rollans did not seek help (from persons or databases) concerning moves of the match or matters of chess history during the years of the match. Witnesses who attest to these circumstances and their continuation from the beginning to the end of the match are Dr. Eisenbeiss, Mrs. Ellen Rollans, Prof. Schiebeler and Mr. Holbe.
>
> Mr. Rollans undertook his part of this endeavour on a voluntary, unpaid basis. His purpose in facilitating this match was his wish to prove that physical death is by no means the end of personal life. Mr. Rollans believed in reincarnation.[47]

Moreover, the style of the game was consistent throughout, and typical of the style of Geza Maroczy. Rollans had first discovered his ability as a medium accidentally while composing a letter at the age of 33, almost 40 years before the chess game began. In addition to working as a musician and composer, he had also been an amateur practicing medium over the intervening years. Rollans did not accept payment for his services as a medium, and was never exposed as a fraud. The supposition that an elderly, frequently ill man with an impeccable reputation for honesty secretly conspired with a living chess master over seven years and eight months in order to mimic the chess ability and style of a deceased grandmaster for no apparent purpose or gain can be safely rejected by all but the most dogmatic skeptics.

But there is even more to this remarkable case than demonstrated high-level chess skills. *Maroczy,* through Rollans, was asked questions about the obscure life of Geza Maroczy. He answered seventy-nine out of eighty-one correctly, or 97.5 percent, for all the authenticated items. Even more remarkable was the accuracy rate for the most difficult-to-retrieve items involving expert knowledge or private knowledge: of these, *Maroczy* answered thirty-one out of thirty-one, or 100 percent correct when answers were authenticated (for two of these items the answers remained unknown).[48]* Many of these answers were so difficult to authenticate that the expert Korchnoi could not answer them, and declined to even try because of the enormous effort involved (in the end a professional historian from Hungary was employed to track down the answers). These considerations make fraud even more unlikely since, as Neppe writes, "It would require major conspiracy involving the librarian, Maroczy's children, Eisenbeiss, plus possibly media involvement too as it was reported in 1987."[49]

The only remaining explanation—besides genuine communication from Maroczy—is that Rollans subconsciously fabricated the *Maroczy* communications using super-ESP. However, the following features of this case create great difficulties for this hypothesis.

---

*Note that Neppe corrected an error made by Eisenbeiss and Hassler: two items thought to be incorrect were reclassified as unsolved.

Romi(h)

Eisenbeiss questioned *Maroczy* about his life, and at one point received a very unexpected answer. Eisenbeiss and Hassler wrote:

> In questioning *Maroczy* about his life, Eisenbeiss had deliberately selected a chess match against a relatively unknown player, but which had included a surprising key-move which might at the time have been so impressed upon *Maroczy*'s memory as still to be recollected now. It was the match against a certain Romi, played in San Remo, Italy in 1930.[50]

In this game *Maroczy* recovered from a seemingly "hopeless situation" and unexpectedly became the winner.

> With this in mind, Eisenbeiss asked *Maroczy* (via Rollans) whether the name "Romi" meant anything to him. In his answer *Maroczy* mocks Eisenbeiss for not knowing the correct spelling of "Romi" which should have been "Romih" (i.e. with an "h"). Eisenbeiss was not aware and had no idea that the name could be spelled that way. So the particular way in which the question was answered came as a complete surprise.[51]

Maroczy's answer was:

> I am sorry to say that I never knew a chess player named Romi. But I think you are wrong with the name. I had a friend in my youth, who defeated me when I was young, but he was called Romih—with an "h" at the end. I then never again saw the friend whom I so admired. In 1930 at the tournament of San Remo—who is also present? My old friend Romih coming from Italy also participated in that tournament. And so it came about that I played against him one of the most thrilling matches I ever played. I suspect that you were thinking about the same person but gave the name incorrectly.[52]

Which was the correct spelling? The historian-researcher found both and could not reach a decision on which was correct. Finally, a copy of the official book from the San Remo Tournament 1930 was obtained, with "Romih" throughout spelled with the *h*.

So, what accounted for the confusion in the spelling?

> With the help of a chess expert from Italy Eisenbeiss learned that the aforementioned Romih was of Slavonic origin, where the spelling with "h" is common. Romih emigrated in 1918 to Italy and after "many many years" . . . (letter to Dr Eisenbeiss, 21st October 1992) sometime in the 1930s, but definitely after the tournament of San Remo in 1930, decided to drop the "h" because it was unfamiliar to Italians. The Slavonic origin of Romih also makes it more probable for Maroczy as an Hungarian to have known Romih, both being subjects of the Habsburg Austro-Hungarian "Dual Monarchy."

> So, because Maroczy claimed to know Romih from his youth, it is logical that he would have known the original spelling of Romih's name and would not have replaced it with the later Italianization. For the super-ESP hypothesis to work, the controlling mind, on perceiving varying references to Romih or Romi, would have to be able to grasp the correct one from Maroczy's perspective, decide to address the situation, formulate a response to the conflict and dramatize it in the context of a teasing dialogue with Eisenbeiss/ Rollans about their ignorance of the correct spelling.[53]

The Vera Menchik Club

Another question put to *Maroczy* was taken from a reader competition in the August 4, 1988, edition of the Swiss chess magazine *Schachwoche*, which Eisenbeiss duly put to *Maroczy* via Rollans. The question was: Who was the Austrian founder of the Vera Menchik Club? Vera Menchik was the first-ever women's world chess champion, and had been a pupil of Maroczy. Membership in the club was restricted to those who had been beaten by Vera Menchik.

On August 8, 1988, Maroczy via Rollans speculates on who the founder was, first naming Rudolf Spielmann and later Ernst Grunfeld. On August 11, 1988, Maroczy confesses he is uncertain about the founder, discusses Professor Albert Becker as a possibility, but in the end rejects Becker. Note that if super-ESP were real and operating, then the medium—posing as Maroczy—should have given the correct name of the founder, because by August 4, 1988, the entire editing team of the Schachwoche knew the answer to the contest.

Maroczy correctly stated in his transcript that he had been a teacher of Menchik, but describes the idea of a Vera Menchik Club as "a silly joke to which he paid no attention." That is given as the reason for his not remembering the founder's name. *Maroczy* wrote that "it's very natural and like your world: what is pleasant and important can be more easily remembered, whilst the unpleasant and inconsequential—sooner or later—get forgotten."[54]

The solution to the question was published in the same magazine on August 18, 1988: Professor Albert Becker. On August 21, 1988, another transcript came from *Maroczy,* in which Albert Becker is again discussed. However:

> He still does not name Becker as the founder of the club, as might be expected under the Super-ESP hypothesis; once the solution was published it should be possible for the medium to access the information, either clairvoyantly or telepathically from the minds of the magazine's readers. But instead of correcting his wrong answer Maroczy quite unprompted comes up with a different story which evidently demanded his attention much more than the "silly joke."[55]

Maroczy went on to relate an amusing story involving a married chess champion, accompanied by his beautiful Russian mistress at a tournament, being so shocked by the unexpected arrival of his wife from Cuba that he lost a game. Eisenbeiss and Hassler conclude:

In our example Maroczy's rationale for forgetting the name of a man whom he would have considered to be merely indulging a pointless joke but then relating an unprompted story about a woman whose beauty had impressed him is plausible, whereas for Rollans the medium it is difficult to understand [if using Super-ESP] why he should be unable to retrieve the name requested, given his ability to convey detailed precise information on other occasions, even less why he should digress to an unprompted narrative thread.[56]

The 1924 New York Tournament

Eisenbeiss and Hassler describe another similar incident, which provides a second example of inferences that can be drawn from information that is not given and the psychological background to this. Maroczy in his transcript talks about the 1924 New York tournament, emphasizing that he achieved a draw against Alekhine, but failing to mention that the tournament was disappointing to him overall, as he finished in sixth place. In the transcript he says: "I once again travelled to America in 1924, again to New York. I had a thrilling game against Alekhine there, ending in a draw. You certainly have observed my trick in saying 'I no longer know which of us won the game.' In doing so I want to bury a failure in order not to have to write so much, because failures are rather common among all chess players. This is a joke only, my dear friends; in fact it is true for me that I am not able to remember everything, most of all whenever winning eluded me.

The facts are correct: Maroczy took part in the New York Tournament in 1924 and had a match with Alekhine, ending in a draw, as confirmed in Lasker (1992). This article confirms that Maroczy finished sixth, well below expectations. The psychological explanation for failure to disclose this in the transcript is given by Maroczy himself (see above). If Rollans were trying to engineer a story with verifiable facts as evidence of survival, he could have inserted Maroczy's final ranking, a checkable fact. Clearly, elsewhere the Maroczy transcripts contain innumerable such verifiable facts. . . . we know Maroczy to have been very ambitious and it is thus entirely in character that he would omit reporting failures or mediocre tournament rankings. Yet for Rollans, whose main objective was to provide convincing evidence to support the survival hypothesis, it would make no sense to censor information concerning Maroczy's failures.[57]

Unless of course, to paraphrase Gauld, we are willing to attribute to Rollans not just super-ESP but super-*guile* as well.

Chess Game with a Deceased Grandmaster: Summary

What is so impressive about this case is the combination of a demonstrated high-level skill (knowing *how*) with vast and accurate details provided of an obscure life in the early twentieth century (knowing *that*), all presented in the style and from the perspective of a deceased chess grandmaster over a period of almost eight years, and enriched by an unanticipated revelation about a minor detail about the spelling of a name (Romi[h]).

Eisenbeiss and Hassler describe the difficulty of using psi to explain the details provided about Maroczy's life:

> None of the persons around Rollans nor Rollans himself knew the many details about Maroczy's life in advance. So the psi faculty required of Rollans would have to be so extraordinary as to permit the extraction of the information which appears in his transcripts from books and magazines in different libraries, against a huge amount of background "noise" from other sources. Certain facts not set down in written form would have had to be collected from the private memoires of living people who were certainly not thinking about these facts at the moment when it was transcribed by Rollans as "automatic writing."[58]

And Neppe describes the difficulty of using psi to explain the chess-playing skill attributed to Maroczy:

Far more so, chess-playing skill requires a further profound leap when applying the super-ESP hypothesis—delving into a Master's (or several Masters') *unconscious* mind(s) is insufficient; their *active repeated cogitation* 47 times (as 47 moves) over many years plus the medium obtaining it all by automatic writing. . . . Merely divining this information from the Master's unconscious would not work, as the responses would require active intervention. The medium would [then] need to be able to record the moves by automatic writing.[59]

As mentioned, an elaborate fraud involving several highly respected people over a period of almost eight years would have been extraordinarily difficult, if not impossible. As for super-ESP, it utterly fails to explain not one but four features of this case. The sole remaining alternative is that the transcripts are in fact what they consistently appear and claim to be: genuine communication from the deceased chess grandmaster Geza Maroczy.

SUPER-ESP: CONCLUDING THOUGHTS

We started out discussing cases in which the flow of information from the medium, ostensibly from a deceased person but possibly from the sitters, seemed to far exceed in *volume, speed, and accuracy* anything seen in experimental or anecdotal cases of telepathy. After this, we discussed cases in which a *purpose,* characteristic of the deceased but contrary to that of the sitters, was displayed. We then examined cases in which the communications seemed unmistakably from the *perspective* of the deceased. Following this, we examined cases in which the *personality* of the deceased was accurately portrayed in the communications. Finally, we examined cases that combined several of the foregoing features with the *manifestation of skills* not possessed by the medium, but known to have been possessed by the deceased.

These five features of the communications progressively stretch the super-ESP hypothesis further and further. The first three stretch it almost to the breaking point; the final two stretch it past that point, simply because there is no independent evidence that extrasensory perception can be used to successfully impersonate an individual whom a person has never knowingly met; and no independent evidence that extrasensory perception can be used to telepathically and instantly acquire skills normally requiring years of practice to acquire. We simply have no reason to think that mere *perception*—extrasensory or otherwise—can be used to impersonate others over a prolonged period well enough to deceive intimate friends and relatives. We also have no reason to think that mere *perception*—extrasensory or otherwise—can be used to instantly acquire the skills of others, skills that required those others years of practice to acquire. Commenting on such cases, Broad wrote:

> It seems to me that any attempt to explain these phenomena by reference to telepathy among the living stretches the word "telepathy" till it becomes almost meaningless, and uses that name to cover something for which there is no *independent* evidence and which bears hardly any analogy to the phenomena which the word was introduced to denote.[60]

Telepathy was a term coined by Frederic Myers and literally means "distant feeling" (from the Greek *tele* meaning "distant," as in telephone and television, and *pathy* meaning "feeling," as in sympathy and empathy). Most examples of telepathy—among both humans and animals—involve hunches, impressions, feelings of distress associated with another, calls for help or to go to a particular place.* Some have argued that communication with the deceased via a medium must also

---

*Typical examples of human telepathy would include a sense of being stared at, or the occasional hunch before a ringing phone is answered that a certain person will be on the line. Biologist Rupert Sheldrake has gathered experimental evidence showing that people can, in fact, perform the first feat at a rate of about 55 percent when 50 percent would be expected by chance, and the second feat at a rate of about 40 percent when 25 percent would be expected by chance (Sheldrake, *The Sense of Being Stared At*).

involve telepathy, as it must involve direct mind-to-mind communication without the use of the ordinary sense organs. Therefore, it is argued, if these cases must involve a form of telepathy, then why can't they be examples of telepathy between the living?

But as Broad wrote, when applied to the most impressive cases this claim stretches the word *telepathy* until it becomes so general that it is almost meaningless. We have examined cases in which the deceased person appears to speak to the medium as though over a telephone line; cases in which the deceased seems to control the medium's hand to rapidly write lengthy and detailed messages; cases of trance mediumship in which the deceased appears to directly control the medium's brain and vocal cords so as to speak directly to the sitters, sometimes in a language unknown to the medium, often with a lifelike manifestation of the personality of the deceased, and sometimes to serve purposes that seem only those of the deceased. In all such cases, both the level and *type* of communication involved seems very different from telepathy between the living. In these cases, the type of communication more closely resembles one person *dictating* a message to a secretary over a telephone, who then immediately repeats it for the benefit of others in the room; or in the case of possession mediumship, it seems that the deceased temporarily takes control of the medium's body. The crucial difference between these cases and telepathy between the living is this: *the active participation of the deceased person's mind* seems to be required, not just merely the gathering of information *about* the deceased. In other words, the best cases require not merely perception, but also communication from the deceased; and in the most dramatic cases of trance mediumship, they would seem to require possession of the medium's body by a disincarnate mind. As Broad remarked, calling what is required to explain such cases "telepathy" stretches the word until it "bears hardly any analogy to the phenomena which the word was introduced to denote."

In the opinion of many who have studied the issue, the cases already covered provide strong evidence in favor of survival, and against the hypothesis that all such cases can be explained by the telepathic and clairvoyant powers of the medium combined with subconscious impersonation. The five features described in this chapter seem to create insurmountable difficulties for the super-ESP hypothesis. However, the final extraordinary set of cases to be considered combines several of the above features, and adds a completely new twist.

FOURTEEN

Cross Correspondences

Frederic Myers died on January 17, 1901. During his life he had been a classical scholar, extremely well-versed in the literature of ancient Greece and Rome. He was also the author of a monumental two-volume work, *Human Personality and Its Survival of Bodily Death,* still considered a classic in the field. In addition, he was one of the founding fathers of the Society for Psychical Research and, at the time of his death, the Society's president. Myers had been intensely interested in the survival problem, and had spent a great deal of time and effort investigating the evidence. However, although he himself came to believe in survival, he also realized that the evidence available at the time was not yet sufficient to compel general belief.

Shortly after Myers died, messages purporting to come from him were received by several mediums in different parts of the world. Most of these messages were received by the technique called automatic writing, in which the medium goes into a trance and writes with pencil or pen on paper. Many of these early messages expressed a passionate longing on the part of the purported Myers to prove his continued existence. For instance, on January 12, 1904, the following message was received by Mrs. Holland in India from an intelligence claiming to be Fred Myers: "If it were possible for the soul to die back into earth life I should die from sheer yearning to reach you to tell you that all we imagined is not half wonderful enough for the truth." And through

Mrs. Piper in Boston: "I am trying with all the forces . . . together to prove that I am Myers." And again through Mrs. Holland: "Oh, I am feeble with eagerness—how can I best be identified? . . . I am trying alone amid unspeakable difficulties."

As a psychic researcher, Myers was fully aware of how difficult it was to find evidence for survival that could not be explained by ESP. The problem is this: most of the evidence for survival coming from mediums consists of communications of knowledge not known to anyone present, but which was, or could very well have been, known to the deceased. Now it is clear that if such communications are to be of any value as evidence, then the information conveyed must be capable of being verified; and this implies that some living person or persons must know the facts, or that some written record of them exists somewhere. But if the knowledge is recorded—either in memories of the living or in writing—then it is always possible, at least in principle, that the knowledge was gained from the telepathic or clairvoyant powers of the medium.

As mentioned, Myers was fully aware of this problem. What makes the cross correspondences so unusual is that they appear to be a method invented by the postmortem Myers in order to overcome this difficulty. In other words, they appear to be a method invented in order to provide evidence of his survival, which would be very difficult—if not impossible—to explain on the basis of telepathy or clairvoyance among the living.

The messages, which became known as *cross correspondences,* were received by mediums in England, the United States, and India during the period 1901–1932. Their distinguishing feature is that they appear to be meaningless when read by themselves. But when combined with messages received by other mediums at about the same time, they show various correspondences, so that when a group of them is considered together they can be seen to clearly refer to some common topic, usually from classical literature or history. They are in the form of literary puzzles, analogous to the pieces of a crossword puzzle—individually meaningless, but when combined can be seen to form a pattern. The nature of these puzzles seems to rule out telepathy between the mediums as their source. After all, if each of the mediums does not understand their own part of the message, then how could they transmit the *corresponding* messages that complete and solve the puzzle?

A further difficulty these puzzles raise for the hypothesis of telepathy is that many of them required knowledge of the classics that far exceeded the knowledge of most of the mediums involved—but not that of the living Myers. In some of the best cases, solving the puzzles required a great deal of study on the part of the investigators. And throughout these investigations, the mediums frequently remained ignorant of what the other automatists had written.

This, then, is the scheme that the messages claim was invented on the other side in order to prove the survival of Myers and his deceased colleagues. There are many passages in the scripts that bear this out. The automatists are exhorted "to weave together" and are told that by themselves they can do little. In the script of Mrs. Verrall we find: "Record the bits and when fitted they will make the whole," and "I will give the words between you neither alone can read but together they will give the clue he wants."[1] It is constantly claimed in the scripts that the enigmatic messages are part of an experiment designed to provide convincing evidence of survival, and that the source of the enigmatic messages is the mind of Frederic Myers or, later, of some of his deceased colleagues.

Also, in several instances there are instructions in the scripts for the automatist to send her script to one of the other automatists, or to one of the investigators. As we will see, it was such instructions that first brought two of the automatists together.

CAST OF CHARACTERS

In addition to Frederic Myers, the communications claimed to come mostly from the two other cofounders of the Society for Psychical Research, Edmund Gurney and Henry Sidgwick. Gurney was Myers's friend and collaborator, and had helped write a book on apparitions, titled *Phantasms of the Living*. He died in June 1888. Sidgwick was a well-known philosopher at Cambridge, and was the first president of the SPR when it was founded in 1882. He died in August 1900. Later communications were received that claimed to come from Dr. A. W. Verrall, a classical scholar at Cambridge who died in 1912; and from his friend Henry Butcher, another classical scholar at Cambridge who died in 1910.

The automatists included the Boston medium Mrs. Piper, whom we have already met. Mrs. Piper was the only professional medium in the group. Most of the other principal mediums were upper-class women, some of them well-known figures in public life who used pseudonyms and kept their mediumship a closely guarded secret, even from their friends. These included Mrs. Verrall, wife of Dr. A. W. Verrall and lecturer in classics at Newnham College; her daughter Helen; Mrs. Holland, the pseudonym of Mrs. Fleming, a sister of Rudyard Kipling who lived in India; Mrs. Forbes, another pseudonym; and Mrs. Willett, a pseudonym for Mrs. Coombe-Tennant, justice of the peace and the first woman to be appointed by the British government as a delegate to the assembly of the League of Nations.*

The chief investigators were Gerald Balfour and J. C. Piddington. Balfour was an expert classical scholar, and Piddington also had sufficient knowledge of the classics to understand the frequent allusions made to them in the scripts. Both men devoted a large part of their lives to the study of the scripts, and the script intelligences took an active interest in their efforts. Others involved in a significant way include Miss Alice Johnson; Mrs. Henry Sidgwick (sister of Gerald Balfour and wife of one of the communicators); physicist Sir Oliver Lodge; Frank Podmore; and Richard Hodgson up to the time of his death in 1905.

---

*At this point the reader may recall with some amusement the remark by "skeptic" Victor Stenger that opened Part III of this book: "Lodge and other nineteenth-century psychical researchers unwittingly allowed themselves to be fooled by the tricks of professional fortune tellers and sleight-of-hand artists posing as spiritualists."

Mrs. Verrall, as a lecturer in classics, filled the dual role of both medium and investigator.

The investigation of the scripts proved to be an enormous task, as they continued to appear for over thirty years, and finally numbered over three thousand. The membership of the group of mediums changed somewhat over the years. In the end, more than a dozen different mediums were involved, from the three countries of England, India, and the United States.

EARLY MESSAGES

Shortly after Myers died in 1901, Mrs. Verrall in Cambridge began to write automatic scripts that were signed "Myers." At first they were rather poorly expressed, but gradually became more coherent. However, the messages remained cryptic, as though their true meaning were being concealed. About a year later, allusions to the same subjects began to appear in the scripts of Mrs. Piper in Boston, and these, too, claimed to come from Myers. Some time later Mrs. Verrall's daughter Helen began automatic writing, and similar oblique references to the same subjects were found in her scripts as well. Starting at this point, the scripts were sent to Miss Alice Johnson, secretary of the SPR.

Soon afterward, Mrs. Holland in India also began to receive messages that purported to come from Myers. On November 7, 1903 the script read, "My Dear Mrs. Verrall I am very anxious to speak to some of the old friends—Miss J.—and to A.W." These initials were taken to refer to Miss Johnson and Dr. A. W. Verrall. This was followed by a largely accurate description of Dr. Verrall, and finally the words: "Send this to Mrs. Verrall, 5 Selwyn Gardens, Cambridge."[2]

Mrs. Holland knew the name of Mrs. Verrall, as it appears in Myers's *Human Personality,* which she had recently read. But she knew nothing about her personally, and most certainly did not know her address, or even if there was such a place as Selwyn Gardens, Cambridge. As such, she did not follow these instructions, but did eventually send the scripts to Alice Johnson, secretary for the SPR, who duly filed them away without suspecting that they contained allusions to the same subjects as the Verrall and Piper scripts.

It was not until 1905 that Miss Johnson realized what was happening. By that time, the scripts contained the astounding claim that the discarnate Myers, Gurney, and Sidgwick had devised the scheme of providing meaningless fragments in the scripts of different mediums, fragments of which would be found to express a coherent idea only when combined. In her article of 1908, the theory of the cross correspondences is fully discussed for the first time. She first describes the nature of the messages:

> What we get is fragmentary utterance in one script, which seems to have no particular point or meaning, and another fragmentary utterance in the other, of an equally pointless character; but when we put the two together, we see that they supplement one another, and that there is apparently one coherent idea underlying both, but only partially expressed in each.[3]

Later, she discusses the apparent origin of the messages:

> Now, granted the possibility of communication, it may be supposed that within the last few years a certain group of persons have been trying to communicate with us, who are sufficiently well instructed to know all the objections that reasonable sceptics have urged against the previous evidence, and sufficiently intelligent to realize the full force of these objections. It may be supposed that these persons have invented a new plan—the plan of cross-correspondences—to meet the sceptic's objections. . . .
>
> We have reason to believe . . . that the idea of making a statement in one script *complementary* of a statement in another had not occurred to Mr. Myers in his lifetime, for there is no reference to it in any of his written utterances on the subject that I have been

able to discover . . . It was not the autonomists that detected it, but a student of the scripts; it has every appearance of being an element imported from outside; it suggests an independent invention, an active intelligence constantly at work in the present, not a mere echo or remnant of individualities of the past.[4]

As we will see later, several of the features discussed earlier that cause problems for the super-ESP theory appear in the cross correspondences. What the cross correspondences add to the evidence from mediumship is *evidence of design*—a design that seemingly could not have originated in the minds of anyone living, but which gives every indication of being designed by the deceased Myers.

It is important to point out that the records of the cross correspondences do not suffer from many of the objections that have been raised against the evidence for deathbed visions, for reincarnation, and for apparitions. The cross correspondences are not the product of eyewitness testimony; they are the product of handwriting performed automatically by mediums while in trance. In other words, the cross correspondences are documentary evidence that is available for anyone to study at any time. They are therefore *permanent and objective,* and cannot suffer from errors of observation or exaggeration.

The cross correspondences gradually became more and more complex, as it became clear that words and topics were not going to be merely repeated in the scripts of different mediums, but that hidden, complementary allusions to the same topic were going to be made. We will first consider two simple cross correspondences, then a complex one, and then another sort of literary puzzle that appeared.

The Case of Thanatos

As Mrs. Piper in Boston awoke from trance on April 17, 1907, a word was spoken that was first heard as *Sanatos,* then repeated as *Tanatos.* Mrs. Sidgwick, the sitter, inserted a note saying that *Thanatos* was probably meant. On April 23, in the waking stage of the séance, the word was correctly pronounced as "Thanatos," and on May 7 "I want to say Thanatos" came through in the waking stage.

Thanatos is the Greek word for "death."

By this time the investigators had learned that the repetition of a word in a disconnected fashion was usually a signal that it is being used in a cross correspondence.

On April 16, 1907, Mrs. Holland in India wrote the following words: "Maurice Morris Mors. And with that the shadow of death fell upon his limbs." It was thought that 'Maurice Morris' were the first attempts at *Mors,* the Latin word for "death." The later occurrence of the English word *death* points to this.

On April 29, 1907, Mrs. Verrall in England wrote: "Warmed both hands before the fire of life. It fades and I am ready to depart . . . *Manibus date lilia plenis* . . . Come away, come away, *Pallida mors.*"

Finally, in the same script came the message: "You have got the word plainly written all along in your own writing. Look back."[5]

"Warmed both hands . . ." is a quotation from a poem by the nineteenth-century English poet Walter Landor. *Manibus date lilia plenis* (Latin for "Give lilies with full hands") is a quotation from a section of Virgil's work *The Aeneid,* in which Anchises foretells the early death of Marcellus. "Come away, come away" is from a song by Shakespeare, and the next word in the song is "death."* *Pallida mors* (Latin for "pale death") are the first two words, in the original Latin, from a line in *Odes* by Horace.[†]

Comments on the Case of Thanatos

In a period of less than two weeks, the same keyword was given by three mediums located in three different countries, in three different

---

*Come away, come away, death,/and in sad cypress let me be laid;/Fly away, fly away, breath:/I am slain by a fair cruel maid (Shakespeare, *Twelfth Night, II*).

†Pale Death, with impartial step, knocks at the poor man's cottage and the palaces of kings (*Pallida Mors aequo pulsat pede, pauperum tabernas regumque turris*) (Horace, *Odes,* 1.4).

languages, combined with indirect references to the same topic. If the occurrence of the same idea in the three messages was due to telepathy among the mediums, it seems surprising that it should take the form of literary allusions typical of a classics scholar.

The Roden Noel Case

On March 7, 1906, Mrs. Verrall's script contained an original poem, which started with the words:

Tintagel and the sea that moaned in pain.

When Miss Johnson read this she was struck by its similarity to a poem by Roden Noel, titled "Tintadgel." To the best of her recollection, Mrs. Verrall had never read this poem.

On March 11, 1906, Mrs. Holland's script contained these words:

This is for A.W. Ask him what the date May 26th, 1894 meant to him—to me—and to F.W.H.M. I do not think they will find it hard to recall, but if so—let them ask Nora.

The date given, which meant nothing to Mrs. Holland, is the date of death of Roden Noel. The initials *A.W.* refer to Dr. Verrall, and *F.W.H.M.* refers, of course, to F.W.H. Myers, both of whom knew Noel, but not very well. *Nora* means Mrs. Sidgwick, which seems appropriate, as Noel was an intimate friend of Dr. Sidgwick.

On March 14, before any of the above facts were known to Mrs. Holland, she wrote, in a trance state:

Eighteen, fifteen, four, five, fourteen, Fourteen, fifteen, five, twelve. Not to be taken as they stand. See Rev. 13, 18, but only the central eight words, not the whole passage.[6]

The whole thing was meaningless to Mrs. Holland, and she did not look up the passage. But Miss Johnson did, and found that the central eight words were: "for it is the number of a man." Taking this to be a hint, she translated the numbers given in the script into the letters of the alphabet, with *d* being the fourth letter, *e* the fifth, and so on. When finished, the letters spelled *Roden Noel*.

There was a further reference to Roden Noel in Mrs. Verrall's script of March 16, 1906, and finally, on March 28, 1906, Mrs. Holland's script contained the name *Roden Noel* written out in full. Hence, the common topic of the scripts was only revealed in a later script, and by the dutiful efforts of Miss Johnson to understand the earlier scripts.

Comments on the Roden Noel Case

In this cross correspondence between two mediums, we find three references to the same person, but given in an indirect manner that did not reveal the chosen topic to the conscious minds of the mediums. This deliberate concealment seems to be crucial to the plan of the cross correspondences: the messages are deliberately enigmatic to prevent the mediums from acquiring knowledge of the topic, in order to rule out the possibility of the mediums helping each other, normally or telepathically.

The following case is a more striking instance of the same principle.

The Case of the Medici Tombs

In 1907, within the space of thirty days, the following messages appeared in the scripts of three mediums, in the following order:

MRS. PIPER: Moorhead. I gave her that for laurel.

MISS VERRALL: Alexander's tomb. Emblem laurels for the victor's brow.

MRS. HOLLAND: Alexander Moors Head.[7]

The third message, written in complete ignorance of the other two, reveals the connection between them. But the common topic was still not apparent. Nearly three years later, in the script of a fourth medium, Mrs. Willett, came the clue: "Laurentian tombs, Dawn and Twilight."

However, the mystery remained, and it was not until 1912 that the riddle was finally solved. It was then realized that the whole series referred to Alexander of the Medici family. The laurel was the family emblem, especially of Lorenzo de Medici. The tomb of Lorenzo has two reclining figures representing Dawn and Twilight. What the investigators learned in 1912 was that Alexander was buried in Lorenzo's tomb in Florence after his assassination in 1537, and so the tomb may also be called Alexander's tomb. He was the son of Pope Clement VII and a mulatto woman, and is shown in his portrait as having a very North African appearance. Because of this, he was known as *Il Moro* (the Moor), and so it is quite accurate for him to be called Alexander, Moor's Head.

Mrs. Piper, who wrote first, knew practically nothing of the Medici or of the Medici tombs, and nothing at all of Alexander of the Medici. This part of the script was simply meaningless to her, and to those who read her script.

Miss Verrall, who wrote second, stated in writing that she had never been to Florence, and so had never seen the Medici tombs. She also had never heard of Alexander of the Medici, and had supposed, quite naturally, that her script referred to Alexander the Great. Those who first read the script also thought it referred to the Macedonian warrior-king.

Mrs. Holland, who wrote last, had been to Florence and did know the tombs. However, the words *Alexander Moors Head* in her script are associated with drawings of masts and the words *The tall mast, but this one not at sea.* This was interpreted by the readers to refer to the tall masts (150 feet high) of the Lodge-Muirhead wireless telegraph apparatus that had been developed recently, and to which references had been made on several other occasions in her script. Consequently, when Miss Johnson first read the script, she had no doubt that "Alexander Moors Head" meant Dr. Alexander Muirhead.

However, in the same script of Mrs. Holland, following the name

"Alexander Moors Head," are quotations from *Othello* ("Antres vast and deserts idle," and "One not easily jealous"). There is no connection between Othello and Dr. Muirhead; but there is a definite connection between Othello, the Moor of Venice, and Alexander the Moor, of Florence. With regard to this script, Miss Johnson commented:

> It looks then as if the "author," out of a number of associations with "Moors Head," has deliberately and carefully selected one that fits in admirably with its special purpose and has influenced the writer to express it, and has then left her subliminal [subconscious] mind free to select another association—"the tall mast"—in order to show what her own subliminal interpretation of the script is.[8]

Comments on the Case of the Medici Tombs

Here we have an example of a cross correspondence involving four mediums in three different countries. Telepathy between the living seems to be clearly ruled out, since no one involved understood the common topic of the messages until 1912. The first message simply seemed meaningless to all concerned. The second appeared to be a reference to the undefeated general Alexander of Macedon, although both messages did include the common word *laurel*, indicating a possible connection between them. The third script clearly illustrates the connection between the first two, but at first appeared to be a reference to a living person—engineer Alexander Muirhead (d. 1920). And finally, in the script of a fourth medium, there appears a clue which finally reveals the common topic: *Alessandro de Medici, Il Moro*.

FIFTEEN

The Lethe Experiment

The final case to be considered is not exactly a cross correspondence, as it was clearly initiated by efforts on "this side." However, this remarkable case is an excellent example of a literary puzzle that took much effort on the part of investigators to solve, and it does share some of the features of the pure cross correspondences.

In early 1908, Mr. G. B. Dorr, a member of the SPR, held a series of sittings with Mrs. Piper in Boston. Dorr had dropped Latin and Greek at eighteen, and had hardly read any Latin, Greek, or translations of the classics since then. Mrs. Piper knew virtually nothing about classical literature. Myers, in his lifetime, had been a classical scholar of repute. So, in order to test the memory of the Myers communicator, Dorr obtained various questions on classical literature, and began to put them to "Myers" when Mrs. Piper was in trance, writing automatically.

On March 23, 1908 he posed this question: "What does the word LETHE suggest to you?" In Greek mythology the River Lethe flows through Hades, and is also known as the River of Forgetfulness. The dead are said to drink from this river to obliterate their memories, before being born again on earth. Dorr was expecting a reply along these lines. Instead, he got the following strange answer:

MYERS: Lethe. Do you refer to one of my poems, Lethe?[1]

Dorr answered in the negative, and pressed the communicator

234

for an answer, getting in response some disjointed words, including "Winds," "Greece," and then:

> . . . It is all clear. Do you remember Cave?
>
> **DORR:** I think you are confused about this. It was a water, not a wind, and it was in Hades, where the Styx was and the Elysian fields. Do you recall it now?
>
> **MYERS:** Lethe. Shore—of course I do. Lethe Hades beautiful river—Lethe. Underground.[2]

Thinking the medium was growing tired, Dorr shortly afterward closed the sitting. As Mrs. Piper came out of her trance (a period called the "waking stage"), she said the following:

> Sybil—Olympus—water—Lethe—delighted—sad—lovely—mate.—
> Put them all together . . .
> Entwined love—beautiful shores . . .
> Warm—sunlit—love.
> Lime leaf—heart—sword—arrow
> I shot an arrow through the air
> And it fell I know not where[3]

Mrs. Piper then described a vision of a woman in the air with a bow and two arrows.

None of this made any sense at all to Dorr. The very next day he held another sitting with Mrs. Piper; at first the control appears to be the deceased Richard Hodgson, who sometimes refers to Myers as *he* and *him*.

> **HODGSON:** Now Myers feels a little distressed because he thinks you did not quite understand his replies to your last question [*i.e.,* the question about Lethe].

DORR: I ought not to have brought any questions up after the letters and the talk they led to. [The early part of the séance the day before was concerned with letters Dorr read to "Myers."]

HODGSON: No, quite right, but he did give you one or two replies which he and I both fear you did not understand.

DORR: No, it wasn't clear. I worked over the sittings yesterday till nearly midnight, trying to straighten things out.

HODGSON: Let Myers explain what he thinks you did not grasp.

MYERS: I wrote in reply to your last inquiry Cave—Lethe.

DORR: I asked him [*i.e.* Myers] whether the word Lethe recalled anything to him.

HODGSON: He replied Cave—Banks—Shore . . . He drew the form—a picture of Iris with an arrow.

DORR: But he spoke of winds.

MYERS: Yes, clouds—arrow—Iris—Cave—Mor MOR Latin for sleep *Morpheus—Cave.* Sticks in my mind can't you help me?

DORR: Good. I understand what you are after now. But can't you make it clearer about what there was peculiar about the waters of Lethe?

MYERS: Yes, I suppose you think that I am affected in the same way *but I am not.*[4]*

After this, some of the words, such as *Iris* and *Clouds,* were spelled out in capitals. Then, as Mrs. Piper came out of trance, she murmured a few words that could not be caught clearly, and said:

Mr Myers is writing on the wall . . . C [a pause] YX.

I walked in the garden of the gods—entranced I stood along its banks—like one entranced I saw her at last . . . Elysian shores.

---

*The major investigator of this case, J. G. Piddington, commented on this line as follows: "The way in which Myers here withheld the obvious and commonplace answer until pressed to give it by Mr Dorr is, I think, deserving of the utmost attention; for this avoidance of the trite and obvious creates a presumption that Myers deliberately preferred so to frame his messages that only study and thought would render them intelligible" (Piddington, "Three Incidents from the Sittings," 91).

At the next sitting, on March 30, 1908, the Myers communicator spelled out CYNX, and after some confused passages, wrote:

We walk together, our loves entwined, along the shores. In beauty beyond comparison with Lethe. Sorry it is all so fragmentary but suppose it cannot all get through.[5]

In the waking stage came several disjointed phrases, including:

Orpheus and Eurydice. It reminds me of them.[6]

At a sitting the next day came the words *Morpheus* and *Eurydice*. In the next séance on April 7 the word *Pygmalion* was mentioned, along with:

A lily came up out of the blood. Don't you remember the flower that grew out of the drop of blood?[7]

On April 21 the séance began:

MYERS: Good morning, friend. Hyacinthus.
DORR: Good. Now what about Hyacinthus?
MYERS: Blood.[8]

After this sitting, Dorr looked up some of the names mentioned in a reference book, to see which authors referred to them. He discovered from the reference book that Ovid wrote about a flower that sprang from the blood of Hyacinthus, and found three other authors from antiquity who wrote about some of the names mentioned in the scripts. In the séance of May 8, 1908, Dorr mentioned three of these authors to the Myers communicator in the following order: Aristophanes, Horace, and Ovid. He then mentioned the Cyclops from Homer's *Odyssey*, to which the Myers control responded:

I remember well OVID.[9]

COMMENTS ON THE LETHE EXPERIMENT

In order to fully appreciate the cross correspondences, some knowledge of the classics is required. This is especially true in the Lethe case, as the solution of the puzzle required a great deal of research and thought on the part of the lead investigator, J. G. Piddington. The solution was by no means apparent from the start, and this is one of the very real strengths of the case: puzzles that are too easily solved can serve no real purpose. So, in order to convey the evidential strength of this case, the relevant classical stories will be presented in summary form when necessary.

At first, the only part of the scripts that seemed to have any connection with Lethe was the reference to "Sibyl" during the waking stage of the first sitting. Mr. Dorr, it must be remembered, did not originally ask what Lethe *was,* but what it *suggested;* and Lethe might well suggest the Sibyl to a scholar intimately familiar with the works of Virgil, which the living Myers most certainly was. In the sixth book of Virgil's *Aeneid* is found the connection between the river Lethe and the Sibyl. For when Aeneas first saw the river of Lethe flowing by the Elysian Fields and the souls about to return to earth drinking of its waters, he was in her company.

But none of the rest made any sense at all to the investigators. Piddington, who eventually became the lead investigator in this case, writes:

In November, 1908, Mrs Verrall went carefully through the records of Mr Dorr's sittings, and she failed to trace any coherence in the answers given to the question about Lethe. Another classical scholar, Mr Gerald Balfour, when he read through the records, likewise saw no sense in these answers. Nor did I, when I first considered them. But I was struck by the way in which Myersp and Hodgsonp [the two communicators through Mrs Piper] at the sitting of March 24, 1908, spontaneously repeated, amplified and emphasized the answers given to the Lethe question on the previous day; and showed themselves apprehensive of its not having been understood, and confident of its relevancy. When confidence of this kind is exhibited by the trance-personalities it is usually well-founded. Accordingly I thought it worth while to search for passages in classical authors which might throw light on the matter; and by good luck came on a passage in the eleventh book, hitherto unknown to me, of the *Metamorphoses* of Ovid, which explains and justifies the main part of the answers given in the trance.[10]

The eleventh book of *Metamorphoses* tells the story of Ceyx and his wife Alcyone. The following summary is adapted from Gauld (*Mediumship and Survival*) and Piddington ("Three Incidents from the Sittings"). The correspondences with the scripts are indicated by capital letters.

CEYX, King of Trachin, was drowned at sea, and Juno sent IRIS, goddess of the rainbow, to Somnus, god of SLEEP, to bid him carry the news in a dream to Alcyone, Ceyx's beloved Queen, daughter of Aeolus, god of the WINDS. Iris clothed herself in raiment of a thousand hues, and imprinting her bended BOW upon the sky, travels along the rainbow thus created to the CAVE of Sleep, hidden by dark CLOUDS. Ovid writes, "From out the ground reek mists and murky fogs, glimmering in a doubtful dusky light . . . Beasts there are none, nor flocks, nor branches waving in the breeze; and never outcry of human voice awakes the echoes. It is the home of silent rest. Yet from the foot of the rock issues the stream of water of LETHE, and as the wave glides purling through the stream among the babbling pebbles, it invites sleep. Before the cavern's entrance abundant poppies bloom and herbs innumerable, from the juice of which Night brews sleep . . . No watchman on the threshold stands; but in the centre is a couch, whereon lies the god himself with limbs in languor loosed." Iris enters the cave, irradiating it with the colors of her apparel, delivers her message to Somnus, and returns to the heavens along the rainbow-path by which she came. From among his thousand sons Somnus chooses MORPHEUS, whose special gift is to mimic the form of man, to impersonate in a dream the dead Ceyx. Alcyone thus learns her husband's fate. In despair, she goes down to the SHORE, and throws herself into the sea, being transformed in the process into a halcyon. But the gods take pity on her SADness, and transform Ceyx into a kingfisher; and thus Alcyone rejoins her beloved MATE. Her nest floats on the sea; and every winter her father Aeolus confines the WINDS for seven days to secure a calm surface for her brood.

The correspondences appear unmistakable. Mrs. Piper knew nothing of Ovid, and did not even know who Ovid was.[11] Dorr claimed to "have never read any Ovid at all." On the other hand, Myers in life was an accomplished classical scholar, and certainly knew Virgil and Ovid well, as the following autobiographical quote of his indicates.

That early burst of admiration for Virgil of which I have already spoken was followed by a growing passion for one after another of the Greek and Latin poets. From ten to sixteen I lived much in the inward recital of Homer, Aeschylus, Lucretius, Horace, and Ovid.[12]

On the surface it seems as though the mind of Frederic Myers was the only plausible source of the association given between the Cave of Sleep and the River Lethe. As an expert in the classics who had studied Ovid in detail, Myers would have been familiar with Ovid's description of the cave as the source of the river in Ovid's story of Ceyx and Alcyone, in which the rainbow goddess Iris visits the god of sleep. On the surface, then, it appears that we can rule out telepathy between medium and sitter as the source of the association.

But the story of Ceyx and Alcyone has often been told in the English language. Perhaps Mrs. Piper or Mr. Dorr had read an English version of the story. After an intensive search, Piddington could find only two books, other than Ovid, from which Mrs. Piper or Mr. Dorr could have derived the details of the story as given in the trance: Bulfinch's *The Age of Fable* and Gayley's *The Classic Myths in English Literature,* the latter based on the former. Mrs. Piper said that she had never read any of these books; and although there was never any real question about her honesty, this was borne out by close questioning of herself and her daughters, and by examination of her bookshelves. Dorr had read Bulfinch's book as a boy; however, the words received in the sittings stirred no recollection of the story in his mind; and when he was handed a copy of the book months after the sitting, he claimed to remember almost nothing about it. The only association "Lethe" had for him was the obvious one: waters of forgetfulness.

It could still be argued that Dorr was the source from which Mrs. Piper telepathically gained her knowledge, even though Dorr retained no recollection of the story and failed to recognize the allusions to it in the trance. However, as Piddington pointed out, this would have been plausible *if the allusions in the trance had been confined only to the story of Ceyx and Alcyone.* But allusions to other stories in the tenth and eleventh book of Ovid's *Metamorphoses* are also mentioned, such as the story of Orpheus and Eurydice, and of Pygmalion. These stories are related to each other in Ovid, but not in Bulfinch or Gayley. Piddington writes:

> The tenth book of Ovid's *Metamorphoses* opens with the death of Eurydice, and Orpheus' descent into Hades in quest of her. Ovid then goes on to relate how Orpheus in his sorrow retires to Mount Rhodope, and there sings of the rape of Ganymede; of the death of Hyacinthus and of the flower that sprang from his blood; of the transformation of the Cerastae into bulls; of the Propoetides changed into stones; of Pygmalion's statue changed into a living woman; of Myrrha; of Venus and Adonis; and of Atalanta and Hippomenes. This completes the tenth book.

The eleventh book opens with the death of Orpheus and his reunion with Eurydice in Elysium. It will thus be seen that the tenth and eleventh books are very intimately connected by reason of Orpheus and Eurydice being a common subject of each. Now the eleventh book contains, besides the death of Orpheus, the story of Ceyx and Alcyone. I think, then, that it is clear that the references made in the trance to Orpheus and Eurydice, to Pygmalion and also to Hyacinthus, are reminiscences of the tenth and eleventh books of the *Metamorphoses,* and not reminiscences of classical dictionaries, or of popular collections of classical myths, or of Bulfinch's *Age of Fable,* or Gayley's *Classic Myths;* for although in these two latter books all the stories in question are mentioned, they are not in any way held together by any common bond, as they are in the *Metamorphoses,* but appear disconnectedly, and without anything being said to suggest a connexion between them.[13]

Could the information have been derived telepathically from one of the *other* investigators or mediums? Piddington ruled himself out, on the grounds that "my first acquaintance with the tenth and eleventh books of the *Metamorphoses* dates from a good many months after the conclusion of Mr. Dorr's sittings." Mrs. Verrall, the only person who doubled as both medium and investigator, seems a more obvious choice, as she was a lecturer in classics at Newham College. However, as mentioned, when she went over the records of Mr. Dorr's sittings with Mrs. Piper—to try to find obscure points in the classical allusions—she completely failed to understand the references to the Cave of Sleep, Iris, Morpheus, and so on.

In a written statement, Mrs. Verrall claimed to have no knowledge of Ovid's *Metamorphoses,* apart from having read the death of Eurydice about four years previous in order to compare it with Virgil's account. And, she added, "I hate Ovid beyond words, and have never read a line that I could avoid." Her daughter, the medium Miss Verrall, also had some knowledge of the classics, but wrote "I am not at all familiar with the works of Ovid."[14]

Also—in spite of these statements—if we were to assume that one of the women had subconsciously known the story of Ceyx and Alcyone and that this knowledge passed from her mind into that of Mrs. Piper, it would still leave Mrs. Piper's knowledge of Orpheus and Eurydice, of Pygmalion, and of Hyacinthus unexplained. It seems hard to believe that Mrs. or Miss Verrall could have read all four stories from Ovid and then have forgotten all of them. On the other hand, if they did read and recall any of the stories, then the references to them in the script would have led Mrs. Verrall to the tenth and eleventh books of Ovid's *Metamorphoses*, and the puzzle would have been solved much sooner than it was.

There seem to be several reasons for concluding that the source of the obscure references to Lethe from Ovid's *Metamorphoses* must have been the mind of Frederic Myers—quite apart from the fact that this claim appears several times in the scripts. First of all, both the allusive answer to the Lethe question, and the nature of the clues in the script that led Piddington to find the puzzle's solution in Ovid, are strongly characteristic of the mind of a classical scholar—one familiar in detail with the works of Ovid. Piddington wrote:

> I consider that the references to Orpheus and Eurydice and to Pygmalion were introduced in order to indicate the source of the allusions to Iris, Cave of Sleep, Morpheus, Ceyx, etc., which constitute the answer to the Lethe question.[15]

This puzzle shows evidence of a design that was not at all apparent to any of the investigators, but it is a design that the living Myers was certainly capable of creating.

The design required detailed knowledge of Ovid, which Mrs. Piper and the others simply did not possess. The associations provided in the script were ones Myers would have naturally made, but associations that at first left Mrs. Piper, Dorr, Piddington, and the other investigators completely baffled.

The other clue was given on May 8. After Dorr mentioned Aristophanes, Horace, Ovid, and Homer, the comment was "I remember well OVID." Piddington noted that this comment came at a particularly appropriate point, just after Dorr had spoken of the Cyclops in Homer. As an expert in Ovid, Myers would have known that the Cyclops is frequently mentioned in Ovid's works. Nothing mentioned by Dorr suggested any connection between the Cyclops and Ovid.

There is no obvious candidate, or set of candidates, from among the living, who had the knowledge of Ovid required to create the puzzle. But, of course, surely there must have been many people in the world who possessed the required knowledge of Ovid, and who could, in principle, have constructed the puzzle. It could be argued that Mrs. Piper telepathically searched the memory of some such person, picking out obscure references to Lethe. Or, it could be argued that Mrs. Piper clairvoyantly searched through Myers's published and unpublished works, noted an interest in Ovid, and then instantly searched through the works of Ovid until an obscure reference to Lethe was found. Either way, the puzzle was then constructed and completed over four or five sittings, under the charade that it was being done by the deceased Frederic Myers.

Apart from the fact that there is virtually no independent evidence that telepathy of the required *degree* ever occurs, we have already noted that both the anecdotal and experimental evidence indicates that telepathy occurs between people who are bonded or linked in some way. We have seen how no living person involved in the investigation seemed to have possessed the required knowledge.

We have also seen that the required knowledge was almost certainly possessed by the mind of Frederic Myers.

IDIOSYNCRASIES IN THE SCRIPTS

There are also certain *personal* touches in the scripts that point to the distinctive character of Frederic Myers as the source of the allusions to Ovid.

First of all, both Virgil and Ovid were objects of Myers's special admiration. So it seems fitting that the word *Lethe* would suggest to Myers, if surviving, stories from these particular authors.

Secondly, three out of the four stories told in *Metamorphoses* X and XI to which "Myers" alluded are also alluded to in three consecutive stanzas of one of Frederic Myers's poems; and Piddington found that the order in which the allusions emerge in the trance and in the poem are the same.

The allusions in question were to Iris, Orpheus and Eurydice, and Pygmalion. They emerged spontaneously in that order in the trances: Iris on March 23 and 24, Orpheus and Eurydice on March 30, and Pygmalion on April 6. And the order in which these three subjects emerged in the trances and in the poem are *not* the order in which they emerge in Ovid's *Metamorphoses;** nor are they the order in which they are mentioned in Gayley's *Classic Myths* or in Bulfinch's *Age of Fable.*†

Piddington also showed that recognizing the allusions to Iris, Orpheus and Eurydice, and Pygmalion in the successive stanzas of the poem would require solid knowledge of the classics. For instance, the subject of the first stanza is a picture by Watts titled *The Genius of Greek Poetry,* with its most prominent feature a rainbow that stretches nearly across the entire picture. The first four lines of the third stanza are:

> *Yet oftenest in the past he walked,*
> *With god or hero long gone by,*
> *Oft, like his pictured Genius talked*
> *With rainbow forms that span the sky.*

---

*In the *Metamorphoses,* the stories appear in this order: Death of Eurydice and Orpheus's descent into the Underworld; Pygmalion and the Statue; Death of Orpheus and his reunion with Eurydice; Iris (Ceyx and Alcyone story).

†In Gayley's *Classic Myths* the stories appear in this order: Hyacinthus, chap. X; Pygmalion, chap. X; Orpheus and Eurydice, chap. XII; Ceyx and Alcyone, chap. XIV.

In Bulfinch's *Age of Fables* the stories appear in this order: Hyacinthus, chap. VIII; Pygmalion, chap. VIII; Ceyx and Alcyone, chap. IX; Orpheus and Eurydice, chap. XXIV.

Piddington commented:

> A classical scholar looking at this picture and knowing its title could
> hardly fail to be reminded of Iris, the rainbow goddess, by the "rain-
> bow-form"; and if, like Frederic Myers, this scholar were at the same
> time an enthusiastic connoisseur of Watts' work, he would almost
> inevitably be reminded of [Watts's other picture] *Iris*.[16]

In the fourth stanza Orpheus and Eurydice are not directly named;
similarly, in the fifth stanza Pygmalion is not directly named, but only
referred to indirectly. Piddington felt sure that Mrs. Piper could not
possibly have recognized the classical allusions.

> I do not believe that it is the kind of coincidence which Mrs Piper
> could consciously or subconsciously have concocted; for, even if
> she had read the poem (which she had not), I do not believe that
> she possesses the classical scholarship requisite to detect the indi-
> rect allusion implicit in the third stanza to Iris, or the allusions
> to Orpheus and Eurydice in the fourth, and to Pygmalion in the
> fifth. Meanwhile, it is precisely the kind of delicate coincidence
> which might be expected to occur, if the communications of Myers$_P$
> are influenced by the mind of the author of *Stanzas on Mr Watts'
> Collected Works*.*[17]

The fourth and last story in *Metamorphoses* X and XI to which
"Myers" alluded is the story of Hyacinthus. Piddington did not think
that this reference spoiled the coincidence, as this reference was given
in response to a question, asked by Dorr on March 31, about a statue
in Greece. Piddington felt that the reference to Hyacinthus would

---

*For instance, in the fourth stanza Orpheus is not named, but is only referred to by his
country of origin, as "the Thracian." Note that Piddington thought that the reference to
Hyacinthus was brought in as an answer to a question asked by Dorr, and not to provide
a clue to the source of the allusions to Iris and the Cave of Sleep.

not have been given if the question about the statue had not been asked.[18]

Finally, the choice of the two myths contained in Books X and XI of the *Metamorphoses* as topics of allusions in response to the Lethe question is entirely appropriate for the mind of Frederic Myers, but not necessarily that of any other classical scholar. We have already covered the story of Ceyx and Alcyone in Book XI, and have noted that the story of Orpheus and Eurydice is the common subject of both books.

Book X deals with the death of Eurydice, and of the song Orpheus sang in his sorrow. In Book XI Orpheus dies, and is finally reunited with his love in the Elysian Fields along the banks of the river Lethe. The reunion of Orpheus with his beloved seems to be the subject of the successive allusions on March 24 and 25.

> I walked in the garden of the gods—entranced I stood along its banks—like one entranced I saw her at last . . . Elysian shores.
>
> We walk together, our loves entwined, along the shores. In beauty beyond comparison with Lethe.

Piddington noted how appropriate these themes were to Frederic Myers.

> It was appropriate to represent Frederic Myers as remembering and utilizing in his communications the stories of Ceyx and Alcyone and of Orpheus and Eurydice. The theme of both stories is *ad finem servatos amores* and the happy reunion of two lovers, "after long grief and pain," in another state of existence; and, as must be apparent to any careful reader of Myers's poems, this was a theme very near indeed to his heart; and the Orpheus and Eurydice story had evidently taken great hold upon him.*[19]

---

*At age thirty, Myers fell deeply in love with a married woman, who loved him in return but stayed loyal to her husband. She died three years later, and Myers never forgot her (Salter, "FWH Myers's Posthumous Message," 6–7).

So, the defender of the ESP hypothesis has to explain not only how telepathy—as the term is normally understood—was employed by a woman almost completely unfamiliar with the classics in order to *instantly* track down obscure classical references from sources with which she had no personal connection. The defender must also explain how the associations specifically chosen from the classics were those that *Myers* might plausibly have made with the name *Lethe*. Saltmarsh has noted the implications these associations have for establishing personal identity.

> Some of the most characteristic individual possessions of the human mind are the associations which it makes between ideas. These associations are the result of past history and are as clear an indication of psychical individuality as finger-prints are of physical. No two persons will make exactly the same associations between ideas, because no two persons have ever exactly the same history.[20]

To sum up: the answers given to the Lethe question appear to have been deliberately chosen so that they would not be initially understood by the investigators; however, after a great deal of detailed investigation, they were found to have all the hallmarks of Myers's unique interests, personality, and classical education. As Ducasse pointed out:

> To account for such an ingenious feat of inventive and constructive activity as the purported Myers performed in this case, something different from ESP *in kind*, not just in degree, is indispensable; namely, either Myers's own mind at work, or else a duplicate of it; which, however, then needs to be itself accounted for.[21]

LODGE CONTINUES THE LETHE EXPERIMENT

And this is not all there is to this remarkable case. At the time Dorr was questioning the Myers who purported to write through Mrs. Piper in Boston, Sir Oliver Lodge was also in Boston, and became interested in the case. He thought that useful evidence might be obtained if the Myers who purported to write through Mrs. Willett in England were asked the same question. So, in September 1909 he wrote the following in a letter, to be read by Mrs. Willett to her Myers communicator.

> My dear Myers, I want to ask you a question—not an idle one.
> WHAT DOES THE WORD LETHE SUGGEST TO YOU?
> It may be that you will choose to answer piece-meal and at leisure. There is no hurry about it.
> Oliver Lodge[22]

It should be stressed that Mrs. Willett in England had no normal knowledge of the question that was asked of Mrs. Piper's Myers control in Boston, nor of the material that had been obtained in reply.

On February 4, 1910, Mrs. Willett sat with pen and paper, and the following was written automatically: "Myers yes I am here. I am ready now to deal with the question from Lodge. Before you open the envelope reread his letter to you the one that accompanied the letter to me."[23]

Mrs. Willett then opened the envelope and read the letter to the communicator who claimed to be Myers. The script began at once.

> Myers the Will again to live
>> the Will again to live
>> the River of forgetfulness
>> . . . the blending of the Essence with the instrument
>> Myers tu Marcellus Eris you know the line you [Mrs. Willet] I
> mean . . . write it nevertheless, and add Henry Sidgwicks
>> In Valle Reducta
>> Add too the Doves and the Golden Bough amid the
>> Shadows add too
>> Go not to Lethe

Myers

Myers there was a door to which I found no key

and Haggi Babba too

This is disconnected but not meaningless

the shining souls shining by the river brim. The pain forgotten

but there

is another meaning another more intimate link and connection

that now I cannot give

it does not escape me I see

the bearing Rose fluttering rose leaves blown

like ghosts from an enchanter

fleeing Myers and Love

Love the essential essence

not spilt like water on

the ground far off forgotten pain

not not [A break and pause here.]

Darien the Peak

in Darien the Peak

Peak PEAK [another pause.]

m Myers I have not done yet

to Lodge this may have meaning

to Lodge this may have meaning

Let him remember the occasion

Myers I am not vague I am not vague

I want an answer to this . . . to this

Script from Lodge

Myers tell

him I want an answer

Does he recognize my recognition

Let Lodge speak . . . enough for to-day Myers[24]

The next day, while reading a newspaper, Mrs. Willett felt an overpowering urge to write. Although other people were in the room, she sat down and obtained the following script.

> You felt the call . . . it is I who write Myers I need urgently to say this tell Lodge this word . . . the word is DORR[25]

None of this made any sense to Mrs. Willett, except that she knew the name *Dorr* as that of an American who had some sittings with Mrs. Piper. She had no normal knowledge of his connection with the "Lethe" question.

The allusions to Lethe in the script of February 4th are obvious. The first sentence, "the will again to live" is from a poem written by the living Myers, and refers to souls gathering on the banks of Lethe, waiting to drink the waters of forgetfulness, and willing again to live on earth.[26]

> *God the innumerous souls in great array*
> *To Lethe summons by a wondrous way*
> *Till these therein their ancient pain forgive*
> *Forget their life, and will again to live*

Recall that the *first response* of Mrs. Piper's Myers communicator in response to the Lethe question had been: "Do you refer to one of my poems?" This answer was thought by Piddington to be confused and inappropriate, as he had failed to discover a mention of Lethe in any of Frederic Myers's original poems.*[27]

The blending of the Essence with the instrument is a paraphrase from Virgil's *Aeneid* in which the deceased Anchises explains to his son Aeneas how souls rejoin mortal bodies after drinking from the River Lethe. *Tu Marcellus eris* is a Latin quote from the *Aeneid;* it is a

---

*Piddington wrote: "Though I have not discovered a reference to Lethe in any of Frederic Myers's *original* poems, one exists in his verse translation of Anchises's famous speech in *Aenid* VI." This paper was not published at the time the question was put to Mrs. Willett, but it seems that Mrs. Willett's *Myers* communicator nevertheless corrected Piddington's mistake.

description of one of the souls on the banks of Lethe who would in time become Marcellus. *In valle reducta* (in a sheltered vale) is the phrase that opens Virgil's description of Lethe. *The Doves and the Golden Bough* are further references to Virgil's story: the golden bough had to be obtained before the gods would allow Aeneas to journey to Hades to visit his father by the River Lethe; and it was the doves who guided him to it.

The subject is then changed, and a quote from Omar Khayyam is given: *There was a door to which I found no key.** This quote has no obvious connection with Lethe, but was followed by what appears to be an attempt at the name Ali Babba of *Ali Babba and the Forty Thieves,* and by the words *This is disconnected but not meaningless.*

On March 7, the Myers communicator wrote: "there was a pun but I do not want to say where." This sent Oliver Lodge on "a long and fruitless hunt for it." On June 5, Lodge told Mrs. Willett's Myers communicator that he could find no pun. In response, he got the following written message.

> Re LETHE . . . I, Myers, made a pun, I got in a word I wanted by wrapping it in a QUOTATION. Later I got the WORD itself.[28]

Oliver Lodge interpreted this as referring to the word *door* in the Omar Khayyam quotation as a pun on the name *Dorr,* the American who first asked Myers the question about the word *Lethe* through Mrs. Piper. The door to the robber's cave in the Ali Babba story only opened with the words *Open Sesame,* and might clearly be described as "a door to which I found no key." The fact that the name *Dorr* was given spontaneously the following day seems to justify this interpretation.

The Myers communicator evidently understood what Dorr and Lodge were trying to accomplish, for in a script on February 10 (five days after he first mentioned the word *DORR* in the script of Mrs. Willet) he wrote, "Dorr's scheme excellent. That I have different scribes

---

*There was the Door to which I found no Key: / There was the Veil through which I could not see. —Omar Khayyam, Rubaiyat, XXXV.

means that I must show different aspects of thoughts underlying which unity is to be found" and "I know what Lodge wants. He wants me to prove that I have access to knowledge shown elsewhere."[29]

The script of February 10 contains various references to Virgil and to Homer, and following the mention of Dorr, the name *Ganymede* is mentioned. Her story is told in Book X of Ovid's *Metamorphoses,* immediately before that of Hyacinthus, which had been introduced by Mrs. Piper's Myers communicator in connection with the Lethe question as put by Mr. Dorr. The name *Watts* is mentioned as well, which seems to indicate knowledge of the connection Piddington had drawn between Mrs. Piper's script and the painter, even though Piddington had not yet published his paper at the time. Whoever the Myers communicator was, it seems that he succeeded in showing that he had access to knowledge shown elsewhere.

It is important to stress that, like Mrs. Piper, Mrs. Willett knew practically nothing about the classics. She had read Church's *Stories from Virgil,* but a study of that book convinced Lodge that the knowledge shown could not have been derived from that source. For one thing, the word *Lethe* is not even mentioned in Church's book (although there is a reference to Marcellus, which justifies the remark, "you know the line"). Lodge also stated that at the time he was not familiar with Book VI of Virgil's *Aeneid,* from which the knowledge shown is derived. Like Piddington before him, he needed to complete a great deal of research before he understood the classical references. But as we have already seen, Myers in his lifetime profoundly admired Virgil. And in the script of February 10 and in the weeks that followed, the Myers communicator shows himself possessed of wide classical knowledge, completely beyond anything that could be attributed to Mrs. Willett or to the physicist Lodge.

Sir Oliver commented on the level of skill shown in the scripts.

The way in which these allusions are combined or put together, and their connection with each other indicated, is the striking thing—it seems to me as much beyond the capacity of Mrs. Willett as it would be beyond my own capacity. I believe that if the matter is seriously studied, and if Mrs. Willett's assertions concerning her conscious knowledge and supraliminal procedure are believed, this will be the opinion of critics also; they will realize, as I do, that we are tapping the reminiscences not of an ordinarily educated person but of a scholar—no matter how fragmentary and confused some of the reproductions are.[30]

As we have seen, much of the cross correspondence messages have a fragmentary, disjointed nature. This contrasts sharply with the passages in which cross correspondences are not being attempted; in these, we often find long coherent passages showing great intellectual sophistication, and an appreciation of the difficulties of communication.

It seems that the cross correspondence messages are fragmentary and disjointed by design; they are deliberately kept enigmatic so as not to reveal their meaning. In the true cross correspondences, this seems necessary in order to eliminate the possibility of one medium communicating—telepathically or otherwise—the true meaning of the fragment to another medium in order to complete the cross correspondence. The messages received through Mrs. Piper in the Lethe case are not true cross correspondences in the narrow technical sense, as the messages delivered through Mrs. Piper did not require the messages delivered through Mrs. Willett to be understood; they only required research, following up on clues provided only in the scripts of Mrs. Piper. However, even in this case, for the puzzle to be effective it was necessary to avoid revealing the true meaning before the investigators had a chance to discover it through their own research, in order to rule out telepathy from the investigators as the source.

There is some evidence that the communicators are limited by the normal contents of the minds of the mediums. For instance, while Greek and Latin quotations are freely given through Mrs. and Miss Verrall, who are thoroughly conversant with these languages, it is very rare to find them in the scripts of Mrs. Holland, Mrs. Willett, and Mrs. Piper, who normally know very little of classical literature. It seems as though—and this is repeatedly claimed in the scripts—the communicators find it easiest to select the words they need from the normal minds of the mediums.

But there is also a certain amount of nonsense in the passages in which the cross correspondences are to be found. The mediums sometimes seem to wander along a train of thought that is their own, and the scripts seem to be modified by the personalities of the autonomists. The communicators themselves often complain that the mediums are very inefficient channels. An early script of Mrs. Holland contains the following message, purportedly from Myers, in which he describes the conditions under which he labors.

> The nearest simile I can find to express the difficulties of sending a message—is that I appear to be standing behind a sheet of frosted glass which blurs sight and deadens sounds—dictating feebly to a reluctant and somewhat obtuse secretary. A feeling of terrible impotence burdens me . . . You need much training before you can ever begin to help me.[31]

Either these difficulties were overcome later, or there is something in the nature of the cross correspondences that adds to the difficulty of communication. Because, as the messages from Myers, Gurney, and the others continued, there were many long coherent passages written that show no confusion or rambling. At any rate, Myers, purporting to write in the 1920s through the medium Geraldine Cummins, described the special difficulties of the cross correspondences as follows:

> The inner mind is very difficult to deal with from this side. We impress it with our message. We never impress the brain of the medium directly. That is out of the question. But the inner mind receives our message and sends it on to the brain. The brain is a

mere mechanism. The inner mind is like soft wax, it receives our thoughts, their whole content, but it must produce the words that clothe it. That is what makes cross-correspondence so very difficult. We may succeed in sending the thought through, but the actual words depend largely on the inner mind's content, on what words will frame the thought. If I am to send half a sentence through one medium and half through another I can only send the same thought with the suggestion that a part of it will come through one medium and a part through another . . . We communicate an impression through the inner mind of the medium. It receives the impression in a curious way. It has to contribute to the body of the message, we furnish the spirit of it. In other words, we send the thoughts and the words usually in which they must be framed, but the actual letters or spelling of the words are drawn from the medium's memory. Sometimes we only send the thoughts and the medium's unconscious mind clothes them in words.[32]

Whatever we may think of this passage, there seems to be nothing fragmentary or disjointed about it.

SIXTEEN

Evaluation of the Cross Correspondences

The summary of each of the four cases presented above has only scratched the surface of the enormous volume of source material on the cross correspondences. Clearly, sophisticated knowledge of classical literature was shown in the scripts, and sometimes substantial research into the classics was required to solve the various puzzles. Both these facts certainly contribute to the evidential strength of the cross correspondences. But, unfortunately, these facts also contribute to the difficulty most laypersons have in evaluating them. In addition, nothing less than a study of the original reports can convey the richness of detail and the element of intention in them. And even that cannot convey the vividness of characterization that so impressed the investigators who had known Myers and his friends.

But, at any rate, there seem to be only four possible explanations for the cross correspondences, and it is to an evaluation of these that we now turn.

CHANCE

It has been proposed that the cross correspondences are simply due to chance coincidence. After all, in scripts full of cryptic literary and historical allusions, we might reasonably expect occasional coincidences of theme and reference. However, an explanation in terms of chance coincidence has several strikes against it.

First of all, Piddington and Dorr tried to generate artificial cross correspondences. Fourteen people were each sent quotations—twelve in all—from Virgil, Homer, Shakespeare, Shelly, Milton, Rostand, Wordsworth, and Coleridge, and were asked to write down words or phrases associated with them. The results were very different from the cross correspondences that appeared spontaneously in the scripts of the automatists. There was no tendency to return again and again to one theme, and Piddington and Dorr concluded that the few cross references that occurred bore no resemblance to the cross correspondences of the scripts.

Second, various experiments may be performed in order to attempt to create cross correspondences. Choose a book by an author with whose works you are well acquainted, and pick a passage at random. Pick another book by the same author, randomly choose another passage, and try to work out a cross correspondence between the two passages. The results (or, more likely, the lack or results) will give a clear indication of how much pure chance is likely to have been responsible for the cross correspondences.

Third, Piddington counted cross correspondence on a large scale, and found that allusions pertinent to a given cross correspondence did not wax and wane haphazardly, but arose during the appropriate period and then largely disappeared. And finally, we have seen that the cross correspondences are accompanied by explicit statements that they are indeed parts of a planned experiment. Here is another example: on March 2 and March 4, 1906, Mrs. Verrall wrote a series of cryptic scripts referring to the main events in the history of the City of Rome, accompanied by a statement that she would receive a message *through another woman*. On March 7, five thousand miles away, Mrs. Holland wrote: "Ave Roma Immortalis. How could I make it clearer without giving her the clue?"[1] Similar remarks occur again and again. For all these reasons, chance coincidence can be effectively ruled out as an explanation.

FRAUD

It also seems that fraud on the part of the autonomists can also be quickly ruled out. All the autonomists were persons of excellent reputation, and no indications of fraud ever came to light. Several of the autonomists did not even know each other; and at important periods, one (Mrs. Holland) was in India, another (Mrs. Piper) was in the United States, and the rest were in Great Britain. It is hard to see how the conspiracy could have been carried out without the aid of the investigators, as the scripts were often written under their own eyes. Moreover, several writers have commented on the enormous amount of work that would have been required to perpetrate such a fraud. For instance, Rosalind Heywood describes a simple experiment that a skeptic can perform to illustrate the amount of knowledge, ingenuity, and research required to create these puzzles:

> To construct an elementary cross correspondence, a topic or quotation from a particular author must be chosen and further quotations collected from his work which allude to this topic but do not mention it directly. Puns are allowed. Finally an independent investigator must find the clue which binds the quotations into a coherent whole. Anyone who tries to construct a cross correspondence of the quality of those which claimed to come from the Myers group will sympathize with the remark in Mrs. Willett's script which purported to be made by Dr. Verrall shortly after his death: "This sort of thing is more difficult to do than it looked."[2]

The case against such a pointless and far-reaching hoax is summed up by Saltmarsh as follows:

> No reasonable person could suggest that a group of ladies of the culture and intelligence of those here involved, would combine together to carry out a scheme of concerted cheating—a conspiracy of fraud,

and persist in the practice for over thirty years. Moreover, it is hard to assign any motive for such conduct: had it been for the sake of a practical joke, it was surely a strange sense of humour which could derive satisfaction from anything so cumbrous and prolonged; had it been for the sake of 'showing up' the investigators, the scheme missed fire for the plot was never divulged.[3]

SUPER-ESP AND SUBCONSCIOUS FRAUD

The only alternative explanation that has been proposed by skeptics willing to examine the record of cross correspondences in detail is a further extension of the super-ESP hypothesis. We have already seen that this hypothesis has been progressively stretched in order to account for other forms of communication through mediums. Most of the objections that were raised earlier against ESP as an explanation also apply in the case of the cross correspondences. In particular, we see in the cross correspondences the manifestation of the personalities of the deceased and, even more pronounced, the display of skills and knowledge far exceeding that of both mediums and sitters, but characteristic of the deceased from whom the messages purport to come.

But the super-ESP hypothesis must be extended even further in order to account for the cross correspondences. Since their production eventually involved several different mediums in three different countries, it is now necessary to account for the *coordination* of the messages received through the various autonomists, so that while the productions of each are individually pointless, taken together they form a meaningful pattern. If the messages did not come from the deceased Myers, Gurney, and others, then one possibility is that the subconscious mind of some living person telepathically directed and coordinated the scripts of the various mediums, in order to pull off a remarkable thirty-year hoax.

The most obvious suspect was Mrs. Verrall. Critics pointed out that she was interested in psychic phenomena; that she knew Myers and

Sidgwick personally; and that she was a very good classical scholar. If it was her subconscious mind that designed the scripts, the degree of telepathy exercised is nothing less than astounding. We would have to suppose that, using various false names, she subconsciously directed the subconscious selves of her scattered pupils, some of whom she did not even know—in order to perpetrate a hoax on their normal personalities, as well as on her own. In cases in which she herself lacked the required knowledge of the classics, she must have obtained it by clairvoyantly scanning the literature, or by telepathically picking the minds of other classical scholars.

But this theory has a fatal flaw. Mrs. Verrall died in 1916, yet the cross correspondences continued on for many years. One case that began in her scripts, the "Palm Sunday" case, continued for years after her death.[4] And some new cases were initiated only after her death, despite the fact that there was no autonomist left who combined her knowledge of the Myers group with the classical scholarship and deep interest presumably needed to induce the subconscious mind to work out such an elaborate plan.

The only other alternative seems to be that the group of mediums obtained the required knowledge of the classics by clairvoyantly scanning the literature, or by telepathically picking the minds of other classical scholars; the messages were then framed in a manner typical of the living Myers by picking the memories of Myers's surviving friends, or by clairvoyantly scanning his works. In other words, the alternative is an unconsciously hatched, telepathically coordinated conspiracy. It must be noted that this alleged campaign of deception was carried on for three decades, despite personnel changes in the group as fresh recruits came in and old members dropped out. There is no independent evidence that telepathy and clairvoyance of such detail and complexity ever occurs. It almost goes without saying that there is also not a shred of independent evidence for unconsciously hatched, telepathically coordinated conspiracies. And if the deception is alleged to be entirely unconscious, then what could such evidence *possibly* consist of?

SURVIVAL

In a 1908 review of some of the earliest cross correspondences, Piddington wrote:

> The only opinion which I hold with confidence is this: that if it was not the mind of Frederic Myers it was one which deliberately and artistically imitated his mental characteristics.[5]

But as the years went on, Piddington, who disliked the idea of survival, was driven more and more to the conclusion that communication from the surviving minds of Myers, Gurney, and the others was the most plausible explanation of the cross correspondences. With very few exceptions, the other investigators also came to this conclusion.

We have seen how the death of Mrs. Verrall in 1916 made very little difference to the content or nature of the scripts. This contrasts sharply with the change in the scripts following the death of her husband, Dr. A. V. Verrall, on June 18, 1912. Within a few weeks of his death, messages purporting to come from Dr. Verrall began to appear in the scripts. There also appeared several striking literary puzzles, purportedly created by Dr. Verrall, which differed sharply in style from those that purportedly came from the Myers group. Like some of the earlier puzzles, they were at first completely incomprehensible to the investigators—including his surviving wife and daughter. But after following up on clues provided in the scripts, solutions were found indicating knowledge that very few living classical scholars possessed—but that was known to be possessed by Dr. Verrall.*

In addition, the accompanying messages displayed many idiosyncratic personal characteristics of the living Verrall. We have seen earlier how his old friend, the Reverend Bayfield, after reviewing these messages, testified that "to me at least it is incredible that even the cleverest

---

*Excellent summaries of these cases can be found in Saltmarsh, *Evidence of Personal Survival,* chapter VI.

could achieve such an unexampled triumph in deceptive impersonation as this would be if the actor is not Verrall himself."

Years of reviewing and researching the cross correspondences eventually convinced Piddington, Lodge, Miss Johnson, Mrs. Sidgwick, Balfour, and others that the cross correspondences were, in fact, what they constantly claimed to be—messages from Myers and his deceased colleagues. In 1932, as the cross correspondences were finally petering out, Mrs. Sidgwick wrote an account of the history of the work of the Society for Psychical Research during its first fifty years. At the time she was president of honor of the Society, and her keen mind and cautious approach were widely respected. At the Society's Jubilee, her paper was read by her brother, Lord Balfour. After he finished, he added a personal comment.

Some of you may have felt that the note of caution and reserve has possibly been over-emphasized in Mrs Sidgwick's paper. If so, they may be glad to hear what I am about to say. Conclusive proof of survival is notoriously difficult to obtain. But the evidence may be such as to produce *belief*, even though it fall short of conclusive *proof*. I have Mrs Sidgwick's assurance—an assurance which I am permitted to convey to the meeting—that, upon the evidence before her, she herself is a firm believer both in survival and in the reality of communication between the living and the dead.[6]

As mentioned, Balfour had come to share this belief. Certainly very few people have been as thoroughly acquainted with the evidence from cross correspondences, and at the same time as objective and keenly critical, as were Mrs. Sidgwick and Lord Balfour.

PART IV

Conclusions

It is a stupid presumption to go about despising and condemning as false anything that seems to us improbable; this is a common fault among those who think they have more intelligence than the crowd. I used to be like that once, and if I heard talk of ghosts walking or prognostications of future events, of enchantments or sorceries, or some other tale I could not swallow, I would pity the poor people who were taken in by such nonsense. And now I find that I was at least as much to be pitied myself.

MICHEL DE MONTAIGNE,
ESSAYS

SEVENTEEN

How the Case for Survival Stands Today

The full case for survival rests, of course, on much more than just the evidence from communication through mediums. It is necessary to take into account all the lines of evidence, including those that had barely been explored during the first fifty years of the SPR.

Because of modern resuscitation techniques, the near-death experience is now a much more commonly reported experience, and the second book of this trilogy, *Science and the Near-Death Experience,* concludes that several features of the near-death experience suggest survival. These include normal or enhanced mental processes at a time when there is every medical reason to believe that brain processes are either severely impaired or entirely absent; accurate out-of-body views of one's own body and the surrounding environment; and the perception of deceased friends and relatives.* ESP—super or otherwise—fails utterly to explain these phenomena. Clairvoyant descriptions are not typically from an elevated position and certainly not from an elevated position directly

---

*When others are reported perceived and identified during an NDE, they are almost invariably deceased. For instance, cardiologist and NDE researcher Pim van Lommel wrote: "I have heard hundreds and hundreds of people telling me about their NDE, and I have more than one thousand written reports of NDE in my files. However, I cannot remember a single report of a meeting with living relatives or friends" (personal communication, September 26, 2010).

above the viewer's own body. Nor do they normally occur when we have every reason to believe the subject's cerebral processes are either severely impaired or entirely absent.

Science and the Near-Death Experience also described death-bed visions in which people have reported seeing deceased friends and relatives that they did not know were deceased. We also saw that ESP also fails utterly to explain these experiences, as there is not a shred of independent evidence that the dying become more clairvoyant or telepathic in the final moments of life, and not a shred of evidence that ESP "dresses up" knowledge of unpleasant occurrences into pleasant hallucinations.

The experiences people have while approaching or during clinical death allow us to conclude that consciousness and perception can continue to function in a normal or even enhanced manner after brain activity ceases, at least temporarily. The overwhelming majority of those who have these experiences are convinced that life continues long after the body ceases to function. However, because these people were not *irreversibly* dead, these experiences provide the rest of us with only suggestive evidence in favor of conscious life after the point of irreversible brain death. This book has been concerned with examining evidence for survival from those who have indeed passed beyond the threshold of death. The three additional lines of evidence considered in this book therefore provide more extensive evidence that consciousness continues long after brain and body cease to function.

When we considered cases other than near-death experiences and death bed visions, we have seen that that only one counterexplanation is still defended as credible by those skeptics who have taken time to familiarize themselves with the evidence. At this point only the inference of super-ESP remains in the field to challenge the inference of survival.

The super-ESP hypothesis is a peculiarly elusive theory, because it involves progressively extending the postulated reach of ESP to cover every new type of evidence for survival. It is typically argued that this elastic hypothesis is justified according to some principle of simplicity or parsimony. We know that ESP exists, so the argument goes, and we also know of the existence of incarnate minds. The survival hypothesis, it is argued, requires us to further assume the existence of discarnate minds. Hence, it is more parsimonious to cast our explanation only in terms of ESP among *in*carnate minds. By so doing, we avoid postulating the existence of a whole new class of entities.

But acceptance of the facts covered earlier does not require that we *assume* the existence of discarnate minds, any more than our acceptance of the fact that Magellan's ship circumnavigated the globe requires us to *assume* the earth is round. Rather, the facts presented earlier provide *evidence* of discarnate minds, just as the success of Magellan's voyage provided additional corroborating *evidence* that the earth is round.

And does the super-ESP theory really have an advantage of simplicity? In our review of the various categories of evidence, we have seen how this hypothesis is continually stretched and extended with auxiliary assumptions in order to cover each new type of case. To explain accurate perception of the environment during near-death experiences, a form of clairvoyant perception is invoked; however, this hypothesized form of clairvoyance *only* operates when near death and when brain function is either severely impaired or entirely absent, and then *only* to provide a view from a position directly above one's seemingly unconscious body. To explain visions of those not known to be deceased during deathbed visions, it is maintained that the dying occasionally have enhanced telepathic perception, but *only* about recently deceased friends and relatives; it is also maintained that this singular perception is then incorporated into a pleasant hallucination involving friends and relatives known to be deceased. To explain the knowledge of a previous life shown in reincarnation cases, telepathy is invoked, but, inexplicably, of nothing more than memories of one deceased stranger; and this knowledge is then required to take the form of personal memories belonging to the living subject. To explain collectively perceived apparitions, it is claimed that hallucinations are telepathically projected and shared, with due allowances for different physical perspectives on the hallucination. To explain the evidence from mediums, it is claimed that human mediums can telepathically gather appropriate information from the minds of strangers at any time, no matter what those strangers may be thinking about at the time; and it is claimed that mediums can clairvoyantly scan volumes of books, including books at unknown locations and on esoteric topics of no personal interest to the medium in her normal state, in order to instantly acquire information that the deceased would have known. Then, the hypothesis of extra-sensory perception is stretched to include powers that involve far more than mere *perception*, but also powers to artfully and deceptively present the gathered information and various comments from the perspective of the deceased and to serve purposes that appear to be only those of the deceased. Attempts are made to stretch the hypothesis even further, in order to grant the medium powers to use telepathy to ingeniously and convincingly impersonate the personality of deceased persons the medium has never met, as well as to instantly (and temporarily) acquire skills that the deceased person purporting to communicate required years of practice to acquire. Finally, in addition to all this, it is even held that telepathy can be used to coordinate complex *subconscious conspiracies of deception*.

It should be clear that there is nothing simple about the super-ESP theory. As philosopher Carl Becker wrote, "Its ad hoc contortions to fit the data deprive it of all simplicity and elegance."[1] By contrast, the hypothesis of survival provides one simple and elegant explanation for all the data we have surveyed, from five very different lines of evidence.

Proponents of the super-ESP theory say that we do not know the limits of ESP or of the subconscious mind, and that the natural, all-too-human fear of death is so deep-seated that the subconscious may go to any lengths to suppress it, even to the extent of using extreme powers of ESP to conduct remarkably elaborate ruses in order to deceive our conscious minds.

However, all experimental and anecdotal evidence indicates that psi is a low-level ability that cannot even be used to beat the casinos. "Skeptics" often ask the naïve question, that if psi is real then why do casinos make money? The answer of course is that the odds in favor of the casinos are so overwhelming that even the most talented subjects in controlled experiments do not come close to displaying powers that can overcome these odds.* This objection cannot be used to defend the existence of super-ESP.

If the function of super-ESP is the use of its virtually unlimited powers by the subconscious mind to surreptitiously protect us from the fear of death by fabricating elaborate evidence that seems in every respect exactly *as if* the deceased are visiting or communicating, then why don't we have evidence of our subconscious minds employing these vast powers to protect us from the *actual* threat of imminent death? That would at least provide a more plausible evolutionary reason for the existence of these powers.

The theory of the unconscious employment of vast powers of ESP would therefore seem to predict that these powers should, at least occasionally, be used to save us not from merely the fear of death, but from actual imminent death. Plenty of potential opportunities can be found in history. Consider only one: the Russian front during the Second World War. Surely there must have been many instances in which Slavs could have saved their lives from the death squads of the SS by using super-ESP to instantly acquire the ability to speak excellent German and thus pass themselves off as captured Germans taken prisoners of war. Answering test questions such as "which city is the capital of Bavaria?" would seem child's play compared to the vast powers of telepathy and clairvoyance the proponents of super-ESP attribute to mediums. There must also have been many instances in which Germans could have saved themselves from Russian work camps by using super-ESP to instantly acquire the ability to speak excellent Russian and thus convincingly pass themselves off as captured Russians.

But we have not one single shred of evidence that unfortunate people on either side were able to save themselves from death or lengthy and brutal incarceration by using these vast hypothetical powers. And if the proponents of super-ESP argue that these abilities only become

---

*This matter is discussed in more depth in my previous book *Science and Psychic Phenomena*, chapter 5.

manifest in a trance state, then we may wonder why trance mediums in heavily-bombed London were not invaluable guides to German plans and intentions. Plenty of other examples can easily be found from WWII in which people could have reduced not merely the abstract fear of death but the threat of actual imminent death by the employment of the vast, virtually unlimited telepathic and clairvoyant powers attributed to mediums by the proponents of super-ESP.*

It should be clear that the theory of super-ESP is magical thinking, an unbridled fantasy without a shred of supporting evidence. Worse yet, it is a fantasy that, whenever challenged, shamelessly cloaks itself with elaborate ad hoc, untestable, auxiliary hypotheses whose only purpose is to render the nonsurvival theory immune from being proven false by the overwhelming evidence against it.

MOTIVE BEHIND THE SUPER-ESP HYPOTHESIS

Of course, the obvious motive behind the super-ESP hypothesis is the perceived implausibility of its main rival. The idea of discarnate survival is held to be so antecedently improbable that *any* alternative explanation in terms of ESP is considered preferable, no matter how far-fetched or unsupported. But we have seen that the idea of survival is *not* incompatible with any of the known facts of physiology. The hypothesis that the brain produces the mind and the rival hypothesis that the brain works as a transmitter-receiver for the mind are both fully compatible with the ordinary facts, and so there is nothing

---

*There are in facts several accounts from WWII of people using psychic abilities to save their lives. One of the most famous involved Winston Churchill, whose life was saved by a feeling that he should not sit in his usual place in a car. "I sometimes have a feeling—in fact I have had it very strongly—a feeling of interference," he told a gathering of miners later in the war. "I have a feeling sometimes that some guiding hand has interfered." Sheldrake also reports the case of a British soldier in Malaya who felt he was being stared at, accompanied by a sense of danger. He turned to see an enemy soldier about 20 yards away, bringing his rifle up to fire. The British soldier shot first, killing his enemy and thereby saving his own life (*The Sense of Being Stared At*, xii). These and other historical accounts do not stretch the original meanings of the words *telepathy* and *clairvoyance*, and can be found in *Science and Psychic Phenomena*, chapter 3.

about the ordinary facts that favors either hypothesis. As such, there is really no antecedent improbability of survival—nor any antecedent probability, either. The issue is entirely one for the testimony of the facts to settle.*

In my previous book, *Science and the Near-Death Experience,* we saw that the theory that the brain works as a receiver-transmitter for consciousness can account for the facts that refute the rival theory that the brain produces consciousness. By contrast, in order to remain worthy of serious consideration, the production theory requires either wholesale ignorance of reams of evidence; or the addition of a contorted and elaborate theory of super-ESP, with its various ad hoc auxiliary hypotheses tacked on whenever required. It is difficult to understand how anyone could argue for simplicity as an advantage of the production-plus-super-ESP hypothesis.

And why is simplicity of value in a scientific explanation? In his groundbreaking work *The Logic of Scientific Discovery,* Karl Popper examined the notion of simplicity as applied to explanations:

> Our theory explains *why simplicity is so highly desirable.* To understand this there is no need for us to assume a 'principle of economy of thought' or anything of the kind. Simple statements, if knowledge is our object, are to be prized more highly than less simple ones *because . . . they are* [more] *testable.*[2]

---

*Skeptics sometimes like to claim that "extraordinary claims require extraordinary evidence" but we need to remember that we have no objective guidelines as to what constitutes an "extraordinary claim." Many claims that were once considered "extraordinary"—such as claims that rocks sometimes fall from the sky, or that the continents drift—became in time to be considered quite ordinary. Also, one could easily argue, as philosopher Neal Grossman does, that "there is absolutely nothing extraordinary about the hypothesis of an afterlife. The overwhelming majority of people in the world believe it, and have always believed it" ("Four Errors Commonly Made by Professional Debunkers"). Finally, we could further remark that several of the best cases—such as *Maroczy versus Korchnoi* or the cross correspondences—certainly do provide extraordinary evidence.

Popper concluded that for most of the earlier writers, simplicity was a concept "partly aesthetic and partly practical."* William of Occam famously wrote, "Do not multiply entities unnecessarily"—or in other words, do not add unnecessary causal factors to explanations. If inertia and gravity are sufficient to explain the orbits of the planets, do not add invisible angels. And if your theory of the planetary orbits is contradicted by the data, then do not add the actions of invisible angels to "explain" the discrepancy between your theory and the data. The only sense in which simplicity is of value in scientific explanation is the sense that we refrain from adding ad hoc auxiliary assumptions to our theories in order to render them immune from data that prove them false, and this is precisely the sense in which the theory of super-ESP violates the principle of parsimony in the use of hypotheses. The "invisible angels" of super-ESP are all the untestable ad hoc auxiliary assumptions that are added in order to immunize from falsification the theory that ESP of the living can explain away the evidence for survival. Any scientist who defended a pet theory that did not fit the data by dreaming up ad hoc excuses to render his theory unfalsifiable would be rightly condemned for practicing pseudo-science.

But Popper sought a more rigorous criterion of simplicity, one that he could incorporate within his remarkable philosophy of science.

From my point of view, a system must be described as *complex in the highest degree* if one holds fast to it as a system established forever which one is determined to rescue, whenever it is in danger, by the introduction of auxiliary hypotheses. For the degree of falsifiability of a system thus protected is equal to *zero*. Thus we are led back, by our concept of simplicity, to the methodological

---

*This is sometimes misunderstood as implying the fallacy that the simplest explanation is most likely correct. Examples that illustrate this fallacy are easy to find: for instance, the quantum mechanical theory of matter is far more complicated than the simple classical theory, but it is now known that the classical theory is grossly and fundamentally incorrect.

principle which restrains us from indulgence in *ad hoc* hypotheses or auxiliary hypotheses: to the principle of parsimony in the use of hypotheses.[3]

For Popper, simplicity in theories is desirable simply because simpler theories are easier to test; that is, simpler theories tend to be more readily falsifiable. However, due its elastic nature, the super-ESP theory is completely unfalsifiable! To account for each new type of case or category of evidence, auxiliary hypotheses *that cannot be tested independently* are added in order to continually prop up the nonsurvival position. The theory of super-ESP is thus, in Popper's words, *complex in the highest degree,* and so constitutes a gross violation of the principle of parsimony in the use of hypotheses. It should be clear that the addition of ad hoc auxiliary hypotheses as required is another example of what Popper referred to as an *immunizing tactic*—a tactic used to immunize a theory from falsification.

By rendering itself unfalsifiable with the addition of supplementary hypotheses that cannot be tested independently, the super-ESP hypothesis may be a logical possibility, but it is clearly not a scientific theory. Rather, it is a metaphysical excuse, invented for the sole purpose of immunizing the production theory from falsification. As such, it is similar to the "last stand" position of those creationists who maintain that God invented the evidence for biological evolution found in the geological record in order to test our faith in biblical stories. This is a logical possibility, of course, but also one that is completely untestable (in addition to being a crass deception unworthy of any Creator). Likewise, the super-ESP theory is the last stand position of those who are opposed to the notion of survival, whether for religious, ideological, or personal reasons. This elastic theory is the only excuse they have left for not abandoning their position of nonsurvival. It should be clear that inventing unfalsifiable ad hoc assumptions to explain away every new category of falsifying evidence is neither science nor skepticism, but merely ideological dogmatism masquerading as skepticism.

It may have occurred to some readers that the statement "Human minds survive bodily death" is not itself falsifiable. After all, *even if* we had absolutely no evidence for survival, it could very well be that consciousness survives the death of the body. We could say we have no evidence; but we could not rule out the possibility on logical or empirical grounds.

But the opposite statement, "Human minds do not survive bodily death" most certainly *is* capable of being proven false by evidence. And it is important to remember that the falsification of a statement implies the truth of its negation, even if its negation is not directly falsifiable. The evidence presented here constitutes a scientific refutation of the production theory, and of its antisurvivalist implications.

The fact that we do have substantial evidence means that the production and transmission hypotheses are more than mere metaphysical theories; in other words, we can choose between them on purely empirical grounds.* And if the proponents of survival respect the scientific method, then they should be willing to drop certain lines of evidence if it can be shown—in cases apart from those providing evidence for survival—that ESP can be used in the manner required by the super-ESP hypothesis. Specifically, if it could be shown that gifted subjects could successfully impersonate a living

---

*The crux of the issue is really the old philosophical question of the true relationship between the brain and the mind. The production theory *predicts* that the mind will not survive the death of the brain (and hence, that no solid evidence will be found for survival). The transmission theory *allows* the possibility of survival (and hence, is consistent with any evidence for survival that is found). We have seen that there is substantial evidence for survival. But, we can immunize the production theory with the addition of ad hoc auxiliary super-ESP hypotheses, in order to explain away the data that threatens to falsify the production theory. In their *testable* forms, the auxiliary ESP hypotheses would predict that evidence of these abilities would be found in cases outside of those in question; that is, in cases that do *not* appear to provide evidence for survival. But such evidence has not been found. If the super-ESP hypothesis is held regardless, then its only purpose is to prop up a dogma—that is, a belief that is held for reasons other than the support of corroborating evidence.

person, whom they had never knowingly met, well enough to convince dozens of their friends that it was really that person, then the record of the GP communications would lose much of their persuasive force. Similarly, if it could be shown that ESP could be used to instantly acquire skills normally requiring years of practice, then the language and chess cases could be set aside. But, as philosopher Robert Almeder asks:

> What evidence—experimental or otherwise—would the proponents of the ESP hypothesis (whether normal or super) accept as good grounds for setting aside the ESP hypothesis? Failure to answer this question puts the antisurvivalist in the position of being dogmatic.[4]

As mentioned in my first book, *Science and Psychic Phenomena,* the criterion of testability is *not* a criterion of meaning, of importance, or of truth. An untestable belief may be true or false; but until it is stated in a testable form, we have no way of learning if it is, in fact, false. Scientific progress is only possible if our scientific theories are testable. Metaphysical theories may be useful as guides to research, and may in time turn out to be testable; this eventually happened with Democritus's theory of atoms. But when the reverse occurs—when a testable theory is rendered immune to evidence with the addition of untestable ad hoc assumptions—then a scientific theory is turned into ideological dogma, that is, into a belief that is held regardless of the evidence.

SURVIVAL: CONCLUDING REMARKS

Philosopher Curt Ducasse uses the following analogy to evaluate the strength of the evidence from mediums. Suppose we learn that a friend of ours was on a plane that was known to have crashed with no reported survivors. Further suppose that sometime later we apparently receive a phone call from our friend, telling us that he survived the crash, and requesting that a sum of money be sent. Or—in a closer analogy with most mediumistic communications—suppose that our friend cannot speak directly with us for some reason, but must speak through a third party, who occasionally appears incoherent. How would we decide whether or not to send money?

Our very first consideration would be whether or not it was *possible* that our friend survived the crash. If, for instance, his dead body had been found and identified beyond question, then the person requesting the money could not possibly be our friend not yet deceased. But if we have no solid evidence that our friend was killed in the crash, then our degree of confidence that the message is really from our living friend must be based entirely on an evaluation of the evidence conveyed to us over the phone.

In our evaluation of the evidence, we must ask ourselves the following questions: is the evidence of our friend's identity abundant, or is it scanty? Does it include a great deal of detail, or not? Is there great diversity in the kinds of evidence the messages supply? Does it consist only of correct memories of personal matters? Or does it also include evidence of purpose typical of our friend? Does it include evidence of idiosyncratic personal characteristics, not only of personality, but also of the associations of ideas that were peculiar to our friend?

Ducasse argues that the same considerations of evidence that we would apply in the above case should be applied to the evidence of personal identity received via human mediums. Specifically, our evaluation should be based on the *quantity, quality,* and *diversity* of the evidence that we get over the mediumistic "telephone."

And these considerations can also be applied to the other lines of evidence we reviewed. More generally, the evidence from near-death experiences, deathbed visions, reincarnation cases, and apparitions of the dead contribute to the quantity of evidence; many of the individual cases are of high quality; and this list indicates the diversity of the factual evidence supporting the idea of survival.

What conclusion, Ducasse then asked, do all the facts dictate?

The conclusion they dictate is, I believe, the same as that as finally reached by Mrs Sidgwick and by Lord Balfour—a conclusion which also was reached in time by Sir Oliver Lodge, by Prof. Hyslop, by Dr. Hodgson, and by a number of other persons who like them were thoroughly familiar with the evidence on record; who were gifted with keenly critical minds; who had originally been skeptical of the reality or even possibility of survival; and who were also fully acquainted with the evidence for the reality of telepathy and of clairvoyance, and with the claims that had been made for the telepathy-clairvoyance interpretation of the evidence, as against the survival interpretation of it.

Their conclusion was essentially that the balance of the evidence so far obtained is on the side of the reality of survival and, in the best cases, of survival not merely of memories of the life on earth, but of survival also of the most significant capacities of the human mind, and of the continuing exercise of these.[5]

The evidence for survival was stronger when Ducasse wrote those words than it was when Mrs. Sidgwick wrote her essay for the jubilee anniversary of the SPR. As I write these words, the evidence is even stronger than it was when Ducasse wrote. And like those before me, I too have come to the conclusion that an impartial examination of all the evidence, without religious or materialistic prejudice, fully supports the reality of survival and continuing exercise of the most significant capacities of the human mind.

EIGHTEEN

Is Survival a Fact?

The whole of the available evidence is explicable only on the hypothesis of the survival of the human soul in a soul body. There is no longer a deadlock or a stalemate on the question of survival. On the contrary, survival is as well established as Evolution.

ROBERT CROOKAL, GEOLOGIST,
THE SUPREME ADVENTURE

I propose three categories of convincing evidence:

1. proof beyond all doubt
2. proof beyond all reasonable doubt
3. preponderance of the evidence

Many writers, such as Ducasse, have argued that the evidence for survival belongs to the third category. I argue here that it belongs to the second.

The first category—proof beyond *all* doubt—is generally agreed to apply only in the fields of pure logic and mathematics. In these fields, we are reasoning from premises accepted merely as axioms; or we are simply expressing the same relationship in a different form. As long as we express our statements consistently—that is, as long as the steps in our reasoning do not contradict our premises—then it is generally agreed that in pure logic and mathematics our conclusions can be proved beyond all doubt. But this is only the case because these fields are not empirical: that is, there is no requirement that the premises need to be based on observation or experiment. Indeed, there is no requirement that the premises and conclusions need to have *anything at all* to do with our world of experience.

The mathematician and philosopher René Descartes was not satisfied with only abstract proofs, and wondered which of his beliefs about the world could be certain, immune to all possible doubt. What about the ordinary facts of his life? No, because he imagined the possibility that an all-powerful, malevolent deity had created his sense perceptions as pure illusion, and therefore the existence of the earth, the sky, other people and his body were not immune to all possible doubt (similar to the computer-generated dream world imagined by the writers of *The Matrix*). Descartes also imagined the possibility that his past was not real, as this demon could have created him moments ago, complete with memories.

However, this malevolent deity could never convince him of the possibility that he does not exist, because if someone is wondering whether or not they exist, that is in and of itself proof that they do exist; hence Descartes's famous dictum: I think, therefore I exist. Descartes concluded that the only belief he knows to be true with absolute certainty is the fact that he exists at this moment, at least as a being of pure thought.

However, it seems extremely limiting to consider this belief to be our only item of knowledge. So, before we can answer the question of whether survival should be considered as a fact, we need to consider the more general question of what exactly is knowledge, and what is a fact.

THEORY OF KNOWLEDGE

I would define *knowledge* as belief that meets the following criteria.

◄ It is justified by the critical evaluation of evidence, and so

◄ we therefore have good reason to think it is true; and furthermore,

◄ we have no good reason to think it may *not* be true.

Consider my belief that I have only one brother. I believe this to be true because I was raised alongside him and never saw my parents bring home and raise another boy. I therefore have good reason to consider this belief true. Furthermore, I have never heard any rumors about my mother giving a boy up for adoption before I was born; nor has anyone, bearing a family resemblance or not, ever approached me claiming to be my long-lost brother. I therefore have no good reason— or any reason at all for that matter—to suspect that my belief may not be true.

Could I *possibly* be mistaken in my belief? Of course! But my point is that I have good reasons to think my belief is correct, and no good reason whatsoever to think it may be false. I therefore consider my belief that I have only one brother to be an item of knowledge.

Some philosophers argue that for a belief to be considered knowledge it must be true. But how do you know with absolute certainty that your empirical beliefs are true? The history of science has shown that we can be mistaken in even our most firmly held beliefs, and that we can never know in what ways our beliefs about the world may eventually have to be revised. If we insist that for a belief to be an item of knowledge it must be held to be true *with absolute certainty,* then, following Descartes, we have to restrict what we call "knowledge" to only our existence as a thinking being at this very moment. Being more generous, we could arguably expand "knowledge" to also encompass the most basic facts of our lives, which we believe to be true with a subjective sense of near-certainty.

I therefore consider knowledge as a *category* of belief: knowledge refers to those beliefs that we have good reason to think are true, and no good reason to think may be false. In other words, knowledge refers to those beliefs that—if our corroborating evidence is solid and our reasoning is valid—are true beyond any reasonable doubt.*

This definition of knowledge allows for the *fallibility* of human belief: if new, unexpected information comes to light, then we may reclassify our beliefs, from knowledge to opinion, or to error.

I equate an item of knowledge with what we consider to be a *fact*. For instance, I consider it a fact that I have only one brother. Let's consider some beliefs that many people consider to be facts, but which others consider to be merely controversial opinions.

In July 2009, *New York Times* columnist John Schwartz wrote, "Forty years after men first touched the lifeless dirt of the Moon, polling consistently suggests that some 6 percent of Americans believe the landings were faked and could not have happened. The series of landings, one of the greatest gambles of the human race, was an elaborate hoax developed to raise national pride."[1]

Most people believe that the moon landings of the late 1960s and early 1970s actually happened, for a number of good reasons: the film evidence, the testimony of astronauts and NASA officials, the moon rocks brought back, the fact that scientists of other nations also tracked the missions, and so forth. On the other hand, there is not a shred of credible evidence to support the view that they were faked in a film studio, and as Schwartz wrote, "The sheer unlikelihood of being able to pull off such an immense plot and keep it secret for four decades staggers the imagination."[2]

Of course it is *logically* possible that the moon landings were faked; that the supporting evidence was fabricated; that hundreds of highly respected scientists, engineers, and other witnesses were bribed

---

*Note that while some beliefs about nature—such as the existence of gravity—may count as scientific facts, our scientific *theories* do not count as knowledge, as they are merely hypotheses—conjectures that are attempts to explain *how certain facts fit together*. The distinction here is between gravity and evolution as facts, and the theories that try to explain how they work. The problem of induction—not to mention the entire history of science—means that we can never consider our scientific theories true beyond all reasonable doubt. This point is elaborated in chapter 15 of my previous book, *Science and Psychic Phenomena*.

or threatened, and so on. But we do not have a shred of credible evidence that *any* of these things happened, so we have no good reason to doubt that the moon landings are anything but actual facts.

The philosopher Neal Grossman has written extensively on this issue, specifically with regard to the evidence for survival. In an article for the *Journal of Near-Death Studies,* Grossman first describes the ideological nature of the belief in materialism.

> I coined the term "fundamaterialist" to characterize a person whose attitude towards materialism is the same as the fundamentalist's attitude towards his or her religion. In each case, the attitude is one of unwavering certainty towards the chosen ideology. For fundamaterialists, materialism does not appear to be an empirical hypothesis about the real world; it appears to be a given, an article of faith, the central tenet of his web of belief, around which everything else must conform.[3]

He then discusses various forms of fallacious reasoning that materialist debunkers frequently employ in their attempts to cast doubt on evidence for survival, and elaborates on the fallacy we have touched on.

> [This] kind of logical fallacy, which I will go into in greater length, involves an equivocation between two very different meanings of the word "possible." I recently asked students in my graduate seminar to say what we mean when we call a theory or hypothesis possible. A philosophy graduate student answered that to say that a hypothesis is possible means that it is consistent, that it can be formulated without self-contradiction. This is the correct conception of logical possibility: a hypothesis is said to be logically possible if it is not self-contradictory. But a psychology graduate student offered a different conception of possibility. She suggested that a hypothesis is possible only if there is some empirical reason to believe that it might be true. Let us call this conception of possibility empirical

possibility. The difference between these two meanings of the word "possible" is enormous, and I will argue that an equivocation between the two meanings allows debunkers to believe they actually have a rational perspective; it is also a main reason that the so-called "superpsi" hypothesis was ever taken seriously. But first I will give some examples to illustrate the two very different meanings of the word "possible."

Consider the following hypothesis: an advanced civilization exists on Mars and is living beneath the surface of that planet. Is this hypothesis possible? The hypothesis is not self-contradictory, so it is logically possible. But there is absolutely no evidence that suggests that the hypothesis might be true. So it is not possible in the sense that there are any reasons to believe it might possibly be true.[4]

Grossman is concerned with drawing a distinction between a hypothesis that is merely logically possible, and a hypothesis that is not only a logical possibility but also actually has the support of evidence. He continues:

Science is concerned with real possibilities only, not with mere logical possibilities, that is, not with hypotheses whose sole virtue is that they can be stated without self-contradiction. Philosophers, on the other hand, do consider what I have called mere logical possibilities, and such consideration is an indispensable and important aspect of a philosopher's training. One such logical possibility, which would be familiar to anyone who has taken an undergraduate philosophy course, is the "evil genius" argument of Descartes. Is it possible, asked Descartes, that a mischievous deity is causing us to have the sense perceptions that we do have, while at the same time there is no external world, and so our belief in an external world is false? Or equivalently, as students today pose the problem, is it possible that we are living in the "Matrix"? This is of course a logical possibility, but it is not a real possibility unless empirical reasons are forthcoming.[5]

Grossman takes pains to explain that it is the confusion between logical possibility and real possibility that allows the claims of debunkers—whether for elaborate fraud or for super-ESP—to be taken seriously. It is worthwhile here to quote from his article at some length. As Grossman points out:

The mere fact [that] a sentence is not self-contradictory is not a reason to believe it might actually be true. This is how we get tricked into taking seriously the debunkers' various claims that "it could be this," or "it could be that." This is to treat a mere logical possibility as if it were a real possibility. It is as if we treated Descartes' "evil genius" argument as a real possibility, and felt we could not assert the reality of an external world until we had "proved" that we were not being systematically deceived. Philosophers love to worry over arguments like this, but they have nothing to do with science, which considers real, that is, empirical possibilities only. No one would ever think of applying for grant money to investigate whether or not we are living in the Matrix.

I wish to mention briefly two historical examples, one famous and the other not, that involve this confusion between logical possibility and real possibility. As is well known, Creationists, when confronted with the data such as fossils that show that the Earth is much older than a literal reading of the Bible would indicate, claim that when God created the world 5700 years ago, he created it with the fossils as we find them. What are we going to believe, asks the Creationist: the testimony of our senses or holy scripture? They then challenge the Evolutionists to "prove" that God did not thus create the world. Is this a challenge that any scientist, or any rational person, ought to accept? The hypothesis "God created the world 5700 years ago with the fossils as we find them" is of course logically possible. But no one reading this seriously believes that evolutionary theory is on less solid ground simply because this logical possibility cannot be refuted. And likewise, no one reading this seriously believes that the independence of consciousness from the brain is on less solid empirical ground simply because the logical possibility of fraud can never be refuted. Neither the Creationists' hypothesis nor the debunkers' various hypotheses represent real empirical possibilities; they were proposed for the sole purpose of ignoring data that contradicted their a priori worldview.

Here is another example that is just as silly, but because its silliness was expressed in sophisticated philosophical jargon, it actually got published in the respectable journal *Philosophia*. Philosopher Robert Almeder (2001), after examining several of the stronger reincarnation-type cases collected by Ian Stevenson, which include verified memories, skills and behaviors appropriate to the purported past-life personality, birthmarks, and so on, concluded that it is irrational not to believe in reincarnation, given the data. But philosopher Steven Hales (2001) argued that it could be the case that these children with verified past-life memories were really abducted by aliens. These aliens, for their own amusement, planted false memories into the brains of the children, so that they would come to believe they had been somebody else. Presumably, the mothers of these children would also have been abducted while pregnant, so that the birthmarks could be planted on the fetus.

This, claimed Hale, would explain everything that needed to be explained, and had the virtue of being consistent with materialism. The aliens, after all, are physical beings, so that there is no need to posit the existence of disembodied consciousness, which very idea was repugnant to Hales, to account for cases of the reincarnation type. The burden of proof was cleverly shifted to the believers in reincarnation to prove that the children had not been abducted by aliens before they can rationally assert the truth of the reincarnation hypothesis.

But this is just sophisticated nonsense that should not be, and should never have been, taken seriously. The alien abduction hypothesis is of course logically possible, but calling it "logically possible" means merely that the sentence "aliens abducted the children and planted memories in their brains" is not self-contradictory. But that is not a reason for serious scientists trying to understand real-life phenomena to take it seriously. Scientists are obligated to investigate real possibilities, not imaginary ones. A logical possibility is imaginary only; that is, anything that a human being can consistently imagine is a logical possibility. The alien abduction hypothesis would move from the realm of the purely imaginary to the realm of the real only if there were some evidence to suggest it might be true. What might count as evidence? If the children were found to have implants in their skulls, or if the children were able to remember being abducted, then the abduction hypothesis would represent a real possibility. But no such data are forthcoming.

Notice, incidentally, that neither Hales nor any other fundamaterialist tries to deduce any observational consequences from their imaginary hypotheses, as I have just done. They are content to merely imagine that everything can be explained away in terms consistent with their materialist ideology; they have absolutely no interest in investigating whether what they are imagining is true. That would take them out of their armchair imaginings and into the real world; and real-world data have refuted materialism over and over again. Hales's concern, like that of the religious fundamentalists, is ideological, not empirical. He wants real scientists, who are trying to account for real data, to take as a real possibility what he himself takes as only a logical possibility, or in other words, merely imagines. The debunker wants us to refute mere logical possibilities before we can legitimately make the inference from the data to survival.[6]

And as for the claim that the survival hypothesis is somehow extraordinary, Grossman replies:

"There is absolutely nothing extraordinary about the hypothesis of an afterlife. The overwhelming majority of people in the world believe it, and have always believed it." On the contrary, it is the materialists' worldview that is truly extraordinary, especially when one considers the ridiculous hypotheses that that worldview advances in order to save itself, such as "superpsi," alien abduction of children who appear to remember past lives, and nonfunctioning brains still somehow producing conscious experience.

Survival researchers are under no obligation to refute every, or even any, logically possible alternative hypothesis. Such "hypotheses" are nothing more than the imaginings of the fundamaterialists; the burden is on them to provide non-ideological empirical support for their hypotheses before scientists should take them seriously. In the absence of empirical support, such hypotheses merely reflect the fantasy life of the debunkers, and science is not obliged to take unsupported imaginings and fantasies seriously.[7]

So, does the belief in survival count as a fact, or does it remain merely a reasonable conclusion based on good evidence?

We have seen that the belief in survival is justified by the logical evaluation of evidence. In this book and in *Science and the Near-Death Experience*, we have seen that the evidence in its favor is vast and varied; it comes from near-death experiences, deathbed visions, children who remember previous lives, apparitions, and communications through mediums. These lines of evidence, all very different from each other, all point in the same direction.

Much of this evidence is also very well-corroborated; since much of it stands up to the most severe critical scrutiny, we therefore have good reason to believe survival of consciousness past the point of biological death may be true. The only question remaining is whether we have any good reason to believe it may *not* be true.

I maintain that we have no such reasons. Consider here only one of the several lines of survival evidence, that of communication from the dead via mediums. For materialists and other doubters of survival, this data is simply inexplicable, except for:

◄ elaborate conspiracies of fraud, or
◄ super-ESP

In order to convict a person of a criminal offense, the law does not require that the prosecutor prove the case beyond all *conceivable* doubt, but only beyond all *reasonable* doubt. But what about fraud and super-ESP? Do these logical possibilities cast reasonable doubt on the idea of survival?

In many of the best cases described earlier, explanations involving fraud would have to involve elaborate conspiracies by highly respected people, including, in many cases, the researchers themselves, some of whom started their investigations as professed skeptics. This purely logical possibility will be considered reasonable by only the most paranoid and dogmatic of materialists. As for super-ESP, we have seen that the degree of extrasensory perception required to explain the best evidence far exceeds anything found in the anecdotal or experimental records. We have also seen that much more than mere telepathy or clairvoyance is required, stretching the definition of ESP until it bears almost no resemblance at all to the ordinary meanings of the words *telepathy* and *clairvoyance.** Something different from ordinary extrasensory perception in both degree and *type* is required.

The super-ESP hypothesis asks us to accept the likely existence of supernormal human powers far exceeding in degree anything observed in other situations—powers that include not merely *perception,* but also brilliant theatrical skills of impersonation; powers that allow people to temporarily and instantly acquire skills they have never developed; to serve purposes that, in some cases, seem to be only those of a deceased person; that enable multiple people to subconsciously and telepathically collude together in elaborate plots; and all with the purpose of carrying out an elaborate deception of everyone involved, including the *self*-deception of those who it is claimed are exercising these vast powers.

The utter lack of evidence for any of these powers, apart from the

---

*The term *clairvoyance* comes from French *clair* meaning "clear" and *voyance* meaning "vision."

survival cases in question, makes super-ESP nothing more than an unsupported logical possibility at best, and magical thinking at worst. The former is also true of explanations involving fraud, since in the best cases, there is not a shred of evidence that elaborate fraud was committed by the highly respected people involved. It is nothing more than a mere logical possibility that can never be refuted with 100 percent certainty. And a mere logical possibility is *not* a good reason to doubt the reality of survival, any more than the mere logical possibility that the U.S. government faked the moon landings in a film studio is a good reason to doubt the fact that men have walked on the moon. Similarly, the mere logical possibility that God created all the geological and biological evidence for evolution merely to test our faith in biblical stories is not a good reason to doubt the fact of evolution. As others before me have concluded, survival of human consciousness past the point of biological death is a fact.

NINETEEN

What the Dead Say

Most of the messages from the dead that we have reviewed so far have either been brief snippets of conversation or enigmatic pieces of literary puzzles. But far more detailed and informative messages have been received through the most powerful mediums. Many people have found these messages to be of great interest, and so we will now consider the content of some of these messages.

Dr. Karl Novotny died in Vienna in April 1965. Two days prior to his death, his friend and former patient, Grete Schroder, had a dream in which a figure told her that Novotny was dying. Although Frau Schroder had no previous contact with mediums, she was persuaded after Novotny's death to visit one; and on her very first visit, Dr. Novotny announced his presence. He described his death as follows:

> It was a lovely evening in Spring and I was spending Easter at my country home. I had not been really well for some time, but was not confined to bed. So I agreed to go for a walk with some friends. As we started out, I felt very tired and thought perhaps I ought not to accompany them. However, I forced myself to go. Then I felt completely free and well. I went ahead and drew deep breaths of the fresh evening air, and was happier than I had been for a long time. How was it, I wondered, that I suddenly had no more difficulties, and was neither tired nor out of breath?

I turned back to my companions and found myself looking down at my own body on the ground. My friends were in despair, calling for a doctor and trying to get a car to take me home. But I was well and felt no pains! I couldn't understand what had happened. I bent down and felt the heart of the body lying on the ground. Yes—it had ceased to beat—I was dead. But I was still alive! I spoke to my friends, but they neither saw me nor answered me. I was most annoyed and left them. However, I kept on returning. To say the least it was upsetting to see my friends in tears and yet paying no attention to what I was saying. It was very upsetting too, to look down at my dead body lying in front of me, while I felt in perfect health.

And there was my dog, who kept whining pitifully, unable to decide to which of me he should go, for he saw me in two places at once, standing up and lying down on the ground.

When all the formalities were concluded and my body had been put in a coffin, I realized that I must be dead. But I wouldn't acknowledge the fact; for like my teacher, Alfred Adler, I did not believe in an after-life. I visited my university colleagues: but they neither saw me nor returned my greeting. I felt most insulted. What should I do? I went up the hill where Grete lives. She was sitting alone and appeared very unhappy. But she did not seem to hear me either.

It was no use, I had to recognize the truth. When finally I did so, I saw my dear mother coming to meet me with open arms, telling me that I had passed into the next world—not in words of course, since these only belong to the earth. Even so, I couldn't credit her statement and thought I must be dreaming. This belief continued for a long time. I fought against the truth and was most unhappy.[1]

A similar message was communicated through the trance medium George Woods. Once in a trance, Woods would apparently be possessed by the communicator, who would then speak directly to the sitters using the medium's vocal cords. Here is a tape-recorded message from a man who identified himself as George Hopkins, a farmer.

I just had a stroke, or seizure, or heart attack. Or something of that sort. As a matter of fact I was harvesting. I felt a bit peculiar, thought it was the sun and went down in the 'edge.' I felt a bit drowsy, a bit peculiar, and must have dozed off. But dear, oh dear, I had such a shock.

I woke up, as I thought. The sun had gone down. And there was me, or what appeared to be me. I couldn't make it out at all, I was that puzzled. I tried to shake myself to wake myself up. I thought, well this is funny. I must be dreaming. I couldn't make head nor tail of it. It never struck me that I was dead.

Anyway I found myself walking along the road to the doctor's. I thought well, perhaps he can help me. I knocked on the door but no one answered. I thought well, I shouldn't have thought he would have been out because people were going in the surgery door.

I saw one or two of my old cronies. They all sort of seemed to walk through me. No one seemed to make any comment about me. I thought this a how-de-do.

I stood there for a bit trying to work it out. Then I saw someone hurrying down the road like mad to the doctor's. He rushed in, pushed past me and everybody, and next moment I heard them talking about me. I thought what the hell's wrong? I'm here! I heard them say I was dead!

Several days later, he attended his own funeral.

They were carrying my body down the old churchyard in the box, and they put me there with the old lady. It suddenly dawned on me about Poll, my wife. I thought, "That's funny. If it's as how I am dead, I should be with her. Where is she?"

I was standing there watching them put this body of mine in the grave. After the ceremony I was walking behind them down the path. There, right in front of me coming up towards me, was my wife!

But not my wife as I had known her, in the last few years of her life. But as I first knew her when she was a young girl. She looked beautiful, really beautiful. And with her I could see one of my brothers who died when he was about seventeen or eighteen. A nice looking boy who was fair-haired. They were laughing and joking and coming up to me. I thought well here I am and there they are, so I'm all right. They're sure to know what to do now.

My wife and brother made a proper fuss of me, saying how sorry they were that they were late. They said, "We knew you hadn't been too well, but we had no idea you were coming as sudden as you were. We got the message but we're sorry we couldn't get here quicker."

I thought that's odd. How the hell do they get about? I knew I'd got about, but as far as I was concerned I seemed to be walking about, same as I did before, except that everything was much lighter. I didn't seem to have any heaviness of the body, and no more aches and pains like I used to have. They started to try to explain things, but they wouldn't say too much. They said I'd got to get sort of adjusted and settled.[2]

The following account was dictated through George Woods by someone who identified himself as Rupert Brooke, but provided no details of when and how he died. Nevertheless, the communicator is clearly of an analytical turn of mind.

I came over in the First World War. It was all very sudden. It seemed as if I was in a body which no longer seemed, at first, to be the same, and yet in appearance it was the same. I just couldn't understand it. I just didn't realize that I had died.

Everything seemed in a sense quite natural, and yet the body I was using seemed quite foreign to me. I didn't feel it had any weight. There was a terrible lightness about myself.

I pinched myself and was startled to find that I did not feel any-thing. That worried me terribly. Then I had one or two shocks when

I realized people didn't see me . . . I thought if I can't feel myself when I pinch myself, why should a person see me who was still on earth in the old body? I thought it must be that I am on some vibrational rate which is not common to Earth, and therefore people can't see me. I could see other people but they couldn't see me. It all seemed so strange.

I remember vividly sitting beside a river and looking at myself, and not seeing myself. I could see no reflection. I thought "That seems most extraordinary. I have a body and yet it has no reflection." I couldn't adjust myself at all. I was going round to various people that I had known, trying to tell them that I was alive and well, and they just didn't realize that I was there.

I realized that the reason they couldn't see me was because if my body didn't have a reflection, it couldn't be solid to them. It just couldn't be on the same vibration: it couldn't be the same sort of matter. I had to adjust myself to the fact that I had a body which was to all outward appearances the same, and yet obviously was not a real body from the point of view of Earth. Therefore I was in what I suppose one would term a spiritual body, and yet I was not particularly spiritual. I was puzzled and bewildered.[3]

During his lifetime, the philosopher Bertrand Russell's attitude toward the survival of consciousness after biological death could be described as something between skeptical dismissal and reluctant agnosticism. It may therefore seem oddly interesting that communications ostensibly from Russell have been transmitted through the medium Rosemary Brown. At any rate, the messages show both an awareness of previous opinions and an open-minded attitude toward change.

I was positive I knew the answers to many questions including the vexing one concerning the probability of taking up a new life after this one has ceased. I use the word probability rather than possibility because I believed in the possibility of many improbable things, and preferred to consider problems in the light of probability rather than in the half-light of possibility. . . . [however] If revelations come which present a challenge to some of our present ideas, we must accept them and designate their position in the scheme of things. All the formulations in the world will not arrest the tide of advanced thinking from sweeping away false conceptions and false gods.[4]

Russell described his own death as follows:

After breathing my last breath in my mortal body, I found myself in some sort of extension of existence that held no parallel, as far as I could estimate, in the material dimension I had recently experienced. I observed that I was occupying a body predominantly bearing similarities to the physical one I had vacated for ever; but this new body in which I now resided seemed virtually weightless and very volatile, and able to move in any direction with the minimum of effort. I began to think I was dreaming and would awaken all too soon in that old world, of which I had become somewhat weary, to find myself imprisoned once more in that ageing form which encased a brain that had waxed weary also and did not always want to think when *I* wanted to think.

Several times in my life, I had thought I was about to die; several times I had resigned myself with the best will I could muster to ceasing to be. The idea of B.R. no longer inhabiting the world did not trouble me unduly. I felt the world had had enough of me, and certainly I had had enough of the world. Now, here I was, still same I, with capacities to think and observe sharpened to an incredible degree. I felt earth-life suddenly very unreal almost as though it had never happened. It took me quite a long time to understand this feeling until I realized at last that matter is certainly illusory although it does exist in actuality; the material world seemed now nothing more than a seething, changing, restless sea of indeterminable density and volume. How could I have thought that that was reality, that last word of Creation to mankind? Yet it is completely understandable that the state in which a man exists, however temporary, constitutes the passing reality which is no longer reality when it has passed.[5]

In addition to this, there are extended remarks on the pursuit of happiness, on personal identity, and even a three-page essay on politics, all in a style characteristic of the living Russell. He admits that some of his opinions have changed, and that "I am far less of a cynic than I was, although I remain to be convinced of many things. I am, however, still very cynical as regards human nature, the more so, perhaps, because I can now see its pettiness in sharper detail."[6] He is also aware that we may not consider him to be the real Russell.

> You may not believe that it is I, Bertrand Arthur William Russell, who am saying these things, and perhaps there is no conclusive proof that I can offer through this somewhat restricted medium. Those with an ear to hear may catch the echo of my voice in my phrases, the tenor of my tongue in my tautology; those who do not wish to hear will no doubt conjure up a whole table of tricks to disprove my retrospective rhetoric.[7]

The musician Sir Donald Tovey also claimed to be one of Rosemary Brown's communicators. At one point he first describes his own death: "I could not myself believe that I had passed through death's door upon my arrival here: the entire process is so natural, so automatic, so serene, and so imperceptible from the soul aspect."[8] He then described what he had apparently learned since then.

> I have watched the coming of souls to my spiritual surroundings, and have seen that they appear to rise through a sea of light, gently and slowly and effortlessly, borne securely in their new bodies which are provided for their souls upon cessation of their physical

existence. In actual fact, those new bodies already existed although merged with the physical bodies and linked to them by the silver cord, as it is known. At Death, this cord is dissolved or severed, and can be compared with the umbilical cord which is also dispensed with after birth. Death, after all, is like another birth into another world, excepting that one's new body is a counterpart of the lately vacated physical body. When you are born on earth, you enter a body provided by your parents; when you are born into the World of Spirit, you emerge in the counterpart of that body at whatever stage it has reached, excepting that is it without defect for defects are characteristics of the world of matter and not of the world of spirit.[9]

So far, we have reviewed five apparently postmortem descriptions of dying, received through three different mediums. There are obvious similarities in the different accounts. The process of dying seems so imperceptible that the recently deceased seem frequently unaware of what has happened; and they seem to be in possession of a new body, although possessing different properties from the one recently vacated.

The medium Jane Sherwood had several communicators; one of these, who only identified himself as "E.K.," discussed at length the relationship between life and matter.

Two systems are interlocked in the organism as you know it. They work together and modify each other and the whole story of the organism is the story of their gradual disentangling. They finally draw away from each other at death. The inorganic body is returned into the downward trend towards entropy and the invisible body of life is set free into the upward trend towards development. Of necessity it goes on to develop higher phases of activity for you must think of this body which is only invisible to you, as being perfectly material on its own plane. Get rid of the notion of the ephemeral stuff of which phantoms are made. Life is simply matter which has been pushed upward into a higher phase of activity and has thus gained the power to exist and continue in another degree of being . . . All living energy systems tend toward greater complexity and the consequent creation of higher forms of activity; all dead systems of activity tend towards greater simplicity and end in stagnation. The organism represents the interaction of both these processes and at its death they draw apart.[10]

E.K. describes the normal experience as follows:

As old age comes on the two forms of being represented in the body begin to draw apart. Failing health and failing senses are the symptoms of this withdrawal. The brain tissues often seem to sever connections first before the other organs of the body are ready. This is the meaning of senile decay. When the final breath is drawn the process of severance is practically complete and rounded off by unconsciousness. Where death comes gradually and naturally like this one wakes quietly in the new conditions after an interval of a few days. . . . death is a kind of birth and it should proceed with a quiet inevitableness and not be accompanied by pain or distress. Much of the apparent suffering of a death-bed is not consciously felt by the sufferer. His real life is already half retired from the mortal body and neither experiences nor records its pangs. Shakespeare is very near to the literal facts when he speaks of "shuffling off this mortal coil."[11]

After this, E.K. then gave an account of his own experience.

I found myself awake in the transition state of which we have spoken. I thought myself still weak and ill, but I arose from my rest feeling marvelously refreshed and happy and I wandered for awhile in the something-nothing surroundings of this queer world and was unable to make any sense of it. The brooding silence drugged me into unconsciousness for a long time, because when next I woke my body felt quite different, no longer frail and weak as I had supposed, but vigorous and ready for anything as though I had suddenly stepped back into youth. . . . There was a feeling of expectation, of waiting for something to happen.[12]

This was followed by a life review, after which he understood the failures and successes of his life. The life review left him saddened and humbled; again he fell asleep, and awoke in another land.

THE WORLD OF THE DEAD

E.K. found himself on a hillside, and described what he saw.

This was no earthly beauty. There was a light *on* things and *in* them so that everything proclaimed itself vividly alive. Grass, trees, and flowers were so lighted inwardly by their own beauty that the soul breathed in the miracle of perfection. . . .

I am almost at a loss to describe the heavens as I saw them from my hillside. The light radiated from no one direction, it was a glowing, universal fact, bathing everything in its soft radiance so that the sharp shadows and dark edges which define objects on earth were missing. Each thing glowed or sparkled with its own light and was lighted as well by the circumambient splendour. The sky, as I looked upward was like a vast pearl gleaming with opalescent colours. There was a suggestion of unfathomable depths of space as the shimmering colours parted their transparencies to show the infinite abyss.

I was awakened from my absorption by the sound of voices. If the loveliness of tree and flower had held me spellbound my first sight of fellow beings gave me more cause to rejoice. Here was another form of life, a more complex one which also emanated its own lovely qualities in visible rays. These people were more than alive; life streamed from them, palpitating with their emotions, lit and splendid with their joy and waxing and waning with its intensity. Here, again, bodies were not defined by shadows and the softer outlines were glorious with the out-flowing life. I trembled at their approach and felt like an interloper from a lower sphere. They came toward me, greeted me and reassured me . . . now I had to realize that I was one of them and was glad to go with them and learn something of the conditions of my new life.[13]

Many other accounts of the afterlife have been recorded by mediums, and most of the accounts show many similarities.* But by far the most detailed and extensive account of the next world purports to come from Frederic Myers.

Myers had been dead twenty-three years before attempts to describe the next world claimed to come from him. He had first been anxious to establish his continuing identity to his living friends and colleagues, by using the cross correspondences. However, by 1924 he seemed ready to at last describe his experiences, and to tell what he had learned since his death. The communications were recorded in two books, both dictated through the amateur trance medium Geraldine Cummins.

Myers first announced his presence to Miss Cummins as a drop-in communicator in November 1924, claiming to be attracted by the unusual power of the medium. Miss Cummins did not know the living Myers, and was only a small child when he died. But the communications received through Miss Cummins impressed those who had known the living Myers. Sir Lawrence Jones, past president of the SPR, accepted the scripts as coming from his old friend, and delivered several lectures on them. Mrs. Evelyn Myers, the widow of the communicator, was so impressed that she bought dozens of copies of the books to give to her friends, and even invited Miss Cummins to live with her on the top floor of her house. Oliver Lodge was similarly

*See, for instance, Barker, *Letters from the Light;* Cummins and Toksvig, *Swan on a Black Sea;* and Hamilton, *Is Survival a Fact?*

impressed. Through Mrs. Leonard he asked Myers about the communications delivered through Miss Cummins, and through Mrs. Leonard received permission from Myers to write a foreword to the first book.

After delivering some cross correspondences between Miss Cummins and Mrs. Leonard, Myers got busy dictating his description of the afterlife. There had been earlier descriptions of the afterlife from other communicators, but these had often been dismissed as ridiculous. Communicators described a beautiful world that was not only similar to Earth, but, some thought, *too* similar. In the next world people played golf, drank scotch, smoked cigars, had sexual adventures, lived in houses, and even went to work! Myers went on to describe realms of existence that were far more strange and exotic, but was also to show why these other descriptions were at least partly right.

Myers's first postmortem book, dictated to and written by the hand of Geraldine Cummins while in trance, is titled *The Road to Immortality*. It begins with a chapter titled "Why? The Riddle of Eternity."

Many wonderful speculations have been made about the whence and whither of man's destiny. Few have directly attempted to discuss why man was created, why the material universe spins apparently for ever and ever through space, its elements ever continuing, nothing lost, seemingly immortal, changing but in its imagery.

"A vast purposeless machine." Such was the epitaph the scientist of the last century wrote of it, and in so doing he declared the faith of the thinking men of his age, namely, that there is no why. There is, therefore, no fulfillment. Matter is the only reality. And this terror, a purposeless mechanical drama of motion and life, must, with ghastly monotony, play on for ever and ever.

Now, truth is far from us all; but it was immeasurably remote from those who came to this melancholy conclusion. However, if mind is accepted as existing apart from matter, there is a very definite prospect of discovering the reason for the strange fantasy of existence.[14]

In his books Myers described a process of gradual development as the individual embarks on a stupendous journey through the astral planes. After most deaths, a period of unconsciousness and recuperation usually occurs, in a place Myers referred to as Hades. The time spent in Hades is said to vary with the needs of the individual, with children often requiring hardly any rest at all. However, for Myers: "I died in Italy, a land I loved, and I was very weary at the time of my passing. For me Hades was a place of rest, a place of half-lights and drowsy peace."[15]

But Hades is described as only an intermediate stage, on the borders of two worlds, in between what Myers refers to as "the plane of matter" and "the Lotus Flower paradise." This paradise seemed to be the heaven for which men have always yearned, and of which their various theologies had told them. Myers had loved this plane, for it could be supremely beautiful. But his own feelings toward it had become ambivalent, for he had discovered that there was a realm beyond it. Once he had developed enough to journey beyond the Lotus Flower paradise, he described it in somewhat negative terms, as "the plane of Illusion."

But in his postmortem books Myers wrote about far more than the various planes of existence. He also claimed to have discovered the reason for existence, the very purpose of our universe.

According to Myers, reality has two fundamental attributes: psychic and physical, or mental and material. Each of us begins as an extremely rudimentary psychic entity, capable of physical embodiment as only a simple form of life. Through repeated incarnations, as plants, insects, fish, amphibians, reptiles, and mammals, the conscious being ascends the chain of living matter, attaining greater and greater complexity. And, according to Myers, human life is far from the ultimate state. After repeated incarnations in human bodies, one finally graduates from the human race. Thus, we are "gods in training," and once we are developed enough to pass beyond the plane of Illusion, there is no need to repeat existence in our world of earthly matter.

An identical claim is made by "Seth," the entity who purported to communicate through the medium Jane Roberts. Sociologist Ian Currie has concisely summarized the essence of Seth's message as follows:

> According to Seth, each individual consciousness must undergo a long period of training and learning through repeated physical embodiments. Being human is simply one "stage" in this process of development, and when, through repeated incarnations, this stage is finished, one passes onward to other planes of existence which offer more exalted opportunities for development. The most crucial "lesson" to be learned is karmic or ethical. Through repeated embodiments, the undeveloped individual treats others with cruelty and hatred, and, in accordance with the karmic process, is subjected to cruelty and hatred in return. The ultimate result of these hard lessons is spiritual development and a passage beyond physical embodiment, giving access to god-like creative powers once the entity is highly evolved enough to use these in a karmically responsible way. While he is still unevolved enough to use these powers to injure, control, exploit or destroy others, he does not have access to them.[16]

Seth had given Jane Roberts and her husband a series of lectures on the nature of reality, and one night a particularly interesting message was received, as Jane describes:

> With all Seth . . . told us about man's potentials . . . we . . . wondered . . . why the race isn't more developed morally and spiritually.
>
> One night before our regular Wednesday session Rob and I were pretty upset over the state of the world in general. We sat talking and Rob wondered why we behaved as we did. "What real sense or purpose is behind it all?" he said. "I don't know," I said. I felt as bad as he did.

That was November 6, 1968, and . . . on that . . . evening . . . Seth . . . came through in his distinct clear voice. Among other things, Seth . . . said: "The human race is a stage through which various forms of consciousness travel. . . . Before you can be allowed into systems of reality that are more extensive and open, you must first learn . . . through physical [life] . . . As a child forms mud pies from dirt, so you form your civilizations . . .

"When you leave the physical system after reincarnations, you have learned the lessons—and you are literally no longer a member of the human race, for you elect to leave it. . . . In more advanced systems, thoughts and emotions are automatically and immediately translated into . . . whatever approximation of matter there exists. Therefore, the lessons must be taught and learned well.

"The responsibility for creation must be clearly understood. [In physical life on earth] . . . you are in a soundproof and isolated room. Hate creates destruction in that 'room,' and until the lessons are learned, destruction follows destruction . . . the agonies . . . are sorely felt . . . you must be taught . . . to create responsibly. [Earth life] . . . is a training system for emerging consciousness.

"If the sorrows and agonies within your system were not felt as real, the lessons would not be learned. . . . [It] is like an educational play."[17]

According to Myers, developing psychic entities

must gather . . . numberless experiences, manifest and express themselves in uncountable forms before they attain to completion . . . Once these are acquired, [these entities] . . . take on divine attributes. The reason, therefore, for the universe and . . . the purpose of existence . . . [is] the evolution of mind in matter.[18]

Myers describes how the process of psychic development relates to life on earth:

Place plants, insects, fish, birds and beasts into their several classes. These resemble the [grades] in a public school. The essences or souls of plants, after dying, gather together in their myriads and in time form one whole. These innumerable little beings . . . go up one step in the ladder then, and are one when they enter the body of an insect. Myriads of insect lives again make one being which, in due course, enters the body of a fish or a bird. And so the process continues . . .

Certain dogs, horses and cats, also monkeys, are possessed of a nucleus of intelligence that resembles, in some ways, the crudest of souls that inhabit the bodies of men. These . . . friends of ours pass into the "land of earthly desire," as some of us call it. . . . they do, very often, exist in a world beyond your world.

. . . in this habitat, old dog friends or cats who were comrades in other days may gravitate again to their masters or mistresses by virtue of their affection for them, that is, if the masters and mistresses are living in this Shadow Land. For we call it "Shadow Land," though it is really far more beautiful than the earth. It is, in truth, the next state, and the journeying soul must pass through it, even though he may not tarry long within its borders. But those animals who come to it cannot journey beyond it. They must, at some time, go back to earth and enter the bodies of human beings.[19]

In between and after each life on the plane of matter is a period of rest on the third plane, described by Myers as "a resting place on the road." From the plane of Illusion humans and some of the higher animals return again to earth. Myers writes:

It must be remembered that we are not merely short stories on the pages of earth, we are a serial, and each chapter closes with a death. Yet the new chapter develops from those which preceded it, and we pick up the threads, continuing a narrative that has always design and purpose though the purpose may be hidden because human beings, as a rule, are only permitted to study the one life, the one period of their history at a time.[20]

Regarding the number of times humans must again become incarnate, Myers adds:

I do not for a moment believe that the individual returns a hundred times or more to the earth. The majority of people only reincarnate two, three or four times. Though, if they have some human purpose or plan to achieve they may return as many as eight or nine times. No arbitrary figure can be named. We are only safe in concluding that, in the human form, they are not doomed to wander over the space of fifty, a hundred and more lives.[21]

After spending time once more in the Lotus Flower paradise, Myers claimed to have passed into the next realm beyond, from which he dictated the chapters of his books. But in addition to descriptions of the various astral planes, Myers also told of what he had learned concerning various topics, some of which may be of interest.

His remarks on the process of dying are very similar to the remarks of other communicators we have examined.

The two are bound together by many little threads, by two silver cords. One of these makes contact with the solar plexus, the other with the brain. They all may lengthen or extend during sleep or during half-sleep, for they have considerable elasticity. When a man slowly dies these threads and the two cords are gradually broken. Death occurs when these two principal communicating lines with brain and solar plexus are severed. . . . The average man or woman when he or she is dying suffers no pain. They have become so dissevered already from the body that when the flesh seems to be in agony the actual soul merely feels very drowsy and has a sensation of drifting hither and thither, to and fro, like a bird resting on the wind.[22]

The remarks on senility of E.K. that we covered earlier echo those of Myers, who wrote:

The very old may, before their passing from earth, in part lose memory or lose their grasp of facts, their power of understanding. This tragic decay all too often causes the observer of it to lose faith in an After-life. For the soul seems, under such circumstances, merely the brain. This, however, is a false conclusion. The soul, or active ego, has been compelled partially to retire into the double during waking hours because the cord between the brain and its etheric counterpart has either been frayed, or has snapped. The actual life of the physical body is still maintained through the second cord and through any of the threads which still adhere to the two shapes. So the aged, apparently mindless man or woman, is in no sense mindless. He or she has merely withdrawn a little way from you, and has no need of your pity.[23]

But according to Myers, the cruel man does not find paradise on the third plane. Instead, he languishes in a state of mental distress, until

this individual faces up to his own misery, to his vice; and then the great change comes. He is put in touch with a portion of the Great Memory . . . the Book of Life. He becomes aware of all the emotions roused in his victims by his acts. . . . No pain, no anguish he has caused has perished. All has been registered, has a kind of existence that makes him sensible of it once he as drifted into touch with the web of memory that clothed his life and the lives of those who came into contact with him on earth.

The history of the cruel man in the Hereafter would make a book which I am not permitted to write. I can only briefly add that his soul or mind becomes gradually purified through his identification with the sufferings of his victims.[24]

Decades later, the musician Donald Tovey made a similar claim through Rosemary Brown.

Each and every soul meets here with its just deserts, not because they are dispensed by a presiding deity, but because it is literally true that one reaps what one has sown. If one has endeavored to make the lot of others easier in earth-life and sought to promote the welfare and happiness of one's fellow-beings, then one finds oneself in a pleasing environment among congenial companions, and able to adapt without difficulty to the new mode of living. But those who have deliberately deprived others of their material rights and human needs, or have wantonly caused suffering, will find themselves in turn deprived and also imprisoned by their own meanness of outlook. This does not mean that they are trapped for ever in a self-made hell; the moment a soul sees and confesses its past misdeeds and attempts to rectify them, the way opens for it to evolve into the light.[25]

Myers describes how the nature of the next incarnation is karmically motivated.

When a soul is born into a defective body it is due to the fact that in a previous existence it committed errors from the results of which it can only escape by submitting to this particular experience.

The . . . soul of an idiot, for instance, functions on the material plane and gathers, dimly, certain lessons from its earth life. Actually, such men as tyrants and inquisitors often reincarnate as idiots or imbeciles. They have, on the other side of death, learned to sympathise with and understand the sufferings of their victims. These are sometimes of such an appalling character that their perpetrator's centre of imagination becomes disorganized and he is doomed to exist throughout his next incarnation in a state of mental disequilibrium.[26]

Like many other communicators, Myers strongly discouraged suicide, because the "despair, terror, or cynical disillusionment which usually accompanies the suicide is greatly intensified . . . the mood that drove him to self-slaughter will envelop him like a cloud from which we, on the other side of death may not for a long while give him release."[27]

However:

> I am not, of course embodying the post-mortem history of every suicide. There are exceptions—cases wherein the man who kills himself is filled with some noble purpose, sacrifices his life in order that, through his death, others may be relieved of want, or of the painful sight of a loved one slowly perishing of an incurable disease. The very mood, then, in which he commits the last dread act, has in it a certain fine fervour, a confidence . . . which redeems him in the black hours after his passing. . . . he is haunted by no inverted despair, no torment of self-pity.
>
> Thus, in discussing the penalties that may be attached to suicide, you must bear in mind the character of the soul, the mood, the motives behind the act, and until these are clearly envisaged you are not in a position to calculate its consequences.[28]

Myers also described the mysterious geography of the world of the dead. Myers only claimed personal experience of the second, third, and fourth planes of existence (the first plane being the world of ordinary matter). He never claimed that his knowledge was infallible, only that it was based on his own experience, and on what those more advanced had told him.

The Plane of Illusion

According to Myers, immediately after the death of the body the individual briefly recuperates in a transitional state he referred to as Hades. After a brief period of rest, one normally wakes in the third plane, which he calls the "Lotus Flower paradise," or the "plane of Illusion."

For most, this first world appears breathtakingly beautiful, but not strange, as their earth lives and dreams have prepared them for it. According to Myers, the plane of Illusion is also made of a form of matter, but one responsive to the deepest subconscious thoughts and desires. Unlike existence in our physical universe:

> On higher planes of being your intellectual power is so greatly increased that you can control form; you learn how to draw life to it. . . . In the first state [beyond death] your vision is limited by your earth experiences and memories, and so you create your own version of the appearances you knew on earth. . . . however, in Illusion-land you do not consciously create your surroundings through an act of thought. Your emotional desires, your deeper mind manufacture these without your being aware of the process.[29]

Myers tells us that communities of like-minded individuals with similar tastes come together and live in mutually constructed environments; those of a more solitary nature may live in an environment completely of their own subconscious construction. Here, food and water are no longer required; sexual desires are in most cases still present, but women do not bear children. Regarding love and marriage, Myers writes:

> In the world after death men are the possessors of bodies which reproduce in shape and in general appearance the discarded physical form, though they are clothed in an ethereal substance.
>
> Women do not bear children though sexual passion may be experienced as long as it is the soul's need. The woman possesses an etheric body so framed that it can serve her as the material shape served her various purposes, wishes, and appetites on earth.
>
> The problem of marriage, of two husbands or of two wives, is usually solved after death by the pull of the stronger, finer affection. Each soul is either drawn to the one who is most akin and

sympathetic to it, or is absorbed by whatever special passion or desire fills its nature.[30]

One question that has frequently been asked about a possible world beyond death is this: Where is it? Myers answers this question, saying that most of the planes of existence occupy the *same* physical space, but are composed of finer and finer forms of matter that, for the most part, never interact with each other. Myers writes that part of our being

> contains the infinite subtlety of atoms that are not destroyed through the death of that crude machine, the body. Actually, though I call them atoms, they would appear to you to be of a fluid character.[31]

Regarding the composition of the next world:

> Our surroundings are of a metetheric character. You ask me to define this. It is exceedingly difficult. But I think I may say that it contains atoms of the very finest kind. They pass through your coarse matter. They belong to another state altogether.[32]

> This world beyond death . . . consists of electrons differing only in their fineness or increased vibratory quality from those known to earthly scientists. These very subtle units are extremely plastic and, therefore, can be moulded by mind and will.[33]

The first two quotes regarding atomic structure were transmitted between 1924 and 1927; the third between 1927 and 1931. They are all the more remarkable when we consider the fact that in the early 1920s some physicists still held serious reservations about the existence of atoms. Quantum physics, born in the early years of the twentieth century, tells us that apparently solid matter is in fact mostly empty space. Much of this empty space is between the mutually repulsive, negatively charged electron shells of atoms; the remaining space is between the electron clouds and the positively charged central nuclei of the atom. If an atom was expanded to the size of the dome of St. Peter's Cathedral in Rome, the nucleus of tightly bound protons and neutrons would be an altar the size of a grain of salt. The electrons would flit like moths around the ceiling of the dome (not revolve in orbit like miniature planets). Because matter is almost entirely empty space, cosmic particles can easily pass through layers of apparently solid rock. It is the reason why trillions of neutrinos—tiny particles without mass or charge that rarely interact with matter—penetrate the earth every second as though it didn't exist (these particles are not affected by the electromagnetic force, and so are not captured or repelled by the electric and magnetic fields of other particles while flying past them).

Physicist Peter Russell has written:

Early in the twentieth century, physicists realized that atoms are composed of even smaller, subatomic particles. An atom may be small, a mere billionth of an inch across, but these subatomic parti-cles are a hundred-thousand times smaller still. Imagine the nucleus of an atom magnified to the size of a tennis ball. The electrons would [be] several miles [away], making the atom itself the size of London or Manhattan. As the early twentieth-century British phys-icist Sir Arthur Eddington put it, matter is mostly ghostly empty space, 99.9999999999999% empty space to be a little more exact.[34]

I wrote Dr. Russell, and found that the figure mentioned above is slightly misleading: his calculation refers to the percentage of *an atom* that is empty space. If we factor in the empty space between the nega-tively charged, mutually repulsive electron shells, then the percentage of matter that is empty space is *even larger* than the figure quoted above.

Science writer Timothy Ferris has illustrated how matter would behave if at least some of it were not affected by the electromagnetic force.

Our mental pictures are drawn from our visual perception of the world around us. But the world as perceived by the eye is itself exposed as an illusion when scrutinized on the microscopic scale. A bar of gold, though it looks solid, is composed almost entirely of empty space. Nor, to return to the old classical metaphor, does a cue ball strike a billiard ball. Rather, the negatively charged fields of the two balls repel each other; on the subatomic scale, the billiard balls are as spacious as galaxies, and were it not for their electrical charges they could, like galaxies, pass right through each other unscathed.[35]

In short, it is certainly logically possible that this universe does contain forms of matter that coexist within the same space and are not affected by each other's force fields. At this point in time the existence of such rarefied forms of matter is of course metaphysical speculation— just as the existence of atoms and neutrinos were, until the twentieth century, purely metaphysical speculations.

So, according to Myers, the third plane is composed of a finer form of matter, responsive to subconscious thoughts and desires.* Myers explains that this is why so many descriptions of the afterlife have seemed so much like a glorified version of the earthly environment. For when the average man on the street finds himself in the after-death state, he at first desires only an environment similar to the one he left behind.

---

*Regarding clothing, Myers writes: "It is necessary for me to emphasise once again the important part our subconscious memory of our past terrestrial life and our creative faculty play in the building up of a new life, a fresh story which, however, for a time, naturally bears a resemblance to the past out of which it has sprung . For instance, we were accustomed to wear clothes that belonged to our particular period. The images of these are deeply marked in our subconscious memory. So our first instinct is to appear to those we love as we were on earth. Our minds, though unconscious of the imaginative act, fashion out of this amazingly plastic ether every thread, every inch of the garments which we habitually wore during our earth-life. Naturally, after a while, we become aware at last of the creative powers of imagination, and devise strange and lovely coverings for our etheric bodies (Cummins, *Beyond Human Personality,* 33). Note that this provides a solution to the problem mentioned earlier regarding reports of appropriately clothed apparitions (see pages 88–89).

However, Myers tells us that far more extraordinary forms of existence are possible.

> The more advanced souls—whom the Church may call the angels and whom I call "the Wise"—can exist in tenuous forms within vast vistas of space and lead within it an extraordinarily vivid existence. [The average newly dead person] is quite incapable of facing such a strange and strenuous state of being.
>
> So we, who are a little more advanced than he, watch by the gates of death, and we lead him and his comrades, after certain preparatory stages, to the dream which he will inhabit, living still, according to his belief, in earth time. He bears within him the capacity for recalling the whole of his earth life. Familiar surroundings are his desperate need. He does not want a jeweled city, or some monstrous vision of infinity. He craves only for the homely landscape he used to know.
>
> The Wise, as I call them, can draw from their memory and from the great super-conscious memory of the earth the images of houses and streets, of country as known to these wayfarers so recently come from the earth. The Wise Spirits think, and thereby make a creation which becomes visible [to the newly dead].[36]

And gradually, the matter on this plane responds to the subconscious thoughts and desires of the newly arrived.

> The large majority of human beings when they die are not prepared for an immediate and complete change of outlook. They passionately yearn for familiar though idealized surroundings. Their will to live is merely to live, therefore, in the past. . . . For instance, the unthinking man in the street will desire a glorified brick villa in a glorified Brighton. So he finds himself the proud possessor of that twentieth century atrocity. He naturally gravitates towards his acquaintances, all those who were of a like mind. On earth he

longed for a superior brand of cigar. He can have the experience *ad nauseam* of smoking this brand. He wanted to play golf, so he plays golf. But he is merely living within the fantasy created by his strongest desires on earth.*[37]

But there is a limitation to this kind of existence. It seems that part of the purpose of the third plane is to exhaust the possibilities of earthly life, so that an individual may develop beyond the limitations it imposes. Eventually, boredom sets in, and the individual longs for some sort of challenge, a new adventure into the unknown. At this stage, the individual has two possible options: he may return to earth for another incarnation in human form; or he may choose to ascend to the fourth plane. If he is highly enough developed, he may enter it.

The Higher Planes

Myers wrote, "[I]f you are a Soul-man—in other words an intelligent, ethically developed soul—you will desire to go up the ladder of consciousness. The longing for a physical existence will have been burned into ashes with, however, a few exceptions."[38] These few exceptions are those who wish to achieve some remarkable intellectual triumph on earth, or who wish to play a notable part in the strife of earth life. But the majority of ethically developed beings no longer wish to live again on earth, and "they are then released from Illusion-land, from that nursery in which they merely lived in the old fantasy of earth."[39]

Myers himself claimed to have ascended to the fourth plane, which he referred to as Eidos, or the plane of Colour. He described the earth as only a poor copy of the fourth plane, in his words, "a copy of a masterpiece."

We dwell in a world of appearances in some respects similar to the earth. Only all this vast region of appearances is gigantic in conception, terrifying and exquisite according to the manner in which it

---

*The appendix contains what Myers claims is a true story of one woman's experiences in the Lotus Flower paradise.

presents itself to the Soul-man. It is far more fluidic, less apparently solid than earth surroundings.[40]

In his second postmortem book, the sequel *Beyond Human Personality,* Myers elaborates on the nature of Eidos; compared to the Lotus Flower paradise, he describes it as

> a loftier world, magnificent, exquisite, full of strange beauties and forms that may still be, in some respects, reminiscent of earth. These are, however, infinite in variety. They are composed of colours and light unknown to man. There, on this level, will be found a perfection in outward form, in surface appearances; a perfection only occasionally realized in the creations of the greatest of earthly artists.[41]

In this world the mind is now endowed with godlike creative powers, and it uses substances and colors unknown on earth to create an infinite variety of forms of unsurpassable beauty. The purpose of existence on this plane is to experience all the possibilities of form, so that the evolving soul may eventually pass beyond all involvement with it.

> On this luminiferous plane the struggle increases in intensity, the efforts expended are beyond the measure of earthly experience. But the results of such labour, of such intellectualized and spiritualised toil and battle also transcend the most superb emotion in the life of man. In brief, all experience is refined, heightened, intensified, and the actual zest of living is increased immeasurably.[42]

The planes beyond the plane of Illusion are progressively more remote from human experience, and words begin to lose the ability to describe them. Nevertheless, Myers tries his best. Beyond the fourth plane lies the plane of Flame, in which the individual "is as an artist who lives in his masterpiece, derives from it, in all its features, in the freshness of its evolving, changing creation, that strange exhalation which may, perhaps, at one rare moment, be known to a creative genius—though very faintly—while he still lives upon the earth."[43]

Beyond the plane of Flame lies the plane of Light, which is described as existence beyond form.

> On this level of consciousness pure reason reigns supreme. . . . the souls who enter this last rich kingdom of experience . . . bear with them the wisdom of form, the incalculable secret wisdom, gathered only through limitation, harvested from numberless years, garnered from lives passed in myriad forms. . . . They are capable of living now without form, of existing as white light . . . as pure thought.[44]

Finally, beyond all the others lies the seventh plane. Myers struggles to convey what others more advanced than he had told him of it.

> The Seventh state . . . baffles description. It is heart-breaking even to attempt to write of it. . . . the passage from the Sixth to the Seventh state means the flight from the material universe . . . You dwell not only outside of time but outside of the universe on this last plane of being.[45]

After he had described the other worlds, Myers summed up the reason why he has struggled so long and hard to communicate.

> Because a man dies, it does not follow that he loses touch with the earth, with that state of Penia—poverty—from which he rose into the delights of the plane named Illusion, from which he penetrated into the world of Eidos, to the human soul the Heaven World, the ultimate goal.
>
> We perceive the strange disorder of the world of men and women. We recognize the causes of that disorder and the purpose behind them. We realize the necessity for such disorder and at the same time we desire to convey some indication of the Great Reality.
>
> For this reason I, Frederic Myers, have endeavored to trace a rough outline of the road man must follow in the After-death if he be a seeker of immortality.[46]

Epilogue

For myself, Birth and Death seem to be respectively the great Exile and the great Returning Home. I expect, when the immediate shock of change is over, to find myself with a body familiar to me (because it has always been a possession without my realizing it), in a country from which come thronging back to me welcoming echoes of old familiarity. It will still be a world of Appearance; but since one veil at least will then have fallen from the face of Truth, I shall expect to find myself more responsive to her Eternal Beauty as I set out again—a pilgrim on an endless way.

RAYNOR JOHNSON,
THE IMPRISONED SPLENDOUR

This is the final work of a trilogy, and not one of my books was written to change the minds of the dogmatic pseudo-skeptics. They were written only as an appeal to those with an open mind on the subjects discussed. Those readers who suppose that the evidence and arguments presented in these books can be used to change the minds of the "skeptics" would be wise to consider the words of surgeon and anthropologist Paul Broca.

A new truth contrary to the prejudices of our teachers has no means wherewith to overcome their hostility, for they are open neither to facts nor to reasoning; it is necessary to wait for their death.[1]

Those words were written in the nineteenth century, and did not specifically refer to what was then called psychical research. But they are every bit as applicable today, to the continuing struggle of parapsychology for recognition and legitimacy. There is something in our nature that resists new ideas that run contrary to our entrenched opinions. Perhaps we all share this characteristic to some degree. And perhaps it is *good* that we do not drop our opinions at the first sign of contrary evidence, without first putting up a vigorous defense. But the so-called skeptics of parapsychology seem to have cultivated this characteristic to an absurd degree.

Psychologist Gary Schwartz has conducted twenty-first century research with mediums, and on numerous occasions he has been forced to defend himself against skeptical attacks. Apparently, on one occasion a prominent skeptic privately made to him a candid confession.

> Professor Ray Hyman, one of the most distinguished academic skeptics, has told me, "I do not have control over my beliefs." He had learned from childhood that paranormal events are impossible. Today he finds himself amazed that even in the face of compelling theory and convincing scientific data, his beliefs have not changed.[2]

We have seen in my first book *Science and Psychic Phenomena* how the so-called skeptics have resorted to every possible trick to discredit psi research. We have seen how, after conducting an experiment that produced results they did not expect, the Committee for Scientific Investigation into Claims of the Paranormal refused to carry out any more "scientific investigation." We have seen how a prominent "skeptic" has conducted research that successfully replicated a psi experiment, and how he then denied and distorted his results in order to avoid admitting he was wrong. We also have seen how the "skeptics" have finally run out of plausible counterexplanations, and how they now are left with little more than empty rhetoric. Psychologist Nancy Zingrone has studied the skeptical movement, and wonders:

> Can it be true that many critics behave as if they have never really noticed how complicated the world really is, as if they have never turned their focus inward? When one reads their writing in a systematic way—from the pages of the *Skeptical Inquirer* to the entries in Gordon Stein's *Encyclopedia of the Paranormal* to their various book-length treatments of the paranormal—one gets the impression that what characterizes the genre is exceptionally superficial reasoning.[3]

As pointed out in the first book in this series, parapsychology is the only branch of scientific research with a body of skeptics actively trying to discredit it. It was also indicated that this opposition can be best understood in terms of the historical struggle of science to escape from the fetters of religion.

Galileo was the first scientist to openly challenge the authority of the church. Like the monk Giordano Bruno before him, he insisted that the earth revolves around the sun; and like Giordano before him, Galileo paid dearly for his heresy. Shortly afterward, the scientific theory of Newton, with its determinism and mechanism, gave certain eighteenth-century philosophers more material with which to shake the complacency of religious beliefs. By this time the church had lost much of its power to silence dissidents. However, it was Darwin who delivered what was for many the decisive blow against the literal truth of scripture, with his argument that both modern animals and humans may have evolved over millennia from simpler creatures, through the mechanism of natural selection operating on random natural variation in the characteristics of offspring. In the 1930s, Darwin's work was combined with the discovery of genes, and the neo-Darwinian theory of evolution was created. In a nutshell, random genetic mutations are thought to occur within an organism's genetic code. Most mutations are harmful, but beneficial mutations are preserved because they aid survival—a process known as "natural selection." These beneficial mutations are passed on to the next generation. Over time, beneficial mutations accumulate and the result is an entirely different organism (not just a variation of the original, but a different species altogether).

It is the assertion that the variation is entirely random, purely a matter of chance, that sticks in the craw of so many people. The Catholic Church accepts evolution as a historical fact, but believes that evolution is guided by the mind of God.* Evolution as a biological fact was accepted long before Darwin, but the modern *theory* of evolution has two main planks: random mutation leading to variety of form, and natural selection operating on this variety in order to perpetuate those mutations that favor survival and reproduction.

Evolution as a fact of nature can hardly be disputed—the evidence for it comes from the geological record; from vestiges of now-useless parts, such as our own tailbones and appendixes; and from phenomena such as strains of bacteria that develop growing resistance to antibiotics. Nor can it be denied that natural selection operates in favor of certain inherited characteristics.

The legitimate source of controversy concerns the first tenet—that is, whether or not all genetic mutation is purely random. In the orthodox view, it has come to be believed that the natural variation found in the offspring of plants and animals arises through chance and natural selection alone, but Darwin himself was in doubt about this. Unlike many modern neo-Darwinians, Darwin was modest and undogmatic in his claims. In correspondence with Asa Gray of Harvard on divine design Darwin wrote to Gray, one year after the publication of *On the Origin of Species*: "... about Design. I am conscious that I am in an utterly hopeless muddle. I cannot think that the world, as we see it, is the result of chance;

---

*In the words of liberal theologian Arthur Peacocke, "God creates the world through what we call 'chance' operating within the created order" (Peacocke, *Theology for a Scientific Age*, 119).

and yet I cannot look at each separate thing as the result of Design." A year later Darwin wrote to Gray: "With respect to Design, I feel more inclined to show a white flag than to fire . . . [a] shot . . . You say that you are in a haze; I am in thick mud; . . . yet I cannot keep out of the question."[4]

Science suggests to us a picture of a universe that is creative; but is this creativity the result of blind chance or of the action of mind? If minds can produce blisters on skin under hypnosis, influence radioactive decay, and possibly collapse state vectors in the brain in a desired direction, then they could conceivably direct mutation by affecting the nucleotides in DNA.[5]

Chance may very well play a large role in evolution, but the hypothesis of directed mutation and the Darwinian interpretations of evolution are not mutually exclusive. The completely random nature of genetic mutation is an assumption, and evidence to the contrary has been found.[*] Since mutation occurs at the atomic and molecular level, it may possibly be influenced by the psychokinetic powers of human or nonhuman minds.[†]

Geneticist Michael Denton refers to the idea of random, undirected mutation as "the fundamental assumption upon which the whole Darwinian model of nature is based," and as "an unquestioned article of faith."[6]

In his remarkable book *Nature's Destiny*, Denton describes in detail how advances in physics, cosmology, and astronomy since the beginning of the twentieth century support the growing opinion within the scientific community that the universe gives every appearance of being specially designed for life.

---

[*]This idea is also known as directed mutagenesis, and John Cairns of Harvard first proposed this hypothesis in 1988. He found that *Escherichia coli* bacteria evolved the ability to metabolize lactose at a rate many times greater than that which would be predicted if the mutations were truly random. Susan Rosenberg at the University of Alberta later corroborated his results. (See Symonds, "A Fitter Theory of Evolution"; and Nash, "Test of Psychokinetic Control of Bacterial Mutation.")

[†]See chapter 4 of my book *Science and the Near-Death Experience* for experimental evidence of this effect, and the relationship of the effect with modern physics.

Several well-known physicists and astronomers, among them Brandon Carter, Freeman Dyson, John Wheeler, John Barrow, Frank Tipler, and Sir Fred Hoyle, to cite only a few, have all made a point in recent publications—that our type of carbon-based life could only exist in a very special sort of universe and that if the laws of physics had been very slightly different we could not have existed. With the evidence as it now stands, it is not surprising that there now exists a significant body of opinion within the scientific community prepared to defend the idea that the universe is in some way profoundly biocentric and gives every appearance of having been specially designed for life.[7]

However, Denton notes that "the life-giving coincidences do not stop at the distribution of supernovae or with the resonances of the energy levels of the carbon and oxygen atoms. They extend on into chemistry, into biochemistry and molecular biology, into the very fabric of life itself." After a detailed review of the long chain of life-giving chemical, biochemical, and biological coincidences, he eventually concludes:

Water, the carbon atom, oxygen, the double helix, and many of the other constituents of life possess unique properties which seem so perfectly adapted to the biological ends they serve that the impression of design is irresistible. Many of these adaptations not only serve the end of microscopic life but also give every appearance of having been adjusted to serve the end of macroscopic terrestrial life forms such as ourselves. This raises the very natural but heretical idea that if the cosmos is fit for the being of higher life forms, then surely it is not inconceivable that an evolutionary mechanism for their actualization could also have been written into the order of things and that perhaps the entire process of biological evolution, from the origin of life to the emergence of man, was somehow directed from the beginning. I believe that our current model of molecular genetics sanctions such possibilities.[8]

The Nobel Prize–winning neuroscientist Sir John Eccles thought that while evolution could account for the development of brains, something else was needed to account for the existence of conscious minds: "The evolutionary origin of our bodies and their building by the unique instructions provided by DNA inheritance is at best but a partial explanation, and certainly not a sufficient explanation of our existence as conscious beings."[9] He referred to neo-Darwinism as a "psuedo-religion" if taken as a complete explanation of life, including conscious life.

Physicists such as James Jeans and Nick Herbert have seriously proposed that modern physics suggests that mind is not derived from matter, but rather that mind is an elemental property of the universe, as elemental as energy and force fields. As Herbert wrote, "In the von Neumann interpretation of quantum theory, consciousness is a process lying outside the laws that govern the material world, and it is just this immunity from the quantum rules that allows mind to turn possibility into actuality."[10]

We may indeed be ghosts in machines, minds out for a spin in material bodies. According to this view, the origins of consciousness lie outside the story of biological evolution. The data we have examined in detail indicates that consciousness emerges into the physical world through the medium of brains, and that spiritual evolution has become intertwined with biological evolution, and that consciousness has used the material world as a springboard for growth.

When considering this idea, it is important to remember that many of our intellectuals are prejudiced in the literal sense: that of being inclined to prejudge. Professor of Medicine Louis Lasagna had this prejudicial attitude in mind when he wrote:

To believe without questioning or to dismiss without investigating is to comport oneself non-scientifically. It is *not* inspiring to read that the audience hissed when the great neurologist Sir John Eccles ended a Harvard lecture by admitting that evolution could account for the brain but not for the mind, and that only something transcendent could explain consciousness and thought.[11]

FINAL THOUGHTS

Perhaps it is time the conventional theorists realized that there is another choice in spiritual matters, something else besides religious or materialistic faith. Perhaps this is one of the finest lessons our history can teach us.

We have seen that the shaman has been found worldwide in hunter-gatherer societies, as the member of the tribe who is thought to act as an intermediary between his or her people and the spirit world. We have also seen that some shamanic practices involved what we would now call mediumship. The very earliest religions of our wandering hunter-gatherer ancestors would have been shamanic, and it seems plausible that early spiritual beliefs grew directly out of the sorts of human experiences that have been described in this book.

With the development of agriculture, our ancestors settled down in communities, and religion became institutionalized. Priestly castes formed, and over the centuries added layers of dogma to the ancient beliefs, according to the circumstances of their societies. Eventually, societies came into contact with other societies, and differences of religious beliefs were sometimes a source of conflict. Of course, within religions there have also been conflicts—sometimes violent—between various factions with different views. By the time humans began to build cities, such beliefs in many parts of the world were no longer based on human experience, but were instead taught by members of the priestly castes, and accepted by their people on faith. Since spiritual beliefs were now a matter of faith, no rational method was available to settle disputes. Unfortunately, by default, violence sometimes became the method of choice for settling religious differences.

It cannot be denied that during the Dark and Middle Ages, people in times of trouble took comfort in the teachings of the church. But the science of Galileo, Newton, and Darwin challenged the faith of many thinking persons, and ushered in a new age of skepticism. However, skepticism—the practice of doubt—turned for many into dogmatism, the practice of disbelief. Science itself became, for many individuals, a new religion, with its own saints, blasphemers, and cherished dogmas. Materialism, once a mere hypothesis, became one of these cherished dogmas, the unquestioning acceptance of which seemed crucial if the human race were not to regress to an earlier age of superstition and religious persecution. It is this attitude that accounts for the continuing refusal to accept the considerable evidence that proves materialism false. The psychology of this reaction to the evidence is perhaps understandable. But it has also left a void in the human psyche.

In the words of John Eccles:

Man has lost his way these days—what we may call the predicament of mankind. He needs some new message whereby he may live with hope and meaning. I think that science has gone too far in breaking down man's belief in his spiritual greatness and in giving him the idea that he is merely an insignificant material being in the frigid cosmic immensity. I think there is mystery in man, and I am sure that at least it is wonderful for man to get the feeling that he is not just a hastily made-over ape, and that there is something much more wonderful in his nature and his destiny.[12]

I believe our species has much growing up to do. Many of us have outgrown the comfortable smugness of the religions developed during the infancy of the human race. Yet we now find ourselves experiencing a rather troubled adolescence, with all its attendant doubt, dismay, and spiritual crisis. In the adolescence of our species we are struggling to find answers to questions that haunt us. But if there is one thing this book should have made clear, it is that the modern choice is not between blind religious faith and the pseudoscientific ideology of materialism. There is a third alternative, one that requires neither a leap of faith nor the denial of evidence. Our science and philosophy have evolved to the point at which they can finally come to grips with some of the deepest questions the human race has struggled with in the dark for thousands of years. Dawn's early light has appeared on the horizon, and the answers we have begun to glimpse appear breathtaking.

> *We are not human beings having a spiritual experience; we are spiritual beings having a human experience.*
>
> *Tielhard de Chardin*

The Dream Child

The following is an account of what the deceased communicator Frederic Myers claims is a true story of one woman's experiences in the Lotus Flower paradise. It is taken directly from the second postmortem book, *Beyond Human Personality*. This account may be of interest to many readers, as it illustrates several aspects of what Myers describes as the next plane of existence and its relationship to this life.

A certain mother longed for a daughter. Sons were born to her, but the little girl she desired so much never appeared in the flesh. Yet she is waiting for her mother in the world beyond death, for her soul has, on two or three occasions, made the attempt to be born but failed in each instance. There is a cogent reason for this failure. The soul of the daughter may not meet the mother in full conscious knowledge until after the latter's death. They meet already, but subjectively, in the manner I have described in a previous chapter. I might call this daughter the "dream-child." She has a lovely soul and if she had been born into this present life would have made a paradise for her mother.

Now during this earth-life, owing to the fact that this particular heart's desire of hers was not granted, the mother has learned much and developed spiritually. The little daughter was bound to absorb her attention, leading her to become selfish and only occupied with the pleasure of motherhood. For the child would have made radiant all her days. Such happiness belongs as a rule to the first heaven-world—to Eidos, and there she will, in due course, experience such joy. In the world of Illusion she will meet this daughter and be so overjoyed at seeing her and having her companionship that the separation from her sons, caused by death, will not inflict the suffering that might otherwise have been her portion.

So, there is providence in the fact that this child has not been given into her charge during her earth life. After death the mother will obtain her longing—a quiet, lovely, country place where her family live and come and go—a nursery where she finds this little daughter who fulfills the dream, is the dream of her imagination, the one she proudly cherishes and shows to her own brothers and sisters and to her parents; the pretty birdlike thing with whom she plays games and thus fulfills her own nature; to her that treasure beyond all treasures—a small girl, dainty and exquisite.

Therefore, the mother's true happiness lies in the world beyond death. Deep down she already knows this little daughter because she has been with the child when she was in deep slumber. But the inexorable supernal law forbids her to bring the memory back to her conscious life, she bears only the ache of parting from the child and this ache is expressed in a vague dissatisfaction—a kind of weariness or feeling of disappointment which she cannot understand and attributes to all but the true cause. After death her memory of these meetings with her daughter will be recaptured by her soul, and so they will meet as adoring mother and child.

But you must not assume that the many years of earth-time affect this child. In the Hereafter there exists a subjective time that may run according to the character of the souls. Appearance and desire will harmonize. At the time of the mother's death and entry into the new life, the daughter will have reached that lovely age when the child begins to talk brokenly, to make brave expeditions—half crawling, half walking—across the vast expanse of nursery floor. All the enchantment of the great, big world for the slowly blossoming intelligence will be per-ceived by the mother when she comes over here: she will find all that she has most desired on earth in the Lotus Flower Paradise which lies beyond tawdry death, beyond the tomb.

You may say that this picture I have drawn of a mother's happi-ness and heaven sounds too good to be true. But bear in mind that fate presents a debit and credit account. The mother, in this case, has known a great deal of unhappiness while on earth—troubles and disap-pointments that torment and take the colour out of life. So, before she chooses to go farther along the road to immortality, her heart's desire is granted and she reaps the full harvest from the grain sown with care and toil and sometimes pain in that terrestrial life of hers.

I was interested in this woman's soul and traced it back to the roots, and so made the acquaintance of the dream-child. I see that she is the outstanding feature in the former's supernal existence. As things are the mother will always be deeply affected by the pull of this other world where lives the dream-child. For where your treasure is there will your heart be also.

I should like to draw your attention to my repeated statements that imagination has extraordinary creative force in some instances, and you must not think it essential that to be an artist it is necessary to paint pictures, or write poems, or compose music. This mother is essentially an artist and such an artist may make a poem of life. If she be a mother she may desire to make a poem of childhood for a small daughter. Pray remember always that, however you are placed, you can make an art of living and thus enrich the lives of those who are of your immediate circle.

Notes

FOREWORD

1. Sidgwick, "Address by the President at the First General Meeting, " 12.
2. Bailey, *Death,* 2.

INTRODUCTION

1. Griffen, *Parapsychology, Philosophy, and Spirituality,* 291–92.
2. Becker, *Paranormal Experience and Survival of Death,* 3.

PSYCHIC PHENOMENA AND THE NEAR-DEATH EXPERIENCE: BACKGROUND

1. Evans, "Parapsychology"; Wagner and Mary Monet, "Attitudes of College Professors Toward Extra-Sensory Perception."
2. Carter, *Science and Psychic Phenomena,* 60, 131–32.
3. Ibid., chapters 4–8. See also Radin, *The Conscious Universe.*
4. Popper, "Replies to My Critics," 983.
5. Carter, *Science and Psychic Phenomena*, chapter 12.
6. Costa de Beauregard, "The Expanding Paradigm of the Einstein Theory," 182.
7. Murphy, "Psychology in the Year 2000," 527.
8. Kurtz, "Committee to Scientifically Investigate Claims of Paranormal and Other Phenomena."
9. Harris poll released January 1978, quoted in Clark, "Skeptics and the New Age," 425.

CHAPTER 1. EVIDENCE FROM INDIA TO ENGLAND

1. Stevenson, *Children Who Remember Previous Lives,* 26.

2. See Almeder, *Death & Personal Survival,* 66–81.

3. Stevenson, *Children Who Remember,* 26.

4. Ibid., 125–26.

5. See Stevenson, "The Evidence for Survival from Claimed Memories of Former Incarnations."

6. Stevenson, *Twenty Cases Suggestive of Reincarnation,* 259–69; Stevenson, *Children Who Remember Previous Lives,* 57–59.

7. Ibid., 71–73; Stevenson, *Reincarnation and Biology,* 2041–62.

8. Stevenson, *Cases of the Reincarnation Type,* 194.

9. This case is described in detail in Stevenson, *Cases of the Reincarnation Type,* 176–205.

CHAPTER 2.
CHARACTERISTICS OF REINCARNATION CASES

1. Stevenson, *Children Who Remember,* 103.

2. Ibid., 248.

3. Ibid., 109–10.

4. Ibid., 115.

5. Ibid., 171.

6. Ibid., 117.

7. Ibid., 117, 160.

8. Ibid., 212.

9. Ibid., 257.

10. Ibid., 258–59.

CHAPTER 3. ALTERNATIVE EXPLANATIONS
FOR REINCARNATION EVIDENCE

1. Stevenson, *Children Who Remember,* 147.

2. For instance, see Brody, "Review of *Cases of the Reincarnation Type,*" 770.

3. Quoted in Matlock, "Past Life Memory Cases," 252.

4. Mills, "A Replication Study," 180–81.

5. Mills, Haraldsson, and Keil, "Replication Studies of Cases Suggestive of Reincarnation by Three Independent Investigators," 217.

6. Stevenson, "Characteristics of Cases of the Reincarnation Type in Ceylon," 34–35.

7. Stevenson, *Children Who Remember,* 215.

8. Mentioned in Matlock, "Past Life Memory Cases," 227–28.

9. Stevenson, *Twenty Cases Suggestive of Reincarnation,* 332.

10. Stevenson, *Children Who Remember,* 147.

11. Brody, "Review of *Cases of the Reincarnation Type,*" 770.

12. Ibid., 771.

13. Ibid., 770.

14. Quoted by Brody, "Review of Cases of the Reincarnation Type," 773.

15. Stevenson, *Children Who Remember,* 150–51.

16. Stevenson, "American Children Who Claim to Remember Previous Lives," 742.

17. Matlock, "Past Life Memory Cases," 238.

18. Stevenson, "Comments by Ian Stevenson," 237.

CHAPTER 4. THE OBJECTIONS OF PAUL EDWARDS

1. Edwards, *Reincarnation,* 255.

2. Ibid., 256.

3. Almeder, *Death & Personal Survival,* 34.

4. Ibid., 35.

5. Edwards, *Reincarnation,* 103.

6. Stevenson, "Cryptomnesia and Parapsychology," 27.

7. Edwards, *Reincarnation,* 103–4.

8. Stevenson, "Comments by Ian Stevenson," 231.

9. Ibid., 232.

10. See Gauld, *Mediumship and Survival,* 106–7, 182; Matlock, "Past Life Memory Cases," 247–48; and Stevenson, "Comments by Ian Stevenson."

11. Matlock, "Past Life," 251.

12. Edwards, *Reincarnation,* 264.

13. Pasricha and Barker, "A Case of the Reincarnation Type in India," 396–97.

14. Ibid., 396–97.

15. Ibid., 399.

16. Ibid.

17. Ibid., 404.

18. Pasricha, "New Information Favoring a Paranormal Interpretation in the Case of Rakesh Gaur," 79.

19. Pasricha and Barker, "A Case of the Reincarnation Type in India," 406.

20. Pasricha, "New Information," 83.

21. Edwards, *Reincarnation,* 264.

22. Ibid., 102.

23. Ibid., 140.

24. Ibid., 268.

CHAPTER 5. REINCARNATION IN REVIEW

1. Sagan, *The Demon Haunted World,* 302.

2. Almeder, *Death & Personal Survival,* 47.

3. Stevenson, "Research into the Evidence of Man's Survival After Death," 165.

CHAPTER 6. STRANGE VISITS

1. Inglis, *The Paranormal,* 186.

2. Ibid., 189–90.

3. Osis and Haraldsson, *At the Hour of Death,* 218.

4. Haraldsson, "Survey of Claimed Encounters with the Dead," 107.

5. Quoted in Currie, *You Cannot Die!* 157–58.

6. Green and McCreery, *Apparitions,* 64–65.

7. Ibid., 194.

8. Ibid., 174.

9. Ibid., 144–45.

CHAPTER 7.
CHARACTERISTICS AND THEORIES OF APPARITIONS

1. Haraldsson, "Spontaneous Cases," 1.

2. Stevenson, "The Contribution of Apparitions to the Evidence for Survival," 345.

3. Haraldsson, *Departed Among the Living.*

4. Green and McCreery, *Apparitions,* 143.

5. Ibid., 143.

6. Haraldsson, "Spontaneous Cases," 3.

7. Green and McCreery, *Apparitions,* 50.

8. Stevenson, "The Contribution of Apparitions," 346.

9. Haraldsson, "Spontaneous Cases," 5.

10. Green and McCreery, *Apparitions,* 188.

11. See for instance Gurney et al., *Phantasms of the Living,* 93–94.

12. As quoted in Lorimer, *Survival?* 182.

13. Gordon, *Extrasensory Deception,* 103.

14. Lorimer, *Survival?*183.

15. Yuille and Cutshall, "A Case Study of Eyewitness Memory to a Crime," 291.

16. Ibid., 299.

17. Gordon, *Extrasensory Deception,* 103–4, emphasis added.

18. Anderson, "Abnormal Mental States in Survivors," 369.

19. Ibid., 375.

20. Ibid., 376–77.

21. Hart et al., "Six Theories about Apparitions," 215–16.

22. Broad, *Lectures on Psychical Research,* 234.

23. As quoted in Hart et al., "Six Theories," 222.

24. Ibid., 223–24.

CHAPTER 8. WHAT UNDERLIES GHOSTLY VISIONS?

1. As reported in Stevenson, "The Contribution of Apparitions to the Evidence for Survival," 349.

2. Hart et al., "Six Theories," 203–4.

3. Morton, "Record of a Haunted House," 313.

4. Ibid., 326.

5. Ibid.

6. Ibid., 314.

7. Ibid., 323.

8. Ibid., 319.

9. MacKenzie, *Hauntings and Apparitions,* 58–59.

10. Morton, "Record of a Haunted House," 311.

11. Lambert, "The Cheltenham Ghost," 267–77.

12. As mentioned in Ducasse, *A Critical Examination of the Belief in a Life After Death,* 155–56.

13. Roll, "A Nineteenth-century Matchmaking Apparition," 404.

14. Ducasse, *A Critical Examination,* 155.

15. Ibid., 155.

16. Lieut, "An Apparition Identified from a Photograph," 54.

17. Ibid., 55.

18. Ibid., 56.

19. Myers, "On Recognized Apparitions Occurring More Than a Year after Death," 27–28.

20. Ibid., 28.

21. Gauld, *Mediumship and Survival,* 235.

22. Ibid., 235–36.

23. Bird, "Two Striking Cases of Collective Apparition," 429–30.

24. Hart et al., "Six Theories about Apparitions," 207–8.

25. Hart and Hart, "Visions and Apparitions Collectively and Reciprocally Perceived," 220.

26. Green and McCreery, *Apparitions,* 180.

27. Jacobson, *Life Without Death?* 110–11.

28. Myers, "On the Evidence for Clairvoyance," 41–46.

29. Kelly et al., *Irreducible Mind,* 395–96, footnote.

30. Hart et al., "Six Theories," 235.

31. Brougham, *Life and Times of Lord Brougham,* 200–203.

32. Gurney, "On Apparitions Occurring Soon after Death," 423.

33. Ibid., 424.

34. Clarke, "World of Strange Powers."

35. Gurney, "On Apparitions Occurring Soon after Death," 413–14.

36. Ibid.

37. "Case of the Will of James L. Chaffin," 519.

38. Ibid., 523.

39. Ibid.

CHAPTER 9. FINAL THOUGHTS ON APPARITIONS

1. Hart et al., "Six Theories," 230.

CHAPTER 10. ANCIENT EVIDENCE

1. Inglis, *Natural and Supernatural,* 40.

2. Gauld, *Mediumship and Survival,* 17.

3. Quoted in Hart, *The Enigma of Survival,* 256–57.

4. Gauld and Cornell, *Poltergeists,* 26.

5. Lorimer, *Survival?* 193.

6. As quoted in Heywood, *Beyond the Reach of Sense,* 53–54.

CHAPTER 11. THE SPR INVESTIGATES

1. Beloff, *Parapsychology,* 57.
2. Hodgson, "A Record of Observations of Certain Phenomena of Trance," 130.
3. Quoted in Gauld, *Mediumship and Survival,* 33.
4. Hodgson, "A Further Record of Observations of Certain Phenomena of Trance," 285.
5. Myers, *Human Personality and Its Survival of Bodily Death,* vol. 2, 239.
6. Hodgson, "A Further Record," 300.
7. Ibid., 300.
8. Ibid., 328.
9. Ibid.
10. Ibid., 406.
11. See Gauld, *Mediumship and Survival,* 47.
12. Sidgwick, "An Examination of Book-tests Obtained in Sittings with Mrs. Leonard," 254.
13. Ibid.
14. Ibid., 255.
15. Ibid.
16. Ibid., 256.
17. Ibid., 257.
18. Ibid., 258–59.

CHAPTER 12. ALTERNATIVE EXPLANATIONS

1. Hodgson, "A Further Record," 296.
2. Ducasse, "What Would Constitute Conclusive Evidence of Survival after Death?" 402–3.
3. Gauld, *Mediumship and Survival,* 39.
4. Soal, "A Report on Some Communications Received through Mrs Blanche Cooper."
5. Markwick, "The Soal-Goldney Experiments with Basil Shackleton."
6. Gauld, *Mediumship and Survival,* 137–38.
7. Harris, *Investigating the Unexplained,* 141.
8. Soal, "A Report on Some Communications," 582.
9. Harris, *Investigating the Unexplained,* 142.
10. Ibid.
11. Markwick, "The Soal-Goldney Experiments with Basil Shackleton," 272–73.

12. Toynbee, Heywood, et al., *Man's Concern with Death,* 233.

13. Hodgson, "A Further Record," 485–86.

14. Gauld, *Mediumship and Survival,* 41.

15. "Note by Professor E. R. Dodds," in Thomas, "A Proxy Experiment of Significant Success," 294.

16. Thomas, "A Proxy Extending over Eleven Sittings with Mrs Osborne Leonard," 502–3.

17. Stevenson, "A Communicator Unknown to Medium and Sitters," 63.

18. Ibid., 54.

19. Myers, *Human Personality,* vol. 2, 472.

20. Ibid., 473.

21. Haraldsson and Stevenson, "A Communicator of the 'Drop in' Type in Iceland," 39.

22. Ibid., 57.

CHAPTER 13. *SUPER*-ESP AS AN EXPLANATION?

1. Sidgwick, "An Examination of Book-tests," 255.

2. Myers, *Human Personality*, vol. 2, 181.

3. Hodgson, "A Further Record," 491.

4. Ibid., 493.

5. Gauld, *Mediumship and Survival,* 42.

6. Ibid., 142.

7. Quoted in Ibid.

8. Thomas, "A New Hypothesis Concerning Trance Communications," 134.

9. Ibid., 135.

10. Ibid., 140.

11. Ibid., 143.

12. Ibid., 142.

13. Hodgson, "A Further Record," 290.

14. Ibid.

15. Bayfield, "Notes on the Same Scripts," 246.

16. Ibid., 249.

17. Ibid.

18. Gauld, "Discarnate Survial," 620–21.

19. Hodgson, "A Further Record," 324–25.

20. Broad, *Lectures on Psychical Research,* 297.

21. Almeder, *Death & Personal Survival,* 219.

22. Heywood, *Beyond the Reach of Sense,* 102.

23. Ibid., 103.

24. Broad, *Lectures,* 313.

25. Almeder, *Death,* 208–9.

26. Edmonds, *Spiritualism,* 45.

27. Edmonds, *Letters and Tracts on Spiritualism,* 70–71.

28. Lomaxe, "Judge Edmonds," 11–12.

29. Almeder, *Death,* 236.

30. Ibid., 206.

31. Dingwall, "An Amazing Case," 302.

32. Ibid., 304.

33. Ibid., 303, 304.

34. Ibid., 304.

35. Eisenbeiss and Hassler, "As Assessment of Ostensible Communications with a Deceased Grandmaster as Evidence for Survival," 70.

36. Ibid., 67.

37. Neppe, "A Detailed Analysis of an Important Chess Game," 146.

38. Ibid., 135.

39. Ibid., 142.

40. Ibid., 135.

41. Ibid., 132.

42. Ibid., 136.

43. Ibid., 142.

44. Ibid., 143.

45. Ibid., 146.

46. Eisenbiess and Hassler, "As Assessment of Ostensible Communications," 66.

47. Ibid., 71.

48. Neppe, "A Detailed Analysis," 145.

49. Ibid.

50. Eisenbeiss and Hassler, "As Assessment," 73.

41. Ibid., 74.

52. Ibid., 74.

53. Ibid., 74–75.

54. Ibid., 75–76.

55. Ibid., 76.

56. Ibid., 80.

57. Ibid., 77–78, 80.

58. Ibid., 79.

59. Neppe, "A Detailed Analysis," 146–47.

60. Broad, *Lectures,* 427.

CHAPTER 14. CROSS CORRESPONDENCES

1. Saltmarsh, *Evidence of Personal Survival from Cross Correspondences,* 36.

2. Ibid., 46.

3. Ibid., 36.

4. Ibid., 36–37.

5. Ibid., 60.

6. Quoted in ibid., 57. For original material, see *Proceedings of the Society for Psychical Research, Vol. XXI.*

7. Johnson, "A Reconstruction of Some Concordant Automatisms," 151–52.

8. Ibid., 154.

CHAPTER 15. THE LETHE EXPERIMENT

1. Piddington, "Three Incidents from the Sittings," 87.

2. Ibid., 87–88.

3. Ibid., 89.

4. Ibid., 90–91.

5. Ibid., 92–97.

6. Ibid., 105.

7. Ibid., 109.

8. Ibid., 110.

9. Ibid., 114.

10. Ibid., 98–99.

11. Ibid., 139–40.

12. As quoted in ibid., 129.

13. Ibid., 117.

14. Ibid., 121, 122, respectively.

15. Ibid., 120.

16. Ibid., 130.

17. Ibid., 131–32.

18. Ibid., 120, see footnote 1.

19. Ibid., 132–33.

20. Saltmarsh, *Evidence of Personal Survival,* 134.

21. Ducasse, "What Would Constitute Conclusive Evidence of Survival after Death?" 406.

22. Lodge, "Evidence of Classical Scholarship and of Cross-correspondence in Some New Automatic Writings," 117.

23. Ibid., 122.

24. Ibid., 122–24.

25. Ibid., 126.

26. Ibid., 132.

27. Piddington, "Three Incidents," 87.

28. Ibid., 128.

29. Saltmarsh, *Evidence of Personal Survival,* 95–96. See also Lodge, "Evidence of Classical Scholarship."

30. Lodge, "Evidence," 172–73.

31. Johnson, "On the Automatic Writing of Mrs. Holland," 208.

32. Cummins, *The Road to Immortality,* 23.

CHAPTER 16. EVALUATION OF
THE CROSS CORRESPONDENCES

1. Saltmarsh, *Evidence of Personal Survival,* 85–86.

2. Heywood, *Beyond the Reach of Sense,* 87.

3. Saltmarsh, *Evidence,* 26.

4. See Balfour, "The Palm Sunday Case," 79–267.

5. Piddington, "A Series of Concordant Automatisms," 243.

6. Balfour, "Remarks," 26.

CHAPTER 17.
HOW THE CASE FOR SURVIVAL STANDS TODAY

1. Becker, *Paranormal Experience and Survival of Death,* 118.

2. Popper, *The Logic of Scientific Discovery,* 142.

3. Ibid., 145.

4. Almeder, *Death & Personal Survival,* 228.

5. Ducasse, *A Critical Examination,* 203.

CHAPTER 18. IS SURVIVAL A FACT?

1. Schwartz, "Vocal Minority Insists It Was All Smoke and Mirrors."
2. Ibid.
3. Grossman, "Four Errors Commonly Made by Professional Debunkers," 231.
4. Ibid., 233.
5. Ibid., 234.
6. Ibid., 235–37.
7. Ibid., 237.

CHAPTER 19. WHAT THE DEAD SAY

1. Lorimer, *Survival?* 272–73.
2. Randall, *Life after Death,* 32.
3. Ibid., 11.
4. Brown, *Immortals by My Side,* 33–43.
5. Ibid., 28–29.
6. Ibid., 170.
7. Ibid., 170–71.
8. Ibid., 104.
9. Ibid., 104.
10. Sherwood, *The Country Beyond,* 55–57.
11. Ibid., 60–61.
12. Ibid., 63.
13. Ibid., 64–66.
14. Cummins, *The Road to Immortality,* 30.
15. Ibid., 38.
16. Currie, *You Cannot Die!* 336–37.
17. Roberts, *The Seth Material,* 275–77.
18. Cummins, *The Road to Immortality,* 31–32.
19. Ibid., 189–90.
20. Cummins, *Beyond Human Personality,* 25.
21. Ibid., 76.
22. Cummins, *The Road to Immortality,* 80–81.
23. Ibid., 88–89.
24. Ibid., 47.
25. Brown, *Immortals,* 105.

26. Cummins, *Beyond Human Personality*, 79.

27. Ibid., 64.

28. Ibid., 65.

29. Cummins, *The Road to Immortality*, 41.

30. Cummins, *Beyond Human Personality*, 36–37.

31. Cummins, *The Road*, 100.

32. Ibid., 110.

33. Cummins, *Beyond*, 40–41.

34. "No Matter."

35. Ferris, *Coming of Age in the Milky Way*, 288–89.

36. Cummins, *The Road to Immortality*, 43–44.

37. Ibid., 49.

38. Ibid., 54.

39. Ibid., 54.

40. Ibid., 57.

41. Cummins, *Beyond*, 46.

42. Cummins, *The Road*, 58.

43. Ibid., 69.

44. Ibid., 71.

45. Ibid., 72–73.

46. Ibid., 77.

EPILOGUE

1. Inglis, *Science and Parascience*, 139.

2. Schwartz, *The Afterlife Experiments*, 224.

3. Zingrone, "Failing to Go the Distance."

4. Quoted in Popper, "Natural Selection and the Emergence of Mind," 142.

5. Firsoff, "Life and Quantum Physics," 116.

6. Denton, *Nature's Destiny*, 285.

7. Ibid., 16.

8. Ibid., 298.

9. Eccles, *Facing Reality*, 62.

10. Herbert, *Elemental Mind*, 172.

11. Lasagna, "Let Magic Cast Its Spell," 10–11.

12. Popper and Eccles, *The Self and Its Brain*, 558.

Bibliography

Addison, James Thayer. *Life Beyond Death in the Beliefs of Mankind.* Boston and New York: Houghton Mifflin Co., 1932.

Almeder, Robert. *Death & Personal Survival.* Lanham, Md.: Rowman & Littlefield Publishers, Inc., 1992.

———. "On Reincarnation: A Reply to Hales." *Philosophia* 28 (2001): 347–58.

Anderson, E. W. "Abnormal Mental States in Survivors, with Special Reference to Collective Hallucinations." *Royal Naval Medical Service Journal* 28 (1942): 361–77.

Bailey, Alice, and Djwhal Khul, eds. *Death: The Great Adventure.* New York: Lucis Publishing Co., 1985.

Balfour, G. "Remarks on Mrs. Sidgewick's Paper on the History of the Society," *Proceedings of the Society for Psychical Research* 41 (1932): 26.

Balfour, J. "The Palm Sunday Case: New Light on an Old Love Story." *Proceedings of the Society for Psychical Research* 52 (1958–60): 79–267.

Barker, David. "Letter to the Editors." *Journal of Parapsychology* 43 (1979): 268–69.

Barker, Elsa. *Letters from the Light: An Afterlife Journal from the Self-Lighted World.* Hillsboro, Ore.: Beyond Worlds, 1995.

Barrett, William. *Death Bed Visions.* London: Methuen, 1926.

Bartley, W. W. "The Philosophy of Karl Popper, Part II: Consciousness and Physics." *Philisophia* 7, nos. 3–4 (July 1978): 675–716.

Bayfield, M. A. "Notes on the Same Scripts." *Proceedings of the Society for Psychical Research* XXVII (1914–15): 244–49.

Beauregard, Mario, and Denyse O'Leary. *The Spiritual Brain.* New York: HarperCollins, 2007.

Becker, Carl. *Paranormal Experience and Survival of Death*. Albany: State University of New York Press, 1993.

Beloff, John. "Mind-Body Interaction in Light of the Parapsychological Evidence." *Theoria to Theory* 10 (1976): 125–37.

———. "The Mind-Brain Problem." *The Journal of Scientific Exploration* 8, no. 4 (1994): 509–22.

———. *Parapsychology: A Concise History*. London: The Athlone Press, 1993.

———. *The Relentless Question*. Jefferson, N.C.: McFarland & Co., 1990.

Bird, J. M. "Two Striking Cases of Collective Apparition." *Journal of the American Society for Psychical Research* 22 (1928): 429–32.

Blackmore, S. "Are Out-of-Body Experiences Evidence for Survival?" *Anabiosis: The Journal for Near-Death Studies* 3 (1983): 137–55.

Blanke, O., S. Ortigue, T. Landis, and M. Seeck. "Stimulating Illusory Own-Body Perceptions." *Nature* 419 (September 2002): 269.

Braud, W. G. "Conscious versus Unconscious Clairvoyance in the Context of an Academic Examination." *Journal of Parapsychology* 39 (1975): 277–88.

Braude, Stephen. *The Limits of Influence*. New York and London: Routledge & Kegan Paul, 1986.

Broad, C. D. *Lectures on Psychical Research*. New York: Humanities Press, 1962.

———. *The Mind and Its Place in Nature*. New York: Harcourt, Brace & Co., 1929.

———. "The Relevance of Psychical Research to Philosophy." *Journal of the Royal Institute of Philosophy* XXIV, no. 91 (October 1949): 291–309.

Brody, Eugene. "Review of *Cases of the Reincarnation Type*. Volume 2. Ten Cases in Sri Lanka." *Journal of Nervous and Mental Disease* 167, no. 12 (1979): 769–74.

Brougham, Henry. *Life and Times of Lord Brougham*, vol. 1. Edinburgh and London: William Blackwood and Sons, 1871.

Broughton, Richard. *Parapsychology: The Controversial Science*. New York: Ballantine Books, 1991.

Brown, Rosemary. *Immortals by My Side*. London: Bachman & Turner, 1974.

Carter, Chris. *Science and the Near-Death Experience*. Rochester, Vt.: Inner Traditions, 2010.

———. *Science and Psychic Phenomena*. Rochester, Vt.: Inner Traditions, 2011. Originally published in 2007 as *Parapsychology and the Skeptics* by Sterlinghouse, Pittsburgh, Pa.

"Case of the Will of James L. Chaffin." *Proceedings of the Society for Psychical Research* 36 (1926): 517–24.

Clark, Jerome. "Skeptics and the New Age." In *New Age Encyclopedia,* by J. Gordon Melton, Jerome Clark, and Aidan Kelly. Detroit: Gale Research, 1990.

Clarke, Arthur C. "World of Strange Powers: Messages from the Dead." Yorkshire Television (1985). Available on Pacific Arts Video.

Collins, H. H. *Changing Order: Replication and Induction in Scientific Practice.* Beverly Hills, Calif.: Sage, 1985.

Cook, E., B. Greyson, and I. Stevenson. "Do Any Near-Death Experiences Provide Evidence for the Survival of Human Personality after Death? Relevant Features and Illustrative Case Reports." *Journal of Scientific Exploration* 12, no. 3 (1998): 377–406.

———. "The Expanding Paradigm of the Einstein Theory." In *The Iceland Papers,* edited by A. Puharich. Amherst, Wis.: Essentia Research Associates, 1979.

Costa de Beauregard, Olivier. "Quantum Paradoxes and Aristotle's Twofold Information Concept." In *Quantum Physics and Parapsychology,* edited by Laura Oteri. New York: Parapsychology Foundation, 1975.

Crookal, Robert. *The Supreme Adventure.* Cambridge, U.K.: James Clark, 1961.

Cummins, Geraldine. *Beyond Human Personality.* London: Psychic Press Ltd., 1935.

———. *The Road to Immortality,* 4th ed. London, U.K.: Lowe and Brydone, 1967. Originally published in 1932. London, U.K.: Lowe and Brydone.

Cummins, Geraldine, and Signe Toksvig. *Swan on a Black Sea.* London: Routledge & Kegan Paul, 1965.

Currie, Ian. *You Cannot Die!* Toronto: Somerville House, 1978.

Dean, Douglas. "20th Anniversary of the PA and the AAAS, Part 1: 1963–1969." *ASPR Newsletter* (Winter 1990).

Denton, Michael. *Nature's Destiny: How the Laws of Biology Reveal Purpose in the Universe.* New York: The Free Press, 1998.

Dingwall, E. J. "An Amazing Case: The Mediumship of Carlos Mirabelli." *Journal of the American Society for Psychical Research* XXXLV (1930): 296–306.

Ducasse, Curt. *A Critical Examination of the Belief in a Life After Death.* Springfield, Ill.: Charles C Thomas, 1961.

———. *Paranormal Science and Life after Death.* Springfield, Ill.: Charles C Thomas, 1959.

———. "What Would Constitute Conclusive Evidence of Survival after Death?" *Journal of the Society for Psychical Research* 41, no. 714 (December 1962): 401–6.

Eccles, John. *Facing Reality: Philosophical Adventures of a Brain Scientist*. New York, Heidelberg, and Berlin: Springer-Verlag, 1970.

——. *The Neurophysiological Basis of Mind*. Oxford, U.K.: Oxford University Press, 1953.

Edmonds, John Edwards. *Spiritualism*, vol. 2. New York: J. Partridge & Brittan, 1855.

——. *Letters and Tracts on Spiritualism*. London: J. Burns Progressive Library, 1874.

Edwards, Paul, ed. *Immortality*. Amherst, N.Y.: Prometheus Books, 1997.

——. *Reincarnation: A Critical Examination*. New York: Prometheus Books, 1996.

Ehrlich, Paul, and Marcus W. Feldman. "Genes, Environments & Behaviors." Daedalus, American Academy of Arts and Sciences (Spring 2007): 5–12.

Eisenbeiss, Wolfgang, and Dieter Hassler. "An Assessment of Ostensible Communications with a Deceased Grandmaster as Evidence for Survival." *Journal of the Society for Psychical Research* 70.2, no. 883 (April 2006): 65–97.

Elitzur, Avshalom, Beverly Sackler, and Raymond Sackler. "Consciousness Can No More Be Ignored." *Journal of Consciousness Studies* 2, no. 1 (1995): 353–57.

Evans, Christopher. "Parapsychology—What the Questionnaire Revealed." *New Scientist* 25 (January 1973): 209.

Eysenck, H., and Carl Sargent. *Explaining the Unexplained: Mysteries of the Paranormal*. London: Book Club Associates, 1982.

Ferris, Timothy. *Coming of Age in the Milky Way*. New York: Harper Collins, 2003.

Firsoff, V. A. "Life and Quantum Physics." In *Quantum Physics and Parapsychology*, edited by Laura Oteri. New York: Parapsychology Foundation, Inc. 1975.

Frazier, Kendrick, ed. *Paranormal Borderlands of Science*. Buffalo: Prometheus Books, 1981.

Gabbard, Glen, and S. W. Twemlow. *With the Eyes of the Mind*. New York: Praeger, 1984.

Gauld, Alan. "Discarnate Survival." In *Handbook of Parapsychology, edited* by B. Wolman. New York: Van Nostrand Reinhold, 1977.

——. *Mediumship and Survival: a Century of Investigations*. London: William Heinemann Ltd., 1982.

Gauld, Alan, and Tony Cornell. *Poltergeists*. London: Routledge & Kegan Paul, 1979.

Gordon, Henry. *Extrasensory Deception*. Toronto: Macmillan of Canada, 1988.

Greeley, A. "Mysticism Goes Mainstream." *American Health* 7 (1987): 47–49.

Green, Celia, and Charles McCreery. *Apparitions*. London: Hamish Hamilton Ltd., 1975.

Greene, John. "The Kuhnian Paradigm and the Darwinian Revolution in Natural History." In *Paradigms and Revolutions*, edited by Gary Gutting. Notre Dame, Ind.: University of Notre Dame Press, 1980.

Grey, Margot. *Return from Death*. Boston: Arkana, 1985.

Griffen, D. R. *Parapsychology, Philosophy, and Spirituality*. Albany: State University of New York Press, 1997.

Grossman, Neal. Letter to the Editor: "Four Errors Commonly Made by Professional Debunkers." *Journal of Near-Death Studies* 26, no. 3 (Spring 2008): 231–38.

———. "Who's Afraid of Life after Death?" *Journal of Near-Death Studies* 21, no. 1 (Fall 2002).

Groth-Marnat, G., and R. Summers. "Altered Beliefs, Attitudes and Behaviors Following Near-Death Experiences." *Journal of Humanistic Psychology* 38 (1998): 110–25.

Gurney, Edmund. "On Apparitions Occurring Soon after Death." *Proceedings of the Society for Psychical Research* (1888–89): 403–85.

Gurney, E., F. Myers, and F. Podmore. *Phantasms of the Living,* 2 vols. London: Trubner, 1886.

Lieut, A. M. H. "An Apparition Identified from a Photograph." *Journal of the American Society for Psychical Research* 20 (1931): 53–57.

Haku, Michio. *Hyperspace*. New York: Doubleday, 1994.

Hales S. "Evidence and the Afterlife." *Philosophia* 28 (2001): 335–46.

Hamilton, Margaret Lillian. *Is Survival a Fact? Studies of Deep-Trance Automatic Scripts and the Bearing of Intentional Actions by the Trance Personalities on the Question of Human Survival.* London: Psychic Press, 1969.

Hansen, George. "CSICOP and the Skeptics: An Overview." *Journal of the American Society for Psychical Research* 86 (January 1992): 19–63.

———. "Magicians and the Paranormal." *Journal of the American Society for Psychical Research* 86 (April 1992): 151–85.

———. "Magicians Who Endorsed Psychic Phenomena." *Linking Ring* 70, no. 8 (1990): 52–54.

Haraldsson, Erlendur. *The Departed Among the Living: An Investigative Study of Afterlife Encounters.* Surry, U.K.: White Crow Books, 2012.

———. "Survey of Claimed Encounters with the Dead." *Omega* 19, no. 2 (1988–89): 103–13.

———. "Spontaneous Cases: Apparitions of the Dead." In *Research in Parapsychology,* edited by Emily Cook and Deborah Delanoy. London: The Scarecrow Press, 1994.

Haraldsson, E., and Ian Stevenson. "A Communicator of the 'Drop in' Type in Iceland: The Case of Runolfur Runolfson." *Journal of the American Society for Psychical Research* 69 (1975): 33–59.

Harman, Willis. *Global Mind Change: The Promise of the 21st Century.* Indianapolis: Knowledge Systems, 1988.

Harris, Melvin. *Investigating the Unexplained.* Buffalo: Prometheus Books, 1986.

Hart, Hornell. *The Enigma of Survival.* London: Rider, 1959.

Hart, Hornell, et al. "Six Theories about Apparitions." *Proceedings of the Society for Psychical Research* 50, part 185 (1956): 153–239.

Hart, Hornell, and Ella Hart. "Visions and Apparitions Collectively and Reciprocally Perceived." *Proceedings of the Society for Psychical Research* 41 (1933): 205–49.

Hebb, D. O. "The Role of Neurological Ideas in Psychology." *Journal of Personality* 20 (1951): 39–55.

Herbert, Nick. *Quantum Reality: Beyond the New Physics.* New York: Anchor Press, 1985.

———. *Elemental Mind: Human Consciousness and the New Physics.* New York: Penguin Books, 1993.

Heywood, Rosalind. *Beyond the Reach of Sense.* New York: E.P. Dutton & Company, 1961.

Hodgson, Richard. "A Further Record of Observations of Certain Phenomena of Trance." *Proceedings of the Society for Psychical Research* 13 (1897–98): 284–582.

———. "A Record of Observations of Certain Phenomena of Trance." *Proceedings of the Society for Psychical Research* 8 (1892): 1–169.

Holden, J. M. "More Things in Heaven and Earth: A Response to 'Near-death Experiences with Hallucinatory Features.'" *Journal of Near-Death Studies* 26 (2007): 33–42.

Honorton, C. "Rhetoric over Substance: The Impoverished State of Skepticism." *Journal of Parapsychology* 57 (1993): 191–214.

Horgan, John. *The Undiscovered Mind.* New York: Simon & Schuster, 1999.

Hutcheon, Pat Duffy. *Leaving the Cave: Evolutionary Naturalism in Social-Scientific Thought*. Waterloo, Ontario: Wilfred Laurier University Press, 1996.

———. "Popper and Kuhn on the Evolution of Science." In *Book Review* 4, nos. 1/2 (1995): 28–37.

Huxley, Aldous. *The Doors of Perception*. London: Granada Publishing, 1984. Originally published in 1954 by Harper, New York.

Inglis, Brian. *Natural and Supernatural*. London: Hodder & Stoughton, 1977.

———. *The Paranormal: An Encyclopedia of Psychic Phenomena*. London: Paladin, 1985.

———. *Science and Parascience: A History of the Paranormal, 1914–1939*. London: Hodder & Stoughton, 1984.

Ingram, Jay. "Why I'm Skeptical—Even of the Skeptic." *Toronto Star* (March 16, 2003): A14.

Irwin, H. J. *An Introduction to Parapsychology*, 3rd ed. Jefferson, N.C.: McFarland & Company, 1999.

Jacobson, Nils. *Life Without Death?* London: Turnstone, 1974.

James, William. *Human Immortality: Two Supposed Objections to the Doctrine*. Boston: Houghton Mifflin, 1898.

Jenkins, Elizabeth. *The Shadow and the Light: A Defense of Daniel Dunglas Home the Medium*. London: Hamish Hamilton, 1982.

Johnson, Alice. "On the Automatic Writing of Mrs. Holland." *Proceedings of the Society for Psychical Research* 21, part LV (January 1908): 166–391.

———. "A Reconstruction of Some Concordant Automatisms." *Proceedings of the Society for Psychical Research* 27, part LXVIII (January 1914): 1–56.

Josephson, B., and F. Pallikari-Viras. "Biological Utilisation of Quantum NonLocality." *Foundations of Physics* 21 (1991): 197–207.

Kaku, Michio. *Hyperspace*. New York: Doubleday, 1994.

Keeton, M. T. "Some Ambiguities in the Theory of the Conservation of Energy." *Philosophy of Science* 8, no. 3 (July 1941): 304–19.

Kelly, E., A. Crabtree, A. Gauld, M. Grosso, and B. Greyson. *Irreducible Mind*. New York: Rowman & Littlefield, 2007.

Kircher, Pamela. *Love Is the Link*. Burdette, N.Y.: Larson Publications, 1995.

Kuhn, Thomas. *The Structure of Scientific Revolutions,* 3rd ed. Chicago: University of Chicago Press, 1996.

Kurtz, Paul. "Committee to Scientifically Investigate Claims of Paranormal and Other Phenomena." *Humanist* (May/June 1976): 28.

Lambert, G. W. "The Cheltenham Ghost: A Reinterpretation of the Evidence." *Journal of the Society for Psychical Research* 39 (1958): 267–77.

Lamont, Corliss. *The Illusion of Immortality*. New York: The Continuum Publishing Company, 1990.

Lasagna, Louis. "Let Magic Cast Its Spell." *The Sciences* (May–June 1984): 10–11.

Lasker, E. "Das New Yorker Turnier von 1924." *Schach Journal* 3 (1992): 47ff.

Laudan, Rachel. "The Recent Revolution in Geology and Kuhn's Theory of Scientific Change." In *Paradigms and Revolutions*, edited by Gary Gutting. Notre Dame, Ind.: University of Notre Dame Press, 1980.

Libet, Benjamin. "Do We Have Free Will?" *Journal of Consciousness Studies* 6, nos. 8–9 (1999): 47–57.

Libet, B., A. Freeman, and K. Sutherland, eds. *The Volitional Brain: Towards a Neuroscience of Free Will*. Thoverton, England: Imprint Academic, 1999.

Lodge, Oliver. "Evidence of Classical Scholarship and of Cross-Correspondence in Some New Automatic Writings." *Proceedings of the Society for Psychical Research*, part LXIII (June 1911): 113–75.

Lomaxe, Paul. "Judge Edmonds: A Psychic Sensitive." New York: General Assembly of Spiritualists, 1945.

Lorimer, David. *Survival? Body, Mind and Death in the Light of Psychic Experience*. London: Routledge & Kegan Paul, 1984.

MacKenzie, Andrew. *A Gallery of Ghosts*. London: Arthur Barker Ltd., 1972.

———. *Hauntings and Apparitions*. New York: Granada Publishing, 1982.

Markwick, Betty. "The Soal-Goldney Experiments with Basil Shackleton: New Evidence of Data Manipulation." *Proceedings of the Society for Psychical Research* 56, part 211 (May 1978): 250–81.

Masterman, Margaret. "The Nature of a Paradigm." In *Criticism and Growth of Knowledge,* edited by Imre Lakatos and Alan Musgrave. Cambridge, U.K.: Cambridge University Press, 1970.

Matlock, James. "Past Life Memory Cases." In *Advances in Parapsychological Research,* vol. 6, edited by Stanley Krippner. Jefferson, N.C.: McFarland Publishers, 1990.

Mattuck, R., and Evan Harris Walker. "The Action of Consciousness on Matter: a Quantum Mechanical Theory of Psychokinesis." In *The Iceland Papers,* edited by A. Puharich. Amherst, Wis.: Essentia Research Associates, 1979.

McClenon, James. *Deviant Science: The Case of Parapsychology*. Philadelphia: University of Pennsylvania Press, 1984.

McGrew, Timothy. "The Simulation of Expertise: Deeper Blue and the Riddle of Cognition," *Origins and Design* 19.1 (1998). Accessed March, 15 2012, from www.arn.org/docs/odesign/od191/deeperblue191.htm.

Mills, A. "A Replication Study: Three Cases of Children in Northern India Who Are Said to Remember a Previous Life." *Journal of Scientific Exploration* 3, no. 7 (1989): 133–84.

Mills, A., E. Haraldsson, and J. Keil. "Replication Studies of Cases Suggestive of Reincarnation by Three Independent Investigators." *Journal of the American Society for Psychical Research* 88 (1994): 207–19.

Milner, Richard. "Charles Darwin and Associates, Ghostbusters." *Scientific American* (October 1996): 96–101.

Morton, R. C. "Record of a Haunted House." *Proceedings of the Society for Psychical Research* III (1892): 311–32.

Murchison, Carl. *The Case for and against Psychical Belief.* Worcester, Mass.: Clark University Press, 1927.

Murphy, G. "Psychology in the Year 2000." In *There is More Beyond: Selected Papers of Gardner Murphy,* edited by Lois B. Murphy. Jefferson, N.C.: McFarland & Co., 1989.

Myers, Frederic. *Human Personality and Its Survival of Bodily Death,* vols. 1 and 2. New York: Longmans, Green, and Co., 1903.

———. "On the Evidence for Clairvoyance." *Journal of the Society for Psychical Research* 7 (1891–92): 30–99.

———. "On Recognized Apparitions Occurring More Than a Year after Death." *Proceedings of the Society for Psychical Research* 6 (1889): 13–65.

Nash, C. B. "Test of Psychokinetic Control of Bacterial Mutation." *Journal of the Society for Psychical Research* 78 (1984): 145–52.

Neppe, Vernon. "A Detailed Analysis of an Important Chess Game: Revisiting 'Maroczy versus Korchnoi.'" *Journal of the Society for Psychical Research* 71.3, no. 888 (July 2007): 129–47.

"No matter." Peter Russell Spirit of Now. www.peterrussell.com/Reality/RHTML/R21.php. Accessed April 20, 2012.

Noble, Holcomb B. *Next: The Coming Era in Science.* Boston: Little, Brown, 1988.

Osis, Karlis, and Erlendur Haraldsson. *At the Hour of Death.* New York: Avon Books, 1977.

Oteri, Laura, ed. *Quantum Physics and Parapsychology.* New York: Parapsychology Foundation, 1975.

Pasricha, Satwant. *Claims of Reincarnation: An Empirical Study of Cases in India*. New Delhi: Harman Publishing House, 1990.

———. "New Information Favoring a Paranormal Interpretation in the Case of Rakesh Gaur." *European Journal of Parapsychology* 5 (1983): 77–85.

Pasricha, Satwant, and David Barker. "A Case of the Reincarnation Type in India: The Case of Rakesh Gaur." *European Journal of Parapsychology* 3 (1981): 381–408.

Peacocke, Arthur. *Theology for a Scientific Age*. London: SCM Press, 1993.

Penfield, Wilder. *The Cerebral Cortex of Man*. New York: The MacMillan Company, 1952.

———. *The Excitable Cortex in Conscious Man*. Liverpool, U.K.: Liverpool University Press, 1958.

———. *The Mystery of the Mind*. Princeton, N.J.: Princeton University Press, 1975.

———. "The Role of the Temporal Cortex in Certain Psychical Phenomena." *Journal of Mental Science* 101, no. 424 (1955): 451–65.

Piddington, J. G. "A Series of Concordant Automatisms." *Proceedings of the Society for Psychical Research* 22 (1908): 19–416.

———. "Three Incidents from the Sittings: Lethe; the Sibyl; the Horace Ode Question." *Proceedings of the Society for Psychical Research* 24 (1910): 86–169.

Pinch, T. J., and H. M. Collins. "Private Science and Public Knowledge: The Committee for the Scientific Investigation of the Claims of the Paranormal and Its Use of the Literature." *Social Studies of Science* 14 (1984): 521–46.

Plato. *Phaedo*. Oxford: Clarendon Press, 1975.

Podmore, Frank. "Discussion of the Trance Phenomena of Mrs Piper." *Proceedings of the Society for Psychical Research* 14 (1898–99): 50–70.

Polkinghorne, J. C. *The Quantum World*. London: Longman Group, 1984.

Popper, Karl. "Autobiography." In *The Philosophy of Karl Popper*, part I, edited by Paul Arthur Schilpp. La Salle, Ill.: The Open Court Publishing Company, 1974.

———. *Conjectures and Refutations*. New York: Harper & Row, 1965.

———. *The Logic of Scientific Discovery*, 2nd ed. New York: First Harper Torchbook, 1959.

———. "Natural Selection and the Emergence of Mind." *Dialectica* 22, no. 3 (1978): 339–55.

———. "Normal Science and Its Dangers." In *Criticism and the Growth of*

Knowledge, edited by Imre Lakatos and Alan Musgrave. London: Cambridge University Press, 1970.

———. "Philosophy and Physics." *Proceedings of the XIIth International Congress for Philosophy* 2 (1960): 367–74.

———. "Replies to My Critics." In *The Philosophy of Karl Popper*, part II, edited by Paul Arthur Schilpp. La Salle, Ill.: The Open Court Publishing Company, 1974.

Popper, Karl, and John C. Eccles. *The Self and Its Brain: An Argument for Interactionism.* New York: Springer International, 1977.

Prasad, J., and I. Stevenson. "A Survey of Spontaneous Psychical Experiences in School Children of Uttar, Pradesh, India." *International Journal of Parapsychology* 10 (1968): 241–61.

Price, George, R. "Science and the Supernatural." *Science* 122, no. 3165 (August 26, 1955): 359–67.

Puharich, A., ed. *The Iceland Papers.* Amherst, Wis.: Essentia Research Associates, 1979.

Putnam, Hillary. "The 'Corroboration' of Theories." In *The Philosophy of Karl Popper,* part I, edited by Arthur Schilpp. Chicago: Open Court Publishing Co, 1977.

Radin, Dean. *The Conscious Universe: The Scientific Truth of Psychic Phenomena.* San Francisco: HarperCollins, 1997.

Randall, Neville. *Life after Death.* London: Hale, 1975.

Rawcliffe, D. H. *Illusions and Delusions of the Supernatural and the Occult.* New York: Dover, 1959.

Ring, Kenneth, and Sharon Cooper. *Mindsight.* Palo Alto, Calif.: William James Center for Consciousness Studies, 1999.

Ring, Kenneth, and Evelyn Elsaesser Valarino. *Lessons from the Light.* Portsmouth, N.H.: Moment Point Press, 1998.

Roberts, Jane. *The Seth Material.* New York: Bantam Books, 1976.

Rogo, D. S. *The Return from Silence.* Northampton, U.K.: The Aquarian Press, 1989.

Roll, Muriel. "A Nineteenth-Century Matchmaking Apparition: Comments on Abraham Cummings' 'Immortality Proved by Testimony of the Senses.'" *Journal of the American Society for Psychical Research* 63, no. 4 (October 1969): 396–409.

Rommer, Barbara. *Blessings in Disguise: Another Side of the Near-Death Experience.* St. Paul, Minn.: Llewellyn, 2000.

Rosenblum, B., and F. Kuttner. "Consciousness and Quantum Mechanics: The Connection and Analogies." *Journal of Mind and Behavior* 20, no. 3 (Summer 1999): 229–56.

Russell, Bertrand. *Portraits from Memory*. London: George Allen and Unwin, 1956.

Sabom, Michael. *Light & Death*. Grand Rapids, Mich.: Zondervan Publishing, 1998.

Sagan, Carl. *Broca's Brain*. New York: Random House, 1979.

———. *The Demon-Haunted World*. New York: Random House, 1995.

Salter, W. H. "FWH Myers's Posthumous Message." *Proceedings of the Society for Psychical Research* 52, part 187 (October 1958): 1–32.

Saltmarsh, Herbert F. *Evidence of Personal Survival from Cross Correspondences*. London: G. Bell & Sons, 1938.

Schoolcraft, Henry R. *Travels in the Central Portion of the Mississippi Valley*. New York: Kraus Reprint Company, 1975. Originally published in 1825 by Collins and Hannay, New York.

Schwartz, Gary. *The Afterlife Experiments*. New York: Pocket Books, 2002.

Schwartz, John. "Vocal Minority Insists It Was All Smoke and Mirrors." *New York Times* (July 13, 2009).

Searle, John R. *The Mystery of Consciousness*. New York: New York Review of Books, 1997.

Serdahely, William. "Questions for the 'Dying Brain Hypothesis.'" *Journal of Near-Death Studies* 16 (Fall 1996): 41–53.

Sheldrake, Rupert. *Can Our Memories Survive the Death of Our Brains?* In *What Survives?* edited by Gary Doore. Los Angeles: Jeremy P. Tarcher, Inc., 1990.

———. *Morphic Resonance: The Nature of Formative Causation*. Rochester, Vt.: Park Street Press, 2009.

———. *The Sense of Being Stared At: And Other Aspects of the Extended Mind*. New York: Crown Publishers, 2003.

Sherwood, Jane. *The Country Beyond*. London: Neville Spearman, 1969. Originally published in 1945, London: Rider & Co.

Sidgwick, H. Address by the President at the First General Meeting. *Proceedings of the Society for Psychical Research* 1 (1882): 7–12.

Sidgwick, Mrs. Henry. "An Examination of Book-tests Obtained in Sittings with Mrs. Leonard." *Proceedings of the Society for Psychical Research,* part LXXXI (April 1921): 242–378.

———. "The Society for Psychical Research: A Short Account of Its History."

Proceedings of the Society for Psychical Research, part XLI (April 1932): 1–26.

Siegel, Ronald. "Hallucinations." *Scientific American* 237 (1977): 132–40.

———. "The Psychology of Life After Death." *American Psychologist* 35, no. 10 (1980): 911–31.

Snow, Charles P. *The Search,* 5th ed. London: Macmillan and Co., 1963. Originally published in 1934 by Macmillan and Co., London.

Soal, S. G. "A Report on Some Communications Received through Mrs Blanche Cooper." *Proceedings of the Society for Psychical Research* XXXV (1926): 471–595.

Sperry, Roger. "Holding Course Amid Shifting Paradigms." In *New Metaphysical Foundations of Modern Science,* edited by Willis Harman and Jane Clark. Sausalito, Calif.: Institute of Noetic Sciences, 1994.

Spraggett, Allen, and William Rauscher. *Arthur Ford: The Man Who Talked with the Dead.* New York: New American Library, 1973.

Squires, Euan. *The Mystery of the Quantum World,* 2nd ed. London: Institute of Physics Publishing, 1994.

Stapp, Henry. "Attention, Intention, and Will in Quantum Physics." *Journal of Consciousness Studies* 6, nos. 8–9 (1999): 143–64.

———. "Theoretical Model of Purported Theoretical Violations of the Predictions of Quantum Theory." *Physical Review A* 50 (1994): 18–22.

Stenger, Victor. *Physics and Psychics.* Buffalo, N.Y.: Prometheus Books, 1990.

———. *The Unconscious Quantum.* Buffalo, N.Y.: Prometheus Books, 1995.

Stevenson, Ian. "American Children Who Claim to Remember Previous Lives." *Journal of Nervous and Mental Disease* 171, no. 12 (1983): 742–48.

———. *Cases of the Reincarnation Type: Volume 1, Ten Cases in India.* Charlottesville: University Press of Virginia, 1975.

———. "Characteristics of Cases of the Reincarnation Type in Ceylon." *Contributions to Asian Studies* 3 (1973): 26–29.

———. *Children Who Remember Previous Lives.* Charlottesville: University Press of Virginia, 1987.

———. "Comments by Ian Stevenson." *Journal of the Society for Psychical Research* 55 (1988): 230–34.

———. "A Communicator Unknown to Medium and Sitters." *Journal of the American Society for Psychical Research* 64 (1970): 53–65.

———. "The Contribution of Apparitions to the Evidence for Survival." *Journal of the Society for Psychical Research* 76 (1982): 341–58.

———. "Cryptomnesia and Parapsychology." *Journal of the Society for Psychical Research* 52 (1983): 1–30.

———. "The Evidence for Survival from Claimed Memories of Former Incarnations." *Journal of the American Society for Psychical Research* 54 (1960): 51–71, 95–117.

———. *Reincarnation and Biology*, vol. 2. Westport, Conn.: Praeger Publishers, 1997.

———. "Research into the Evidence of Man's Survival After Death." *Journal of Nervous and Mental Disease* 165, no. 3 (1977): 153–83.

———. *Twenty Cases Suggestive of Reincarnation*. Charlottesville: University Press of Virginia, 1974. Originally published in 1966.

Stokes, Douglas. "Theoretical Parapsychology." In *Advances in Parapsychological Research*, edited by Stanley Krippner. London: McFarland & Company, 1987.

Symonds, Neville. "A Fitter Theory of Evolution?: Biologists Have Always Denied That Organisms Can Adapt Their Genes to Suit a New Environment. But Some Startling Discoveries about Bacteria Are Making Them Think Again." *New Scientist,* issue 1787 (September 21, 1991). Accessed June 10, 2007 from www.newscientist.com.

Teuber, Hans-Lukas. "Recovery of Function after Brain Injury in Man." In *Outcome of Severe Damage to the Central Nervous System,* edited by Ruth Porter and David Fitzsimons. Amsterdam: Elsevier, 1975.

Thomas, C. Drayton. "A New Hypothesis Concerning Trance Communications." *Proceedings of the Society for Psychical Research* XLVIII, part 173 (1949): 121–63.

———. "A Proxy Experiment of Significant Success." *Proceedings of the Society for Psychical Research* XLV, part 159 (1938–39): 257–306.

———. "A Proxy Extending Over Eleven Sittings with Mrs. Osborne Leonard." *Proceedings of the Society for Psychical Research* XLIII, part 142 (1935): 439–519.

Thouless, R. H., and B. P. Wiesner. "The Psi Processes in Normal and Paranormal Psychology." *Proceedings of the SPR* 48 (1949): 177–96.

Toynbee, Arnold, R. Heywood, et al. *Man's Concern with Death*. London: Hodder & Stoughton, 1968.

Utts, J. M. "An Assessment of the Evidence for Psychic Functioning." *Journal of Scientific Exploration* 10, no. 1 (1996): 330. Also published in *Journal of Parapsychology* 59, no. 4 (1996): 289–320.

———. "Response to Ray Hyman's Report of September 11, 1995, 'Evaluation of Program on Anomalous Mental Phenomena.'" *Journal of Scientific Exploration* 10, no. 1 (1996): 59–61. Also published in *Journal of Parapsychology* 59, no. 4 (1996): 353–56.

Valarino, Evelyn Elsaesser. *On the Other Side of Life*. Cambridge, Mass.: Perseus Publishing, 1997.

Vallee, Jacques. *Confrontations: A Scientist's Search for Alien Contact*. New York: Ballantine Books, 1990.

Vandenberg, Philipp. *The Mysteries of the Oracles*. New York: Macmillan Publishing Company, 1979.

Wagner, Mahlon, and Mary Monet. "Attitudes of College Professors toward Extra-Sensory Perception." *Zetetic Scholar* 5 (1979): 7–16.

Walker, E. H. "Consciousness and Quantum Theory." In *Psychic Exploration*, edited by J. White. New York: G. P. Putnam's Sons, 1974.

———. "Measurement in Quantum Mechanics Revisited." *Journal of the American Society for Psychical Research* 81 (October 1987): 333–69.

———. "The Quantum Theory of Psi Phenomena." *Psychoenergetic Systems* 3 (1979): 259–99.

Wheeler, John, and Wojciech Zurek, eds. *Quantum Theory and Measurement*. Princeton, N.J.: Princeton University Press, 1983.

Wigner, Eugene. "Remarks on the Mind-Body Problem." In *Quantum Theory and Measurement*, edited by John Wheeler and Wojciech Zurek. Princeton, N.J.: Princeton University Press, 1984.

Yuille, J., and J. Cutshall. "A Case Study of Eyewitness Memory to a Crime." *Journal of Applied Psychology* 71, no. 2 (1986): 291–301.

Zingrone, Nancy. "Failing to Go the Distance: On Critics and Parapsychology." Parapsychology Foundation, 1997.

Zollner, Friedrich. *Transcendental Physics*. Boston: Colby & Rich, 1888.

Zollschan, George, John Schumaker, and Greg Walsh, eds. *Exploring the Paranormal: Different Perspectives on Belief and Experience*. Dorset, U.K.: Prism Press, 1989.

Zorab, George. "Review of *The Enigma of Daniel Home: Medium or Fraud*." *Journal of Parapsychology* 49 (1985): 103–5.

Index

BOOKS OF RELATED INTEREST

Science and the Near-Death Experience
How Consciousness Survives Death
by Chris Carter

Science and Psychic Phenomena
The Fall of the House of Skeptics
by Chris Carter

Morphic Resonance
The Nature of Formative Causation
by Rupert Sheldrake

The Presence of the Past
Morphic Resonance and the Memory of Nature
by Rupert Sheldrake

Science and the Akashic Field
An Integral Theory of Everything
by Ervin Laszlo

The Akashic Experience
Science and the Cosmic Memory Field
by Ervin Laszlo

Where Does Mind End?
A Radical History of Consciousness and the Awakened Self
by Marc J. Seifer, Ph.D.

Forbidden Science
From Ancient Technologies to Free Energy
Edited by J. Douglas Kenyon

INNER TRADITIONS • BEAR & COMPANY
P.O. Box 388
Rochester, VT 05767
1-800-246-8648
www.InnerTraditions.com

Or contact your local bookseller